Life Is Sales

Life Is Sales

Gary L. Ford and Connie Bird

INSOMNIAC PRESS

Library and Archives Canada Cataloguing in Publication

Ford, Gary, 1946-
      Life is sales / Gary Ford.

ISBN 978-1-897178-57-7 (pbk.)

      1. Success--Psychological aspects. I. Title.

BF637.S8F657 2008   158.1   C2008-901009-4

The publisher gratefully acknowledges the support of the Department of Cana-dian Heritage through the Book Publishing Industry Development Program.

Printed and bound in Canada

Insomniac Press
192 Spadina Avenue, Suite 403
Toronto, Ontario, Canada, M5T 2C2
www.insomniacpress.com

Canadä

Life Is Sales is dedicated to everyone who faces this harshly competitive world and wakes each morning and takes control of their life. Your powerful self-talk, persistence, and commitment to being of service to others makes a difference for millions.

To all our workshop participants, we love your enthusiasm, generous listening, and playful participation. Your hunger to learn, your courage to try something new, and your commitment to creating the right solutions for your clients are why we do this work. We celebrate your successes and honour you in these pages.

Enclosed you will find the keys to creating meaningful conversations, making powerful requests, and becoming more persuasive. As you ponder these pages, we invite you to highlight your "ah-ha" or "light bulb" moments and your new insights. Each time you read this book, you will discover new ideas and approaches to getting to "yes." You will be inspired to take new actions. Read it, play with it, practice it, and tweak it to fit into your life. We promise you amazing results. Learn with *Life is Sales* and your accomplishments will surprise you. You can get what you want! It is there, just for the asking.

Acknowledgements

This book is the product of many great minds, conversations, and experiences. We want to acknowledge all of you—teachers, friends, colleagues, clients, participants, and audiences—for your contributions. It's such a pleasure to learn and grow with you. You enrich many lives by sharing your challenges and successes. Keep saying what you truly mean, having faith in yourself, and asking for what you want!

Our thanks to:

To Robert Cialdini, Regents' Professor of Psychology at Arizona State University, for sparking our passion for persuasion. Thank you for your wisdom.

To Graham McWaters, for your earlier partnership and introduction to our publisher.

To Insomniac Press, for making *Life Is Sales* a dream come true.

To Betty Vosters-Kemp, Michael Kemp, Julia Jones, and Judy Malone, for your feedback and editorial suggestions.

To our thousands of workshop participants for providing feedback, suggestions, and real-life examples that formed the basis for our book.

To our colleagues at First Canadian Title, for your support in bringing this work to the worlds of finance, sales, product, customer service, and relationships.

To our many executive business partners, for providing the space to practice and the opportunity to work and perform research with your people.

To our parents, for teaching us, "You can do anything you set your mind to!"

To our families, for their support and encouragement as we plugged away at our laptops.

Finally, to those of you turning these pages, whom we have not yet had the opportunity to meet. Our heartfelt thanks for buying our book and starting out on the *Life Is Sales* journey with us.

Table of Contents

Chapter 1
Life Is Sales

Why is it that some people are so successful at sales and others are not? Why is it that some can persuade others to their way of thinking and others simply go along with the crowd? Why is it that some can be influential with those in their lives and others are being influenced? The answer lies in our ability to get what we want and need in such a way that everyone wins.

Gary: Two years ago, my first beautiful granddaughter, Avery, was born. As a doting grandparent, I spent considerable time playing and observing Avery's every action as a newborn. It was interesting to note that she was influencing her parents and her grandparents to get what she needed within mere minutes of her birth. When uncomfortable or tired, she would cry and would get the immediate attention she demanded. When she was hungry, she could communicate her desire for food, and her mother would comply. She communicated to her parents in the only way she could: by crying. Her behaviour was reinforced, as she got what she "asked" for. As the days and months passed, Avery's needs expanded and so did her sales skills in getting what she needed and wanted.

Avery has a unique way of communicating her

dislike for certain foods. She likes potatoes and so will eat off her plate just fine, but stick anything green on the plate and it immediately goes over the side of her high chair onto the floor for the dog. This is a more forceful sales technique in communicating what she doesn't want, which gets her more of what she does want. Her mother tries to camouflage the green vegetables but to no avail—Avery can find them again and again, and over the side they go. Is Avery training her mother through influencing techniques? It certainly appears so.

The minute we are born, we begin learning how to get what we need to survive. Babies are at the mercy of their parents, as they are unable to fend for themselves. The only communication tool they have available is their voice, and so they use it to communicate what they require. When hungry, a baby cries; when thirsty, the cry will be a little different; and when a diaper needs changing, they will cry yet another way. Parents learn very quickly the communication techniques of their children. Even at this early age, babies learn sales skills to help them get what they want and need. As we grow older, our wants and needs expand, as do our skills in obtaining these things from those around us. We first influence our parents and grandparents; soon it becomes teachers, friends, and other family members.

In time, we are influencing fellow employees at work, customers, bosses, spouses, and our own children. Influencing and persuading prospects to become clients and purchase our wares is the objective in all sales roles. That's right, "Life Is Sales"—and the more effective we are at influencing and persuading others, the more successful we become in getting what we want and need.

A good definition for *sales* might be: "Getting what you ask for." We really do want to change the actions and behaviour of those we wish to influence rather than just have them think about our proposal in a positive way.

Who are the very best closers and salespeople in the world?
1. They are the most successful.
2. They are the most tenacious.
3. They always ask "one more time."
4. They always have more than one way of asking.

The answer? Your kids.

That's right, your kids! If you have children, you know exactly what we mean. Why do they lose this amazing skill as they get older? Why can't we recapture the exuberance of our youth in making powerful requests and being persistent in getting what we ask for and what we want without being childish?

This book will explore the human condition and what influences others to say yes to requests. Armed with this knowledge, you will discover new and effective ways to be more influential and persuasive with those around you, enabling you to get more of what you want. As we mature, we seem more afraid to ask for what we want. We instead hint at what we want, which is really not asking at all. We seem to be afraid of hearing the word *no*. Asking for what you want and making powerful requests will make you more successful than those who only hint. This book will show you how!

Sales isn't a bad word; it doesn't mean "manipulation" but rather an effective way to move people in the direction you would like them to take. Parents use sales techniques to grow and develop their children. Parents want their children to have certain social skills and achieve certain academic standards. Children, on the other hand, use sales techniques to get their parents to buy them the things they want and, as they get older, to gain the independence they need to grow and mature. Boys and girls, men and women all use sales techniques to attract their future mates. Sales are used in the workplace to build a better team, to get a promotion, to gain opportunities, and, of course, to actually sell products and services to others.

In the past fifty years, there has been significant psychological research that provides clues as to why people say yes to requests.

We will review this research in some detail and then take these findings and apply them to what we all do every day in our lives as we strive to be more successful. We will review what Robert B. Cialdini calls "the six principles of influence" in his book *Influence: Science and Practice* and discover ways to apply these principles to enhance your success, in all areas of your life. We will also review the other criteria for success, such as honesty and integrity, how to deal with rejection, and what personality traits lead to greater success.

The seven principles we will discuss in some detail are reciprocity, concessions, commitment/consistency, authority, consensus, scarcity, and liking. If used effectively, each of these principles will have a significant impact on your life and allow you to be more successful in getting what you ask for. We will also investigate other influence tools and human qualities that allow you to be more effective and successful. The first and perhaps most important quality any person brings to a relationship is honesty.

Honesty and Integrity

"Honesty is the best policy." —Robert Ingersoll

Significant research has been done on what employees look for in a leader. The number one item listed in literally every research program has been honesty. People want to know that their leader is an honest individual. We all want to work with people we can trust. The best way to achieve trust is to be honest—honest with our strengths and our shortcomings. Yes, admit to our own shortcomings.

This honesty factor is evident in all walks of life. Employees need to be able to trust their supervisor, managers need to be able to trust their employees, parents need to be able to trust their children, and customers need to be able to trust the person who is selling them a product or service.

Honesty leads to a feeling of trust between individuals, and trust builds a relationship of integrity. It's what we all want in a relationship. Trust and integrity are at the basis of all human interaction. Relationships are built with trust as the foundation. In selling, trust is the basis for all win/win relationships. A win/lose relationship might result in one sale but will not likely lead to future business or referrals. Life is for the long term and therefore must be based on honesty and integrity. When the honesty disappears, friendships, marriages, and businesses quickly dissolve. Trust must be established in any business or personal relationship before persuasion can be effective and long-lasting.

It is credibility we all crave when making any buying decision. When we look at buying any major item, we want to know whether the person explaining the product or service is telling us the truth. Would you buy anything from a salesperson you knew was lying about the product's features and benefits? Would you want to work for a supervisor who continually lied to you about the priorities of the company or your career future? Would you remain married to a spouse who continually lied to you about their activities? We need to be in a trusting relationship if we are to move forward in any meaningful way.

Honesty is the cornerstone for your career and your life, and this cornerstone will assist you in becoming more influential and successful. Sometimes the appearance of honesty alone will win a sale, but in the end, the full truth always comes out: your reputation will be sullied in the marketplace and your future success will be severely limited. Being honest allows trust to grow so that what you say next will be appreciated as the truth. Truth is a powerful persuasive quality. Honesty, truth, and integrity all work in unison to enhance relationships and enhance the ability to be influential.

There have been countless books written about sales techniques and approaches that will guarantee success. These skills will only work if the basis of the relationship is built on mutual trust. It is your personal choice to be honest, and we all need to look deep within our souls to find that seed of truth and nurture it into full bloom. Research has indicated that most of us lie once every twenty minutes, so it is an uphill battle for all of us, but a battle well worth fighting and a battle well worth winning. How many times do we say things we really don't mean? "Give me a second" really means at least five minutes. "I will be right down" means fifteen minutes.

Later in this book, we will be discussing various strategies you can implement that will showcase your honesty, integrity, and trustworthiness early in the sales process. This, in turn, will significantly enhance the closing ratio of every sales conversation. It is really up to each individual to decide to be honest in building relationships for success. This doesn't come easy, as the desire to close a sale sometimes overpowers our desire to be honest. But it is quite clear: People want to deal with those they trust.

To illustrate this point, just shift the perspective for a moment and put yourself in the customer's shoes. You're buying a new big-screen TV at a price of $4,800. You have done some research online and you therefore know some of the strengths and weaknesses of this TV already. The salesperson you're dealing with works on straight commission and proceeds to lay out all the features and benefits and stretches the truth about the quality and guarantees. Your immediate reaction is to question everything else the salesperson has told you, and you begin to wonder if they even know how to install the TV properly and hook it up to the surround sound system.

Gary: This exact situation happened to me. I was convinced by the sales skills of the individual that they were trustworthy and reliable and I was getting the very best deal in the city. The price was the best in comparison to others, so I bought the whole package: a plasma TV and surround sound system with five speakers for a cost of $10,000, and I had them install it for yet another fee. Well, it didn't work after a week. I noticed that I couldn't get screen-in-screen TV, so I couldn't watch two programs at once, which was one of the features the salesman explained to me. The surround sound didn't work for the TV on pay-per-view television, but did work for the DVD player. I looked behind all the equipment and the maze of wires told me this was a job for a professional, certainly not an inept technician such as me. If you own one of these surround sound setups, take a few minutes to pull the unit out from the wall and you will see what I mean. Wires running everywhere.

When I called the salesperson on the phone, they were not all that co-operative but did say someone would call from technical support. I waited two weeks—and no call. I called back, and this time I asked for technical support only to discover that they didn't have a technical support department at the store and I was on my own to hire someone to come and look at the setup. Fib number one. I never read manuals, but I attempted to find my problem in the 100-page booklet that came with my system. Needless to say, I was just as confused after I read the chapter on setup as I was before. Fib number two. It is easy to setup, just follow the simple directions and diagrams.

I called the salesperson and managed to get through. They confirmed I was on my own with this purchase. Fib number three. He had said they would provide after-purchase service. The after-purchase service had to go direct to the manufacturer, who was located in Korea. I finally hired a friend of a friend who did fix all my problems except the picture-in-picture, which was not actually a feature of this television unless I purchased another add-on. Fib number four.

So, what did I think of this salesperson, this company, and this manufacturer? Did I trust them? What were my actions after all these negotiations? My actions were to tell everyone the story of my problems with this store. I would never purchase anything else from this store, and I would recommend that all my friends and acquaintances buy elsewhere. The salesperson made one sale, but lost countless others because of the trust component. A year later, the store had gone bankrupt, which meant the salesperson was out looking for work. They missed the importance of honesty and integrity in building relationships and creating a win/win for customers and the store. That is how powerful honesty and integrity are in the world we live in today. Successful people and businesses thrive when honesty and integrity are the backbone of their philosophy. Relationships thrive when honesty and integrity are the basis of that relationship. Lose honesty and lose business.

Persistence, Initiative, and Assertiveness

We call these three qualities "PIA." Actually, it was our friend Deb Shepherd who used this acronym to help her remember the three qualities, and now we use it too. These three qualities are attributes of every successful person in the world today. When built upon the foundation of honesty and integrity, these three qualities ensure success in all walks of life. When hiring people, we have always believed that these three qualities are absolutely necessary for any new hire, especially in a sales role.

Persistence

"Many of life's failures are people who did not realize how close they were to success when they gave up."
—Thomas Edison

"Never give up" is the key to success for so many of the world's top performers. Athletes live by this mantra. Vince Lombardi once said, "Winners never quit, and quitters never win." Just look at how many hours an Olympic athlete puts in as training for just one event. Their commitment to persistence is amazing to behold. The athlete overcomes fatigue, boredom, pain, and injury as they persist for countless hours every week for years in preparation for that one day on the Olympic field of competition.

Most successful businesspeople are also known for their persistence. Colonel Harland Sanders is an outstanding example of persistence in action.[1]

Colonel Sanders was born in 1890 and actively began franchising his chicken business at age sixty-five. Most of us are retired, playing golf, fishing, and travelling, but here is a man at the age of sixty-five starting a new business!

Sanders held a variety of jobs in his youth, including railroad fireman and insurance salesman. He operated the Ohio River steamboat ferry, sold tires, and operated service stations. He even studied law by correspondence. When he was forty, he started cooking for travellers at his service station in Corbin, Kentucky. He didn't have a restaurant then but served the guests at his own dining room table. As more people started coming just for the food, he moved across the street to a motel and restaurant that seated 142 people. Over the next nine years, he perfected his secret blend of eleven herbs and spices and the basic cooking techniques that are still used today.

In the early '50s, a new interstate highway was planned to bypass the town of Corbin and the Colonel's restaurant. Seeing the end in sight, he auctioned off his operations, and after paying all of his bills, he was reduced to living on a $105 social security cheque each month.

Confident of the quality of his fried chicken recipe, the Colonel devoted himself to the chicken franchising business that he started in 1952. He travelled across the country by car from restaurant to restaurant, cooking batches of chicken for restaurant owners and their employees. If the reaction was good, he would enter into a handshake agreement on a deal that stipulated a payment to him of a nickel for each chicken the restaurant sold. Legend has it that the Colonel was turned down over 900 times before he made his first sale, but he persisted, and in 1955, the governor of Kentucky made him a Kentucky Colonel in recognition of his contribution to the state's cuisine.

By 1964, the Colonel had 600 franchised outlets, and in 1971, when the company was sold, there were 3,500 franchised and company-owned restaurants. The company was sold to Heublin, Inc. for $285 million. In 1986, the company was acquired by Pepsico for approximately $840 million, and by 1997, there were 29,500 restaurants worldwide in nearly 100 countries.

In 1976, an independent survey ranked the Colonel as the world's second most recognized celebrity. Santa Claus beat him out.

Let's look a little closer at the Colonel's success. He actually demonstrated all three of our key criteria for success with persistence being the number one key to his success.

At age sixty-five, Colonel Harland Sanders became an American fast-food pioneer. Most people would have given up after one month of rejection, and others would have given up after six months of rejection. But not the Colonel. Persistence in the face of overwhelming odds and constant rejection turned a one restaurant operation into a 29,500 unit chain worldwide.

The power of persistence is an amazing force that is available to all of us. We just need to choose fight over flight. This power is well within your grasp. Failure was not an option for the Colonel, and with each rejection, he became more persistent in accomplishing his task. It seemed that rejection fuelled his ardour to continue in his quest to bring his chicken recipe to America.

Did the Colonel demonstrate initiative? Absolutely. Here is a man sixty-five years of age with no real experience in franchising a chicken operation across America. He knew he had a winning chicken recipe with his secret blend of herbs and spices, but he took it to the next step—the critical next step—and demonstrated the initiative to actually go out and attempt to persuade perfect strangers to buy into his chicken recipe. It is this initiative that got the sixty-five-year-old Colonel out of his rocking chair and into his car to tour America to build a fast food empire.

Did the Colonel demonstrate assertiveness? Absolutely! Here is a man sixty-five years of age with minimal sales training and experience, persuading a nation to buy into his chicken franchise operation. Can you imagine running a small restaurant and this guy with a white suit and white goatee comes to your restaurant wanting to sell his chicken recipe? We expect it was quite an experience for those early converts to see this man in action. He convinced these small private restaurant owners to allow him to cook for them and demonstrate the quality of his product. They didn't agree at first, but over time they did. The Colonel didn't take no for an answer, and his assertiveness was based on his conviction that his product would help his potential customers be more successful. A win/win situation for both the restaurants and the Colonel. The honesty component was clearly identified, as the Colonel would seal the deal and the arrangements with a handshake. Trust on both sides of the counter helped build his reputation across the country.

This is an extraordinary story of success, but the Colonel is not the only highly successful individual to overcome extreme odds to take a place in the history books. Review this history and see if you can identify this man:

At age 23 – Ran for state legislature, but failed to get elected
At age 24 – Failed in business
At age 26 – Sweetheart died
At age 27 – Had a nervous breakdown
At age 29 – Defeated for Speaker
At age 34 – Defeated for nomination for Congress
At age 37 – Elected to Congress
At age 39 – Defeated in re-election bid for Congress
At age 45 – Defeated in Senate race
At age 46 – Defeated for nomination for Vice President of the United States

At age 49 – Defeated in Senate race
At age 51 – Elected President of the United States

Answer: Abraham Lincoln[2]

Yes, Abraham Lincoln was persistent, even though he had suffered tremendous defeats both professionally and personally. Perhaps these failures better prepared him to be one of the finest presidents in the history of the United States. Getting back up after a defeat is the measure of a truly successful person. Wallowing in the pain of defeat and blaming others for your misery is a surefire way to limit your success. This is really the magic of persistence. If you never try again, you will be assured of never achieving success. It is only those who actually continue in their quest who even have a chance at it.

The phrase "If at first you don't succeed, try, try again" has been around for decades for a reason. W. C. Fields once said, "If at first you don't succeed, try, try again. Then quit. No use being a damn fool about it." But W. C. Fields was a great comedian, not a great philosopher. The power of persistence is at your command only if you choose to invoke it.

Think back to when you learned to ride a bicycle. Did you master the art of balancing on two wheels as a youngster on the very first try? Not likely. Most of us fell off many times and had the skinned knees and elbows to prove our persistence in learning to balance and steer at the same time. Did you give up after your first failure and simply say, "I can't do it," and return to the tricycle, or did you climb back on the bicycle and give it another try? We all continued until we had mastered the art of the bicycle and felt proud of our accomplishment, with a big smile at our parents and friends as we circled the neighbourhood. Persistence is a way of life for children as they learn new skills, and yet somehow, as we get older, we lose that drive to overcome failure. We lost that "can do" attitude and it was replaced with fear of failure and embarrassment. Truly successful people return to their childhood roots and never give up until success is attained.

Most of us have heard of Dr. Seuss and probably read children's books by this famous author. Theodor Seuss Geisel, who wrote under the pen name Dr. Seuss, had his first personally written and illustrated book rejected twenty-seven times by publishers until it was finally accepted by Vanguard Press. Persistence in the face of continual rejection is one of the key criteria for success for so many amazing people. Dr. Seuss books have now sold over two hundred million copies in over fifteen different languages. How would you feel if you were one of those publishers who declined to publish that first book by Dr. Seuss? How different would our world be if Dr. Seuss had given up trying to publish after twenty-seven individual rejections? There would be no *Cat in the Hat* to read to our children and grandchildren. But Dr. Seuss persisted and we are all richer in our lives for his persistence.

Warren Buffet, perhaps the most successful investor of all time, is a living example of persistence. His buy-and-hold strategy exemplifies the ability to be persistent when investing in quality stocks. His strategy of buying and persistently holding quality companies through the vagaries of the market has proven to be the most successful over time.

We will discuss specific strategies later in the book on how you can unleash the power of persistence within you to achieve greater results. We all have the ability to persist, but we often decide to give up instead. We follow the W. C. Fields quotation. Persistence and stubbornness are close cousins and we will discover the difference so you will become more successful in all aspects of your life.

Initiative

"Screw it, let's do it." —Richard Branson

With his book *Screw It, Let's Do It: Lessons in Life,* Richard Branson is a perfect example of initiative in action. He states that the best lesson he ever learned was to "just do it." It doesn't matter what it is, or how hard it might seem, as the Greek philosopher Plato said, "The beginning is the most important part of any work."

This second key attribute of success is closely linked to persistence. Initiative is the driver that allows successful people to ask for the business. Initiative is what opens doors; it allows salespeople to make cold calls. To benefit from persistence, you must make the first effort, and that is where the attribute of initiative comes in. The beginning is indeed the most important part of any work. After all, if you don't begin, finishing something isn't even possible.

Children seem to be born with the skill of being able to ask for what they want, which is an important characteristic of taking initiative. They have no fear in asking for what they want and no fear in asking many times in many different ways. They don't seem to be influenced by social pressures and norms and just go ahead and do things. They don't wait for instructions and just decide for themselves what is important. This ability is somehow lost as we get older. For example, asking for the business is always mentioned in literally every sales book and sales seminar on the planet, and yet most of us don't follow this advice. Why are we hesitant about asking for what we want? We are humble by nature, so we prefer to hint at what we want.

This is partly a result of our socialization. The teenage years begin the transformation of adjusting behaviour due to peer pressure. Fitting in becomes more important than personal initiative as social skills are developed during this period. Being part of the group becomes a paramount driver for teens. Their interpretation of being unique means being different from parents but the same as friends. This trend continues through high school and university.

It's when we get into corporate life that the real damage is done by managers who want to sap the life right out of new hires. Following procedures and guidelines begin in our school system, are reinforced in business, and rob us of our youthful initiative and creativity. Company policies become mantras, and micromanagement the norm. No wonder we find so few in business with the kind of initiative that creates innovation and success. Managers spend far more time discovering what's wrong than they do discovering what's right with employee performance. The results in changing behaviour are obvious. We all become hesitant to take initiative for fear of being rejected or blamed. We hint at asking for the business rather than make powerful requests. We all have been subjected to this compliance training. The successful salesperson recognizes this and learns how to overcome the socialization to try new and exciting approaches outside the norm. They have the initiative to drive their own personal success rather than be a part of the compliant group and be held back by the status quo.

One of the finest examples in our generation of a man who has the initiative to drive his own personal success rather than be part of a compliant group is Steve Jobs of Apple.[3]

Steve Jobs started his career designing computer games for Atari. He and his friend Steve Wozniak created the first Apple computer in Jobs' garage when he was only twenty-one years of age. From there, they built the company into the mega company it is today. In 1980, Apple went public at a price of $22 per share, giving the company a market value of $1.2 billion.

Jobs was a radical leader and creative genius. His moves were fast and furious. He had initiative and drive. The company grew and prospered under his leadership. However, with the introduction of the Macintosh, the then president John Sculley felt Jobs was hurting the company with his unusual approach and persuaded the board of directors to strip Jobs of his power.

Sculley had tried to change the culture of the company with strict discipline, controlling costs, reducing overhead, and rationalizing product lines within an organization that had been previously undisciplined by nature. Sculley came to the conclusion that they "could run a lot better with Steve out of operations."

The man who had started the company was being ousted by the board of directors and relegated to a meaningless role. Jobs couldn't function like this, so in 1985, he resigned as chairman and went off to start the NeXT Computers company. In 1988, his company launched the NeXTSTEP operating system.

Under the bureaucratic leadership of Sculley, Apple soon began to lose its edge. Initiative was replaced with "followership" and company protocol. Sales declined, and the stock price suffered. This is one of the finest examples of taking a company built on wild and crazy ideas, innovative skunk works, and a corporate culture of initiative and encouraging mistakes to one of complete compliance to company policy and expense control. It was stunning how quickly the corporate culture changed under the micromanagement of Sculley and his team.[4]

It took a while, but Steve Jobs is now back at the helm of Apple, and the results are quite clear. Apple purchased NeXT and used OPENSTEP—a descendant of NeXTSTEP—as the basis for their current operating system, OS X. And Apple is once again at the forefront of innovation and initiative with the iPod, iTunes, and the iPhone.

Steve Jobs, a college dropout, was an unlikely candidate to have become the prototype of America's computer industry entrepreneurs. He is a perfectionist, an inspirational leader, and a visionary. He demonstrates the three attributes of all successful people: persistence, initiative, and assertiveness (PIA).

When it comes to pulling all three attributes together, Benjamin Franklin said it best: "Never leave till tomorrow what you can do today." The procrastinator never wins and never gets started. It seems getting started is a key to success that all of us should heed.

Assertiveness
"Never allow a person to tell you no who doesn't have the power to say yes." —Eleanor Roosevelt

Assertiveness is the final component of our PIA acronym. This particular trait is a favourite one for self-help books, psychotherapists, and personal development coaches. Assertiveness is really all about the individual. It is closely tied to self-confidence and self-esteem.

Hinting at the business is the approach used by salespeople who don't know the assertive technique. Their self-confidence might be at a low ebb and they might fear rejection, so it becomes easier to hint rather than ask. The self-confident individual makes a powerful request and doesn't fear rejection. Later in the book, we will go into much more detail about handling the word *no* and how a response of "no" can really be a tremendous opportunity to close a sale.

In communication, assertiveness is sometimes confused with aggression. The aggressive or pushy approach becomes too demanding and could result in resentment and rejection. It could even damage the relationship, causing you to be less influential and persuasive. Assertiveness is the ability to express yourself positively without violating the rights and sensitivities of others. It is direct, open, honest, and respectful.

Assertive people use phrases such as "I want to…" "Would you…?" or "I recommend…." These phrases are direct and to the point. Words spoken by a less assertive individual might include "if," "maybe," or "perhaps." The difference is clear. The assertive approach takes ownership of the conversation and makes powerful requests.

Acting assertively enhances self-esteem and gains the respect of others. It increases the likelihood of developing honest relationships and in turn increases the effectiveness of sales presentations. Assertive people have an aura of authority around them, which is one of our principles of influence we will discuss in more detail. When asking for the business, be assertive so people understand your request.

We were recently hired by a company to conduct a training session on asking for referrals from satisfied clients. We were surprised by the number of people demonstrating the passive approach. When asking for a referral, most of the participants would respond with, "If you have any family or friends who would be interested in my services, could you give them one of my business cards?" At first blush, this might seem okay, but the documented results of this approach were not meeting expectations and the company required a better payback from satisfied customers by getting additional referrals. The company asked us to do some further research and analyses on the approach used to gain referrals.

In future sessions on referrals, we decided to restate what we had just heard but inserted a pause in the sentence to help create some dramatic effect. We inserted a pause as follows: "If you have any family or friends (pause)...." The participants laughed immediately. The longer the pause, the more people understood the impact of what they were really saying to a client. Light bulbs popped on all over the room for these salespeople. They finally realized what they had been saying to clients. They might appear to be questioning whether their clients even had any family or friends. Now why would any salesperson question whether a satisfied client "had any friends or family"? We would look at one of the participants and say, "I doubt it very much if you have any family or friends, you look like an orphan and I can see why you would have no friends." They all laughed again but admitted to being unassertive. We back off a little and give the client an easy out because we are afraid. We are often afraid they will say no.

Referral success ratios increased immediately once the staff simply assumed the client had some family or friends and changed their referral request to reflect this new approach. This is what they said: "Here are five of my business cards. Will you pass them out to your family and friends who would be interested in our products?" It's so simple to shift the emphasis to getting referrals rather than using the word *if*. But we weren't finished yet.

The next important step was to find out what the salesperson really wants this happy client to do. They usually say "more business" or "hand out their cards" or "talk about them with their friends." Sometimes it takes ten minutes to get them to tell us what it is they really want, which is an introduction to a friend or family member. There is no better referral than when a satisfied customer actually brings in a friend and introduces them to you. The sale is virtually assured, and yet we never make this powerful request. We don't ask because we haven't fully developed the assertive quality in our sales presentations.

We will learn more about this assertiveness quality later in the book. We will discuss specific examples and tips on how to make powerful requests more comfortable for you and significantly increase the chances that your client will say yes. We are generally humble people and don't have the self-confidence to make these powerful requests. When you have completed this book, you will be amazed at how much more comfortable you will feel with the sales process. You will be much more effective at influencing others around you and be more in control of your life and your business.

A good analogy to put the three attributes of persistence, initiative, and assertiveness into perspective is the game of golf. Now, for those of you who enjoy golf, you will be familiar with the terms, challenges, and frustrations of the game. For those of you not familiar with the game, golf is a game that, like life, requires all three attributes and all three are demonstrated in most rounds of golf. The average golfer rarely breaks 100 on a decent golf course, so these three skills, or lack thereof, can be quite evident.

Persistence is an absolute must, given the fact that we rarely break 100 and shot after shot is simply not up to our expectations. We stand up to the tee and pull out the big driver with all the confidence in the world. We do a little wiggle before pounding the ball straight down the fairway—for about 100 yards until a funny thing happens: The ball seems to have a mind of its own as it suddenly veers off to the right and heads straight for the trees. We call this a slice. If persistence wasn't at play, the average golfer would call it quits after one round of eighteen holes. But, oh no, we continue to pound away at that little white ball and continue to drive it into the woods, into the water, or sometimes right into the ground, and it dribbles forty or fifty yards down the fairway, day after day all summer long. This game is loaded with rejection, and yet we come back for more and more. We pay for lessons to fix that slice; we think we can buy a better game, so we invest in the new golf technology with a larger sweet spot on the driver or the latest putter, but to no avail.

What keeps the golfer coming back again and again? It's persistence and that sweet taste of success when once every twenty shots or so we find the perfect backswing, the club face hits the ball in that tiny sweet spot, and we watch the smooth arc as the ball explodes from the ground and lands softly on the green. It's the chance for immediate gratification after a perfect shot and the feeling of success that feeds that persistence. If we could only hit the ball like that every time, we would master the game of golf. Needless to say, it rarely happens, but we persist in our quest for the perfect round of golf. This is persistence at its finest. Failure after failure, and yet there we are on Saturday again, out on the links, searching for that perfect shot that we know is there just waiting to appear.

It's not just persistence, it's also initiative at work here. We need that drive of initiative to get out of bed in the morning and pack up the car with clubs and shoes and head off to the course. We need initiative to take those lessons and we need initiative to search golf shops across the country for that perfect club fit and that huge sweet spot on the driver. Without initiative, all mediocre golfers would stay in bed and cut the grass Saturday morning.

Finally, assertiveness has perhaps the most powerful impact on a game of golf. Have you noticed that golfers speak forcefully to their clubs and to the ball and sometimes to the actual golf course itself? Watch professional golf. Even the fans get into this assertive approach as they forcefully instruct the ball to "get in the hole." We don't have any statistics on the merits of this approach to verbally encourage the ball into the hole by fans, but we do know it is widely used.

We suspect the ball responds better to the actual owner rather than a fan. We've often instructed our own balls to avoid the water and have even lied to them about it. We hate to admit it, but when water is nearby, we will tell the ball and sometimes the club that there's no water in sight. We believe this technique has merit.

The assertive approach of yelling at the ball in mid-flight— "*No! No!* Not the trees!"—has an effect of causing the ball to actually hit a tree and bounce back on the fairway. This is a clear indication that an assertive approach does work. Assertive body language also works, as a good golfer will twist in various gyrations to influence the mid-air flight of the ball. Apparently, the ball does have eyes in the back of its head, as most golfers use this technique. On the green, we will demand that the ball stop rolling if past the hole, and on occasion we will use the body language technique to assist with a break in the green to have the ball get even closer to the hole.

Golf is indeed a marvellous game and a perfect analogy for the three attributes of all successful people. If only we would apply these techniques in the same degree to our business and personal lives, where it would actually have an effect. We would all be amazed at the results and have a lot more fun at the same time. We personally intend to continue our PIA exercises on our golf game until finely honed and then unleash them on the world of business. Colonel Sanders will have nothing on us—or you—if we decide to develop these three attributes.

Self-Fulfilling Prophecy
"You get what you settle for." —*Thelma and Louise*

We have talked about getting what you ask for as a key indicator of success. The challenge for all of us is to discover what it is we really want. As the saying goes, "Be careful of what you wish for, you just might get it." If you don't know what you want, then you end up getting what you settle for.

"Self-fulfilling prophecy" is a term coined by Robert K. Merton in his book *Social Theory and Social Structure*. The concept is quite simple. Once a prediction is made, the prediction actually causes itself to become true. In other words, if a false prophetic statement is declared as the truth, the statement will influence people so that their actions ultimately fulfill the false prophecy. If we believe something, we have a tendency to create activities that will make that belief come true. Unfortunately, the self-fulfilling prophecy dictates that if we believe we will fail, then we will put into motion activities that will ensure failure.

It would appear that we prefer other people to behave as we expect them to behave and we will change reality until it conforms to our expectations. People meet our expectations not just because they want to but because we create the environment for them to meet those expectations. The interesting aspect of this is that we do it and don't even realize we are doing it. A key study on this philosophy was published in the book *Pygmalion in the Classroom.* Pygmalion is from Greek mythology—he was the sculptor who carved the statue of a beautiful woman and then fell in love with it. He believed so strongly that the statue could come to life that it finally did come to life.

Harvard professor Robert Rosenthal collected the results of over 300 studies showing the self-fulfilling prophecy in action.[5] In classroom experiments, a group of children were divided into two classes. One class was given a teacher who was told that the students were high achievers and should do well. The other teacher was told that her class was composed of underachievers who needed help.

At the beginning of the school year, there was no difference between the two groups of children in terms of ability. By the end of the school year, the class that was labelled "high achievers" was doing above-average work. The class that had been labelled as "underachievers" was doing below-average work.

In addition, the study revealed that children who made gains in the "high achiever" group were generally better liked by the teacher, but the children who made gains in the "underachiever" class were generally less liked by their teacher.

It can be said that people prefer those who live up to their expectations, and that people unconsciously create situations that encourage the expected behaviour. If the expectations are positive, people are encouraged to behave positively. If the expectations are negative, people are encouraged to behave negatively. This has huge ramifications in all aspects of our lives.

Think of this in terms of your own children and the expectations you have as a parent. Think of this in terms of your employees and the effect this might have on them. Finally, think of this in terms of the expectations or lack of expectations you place on yourself and how this can affect your performance. What you expect to come true is often what you make come true. We all know the pessimist at work who is always complaining and for good reason. Bad things always seem to happen to this person, or at least they perceive bad things. How much fun are they to work with every day? We also know the optimist at work who always sees the bright side of issues and opportunities. They are generally better performers and a lot more fun to be around.

It seems that even a name can invoke the self-fulfilling prophecy. It is common folklore that teachers believe boys named Mike are troublemakers, and sure enough, they can tell countless stories of boys named Mike who get into trouble. Is it because they are troublemakers or is it because the teacher believes a boy named Mike will get into trouble? This was an especially interesting question for Gary and his wife, Jan. They named their son "Michael" and did their best to ensure everyone called him "Michael" rather than "Mike." It didn't matter—he still got into trouble, and to this day, they aren't sure if it's because of his name or their parenting skills. The fact remains: we judge based on minimal knowledge and then create the environment to prove ourselves correct.

This self-fulfilling philosophy has been around since the dawn of time. The philosophy works in two ways. If you think you can, you will have a much better chance of being successful. "What we think, we become," said Buddha. But on the other hand, Henry Ford once said, "Whether you think you can or think you can't, you're right."

The Little Engine That Could by Watty Piper, published in 1930, is a classic children's story illustrating the self-fulfilling prophecy as its basic theme. Read it to your children; it really does teach valuable life lessons for young people. If you recall, a little train engine was relegated to moving train cars in the yard, as it was too small to handle the long haul routes. One day, a big train with many cars came into the yard and the engine was broken down. The train was full of animals and rides for little children. This train was to be in the neighbouring village the next day for a circus for all the children. The village was on the other side of the mountain range, and the old engine couldn't make it. The only available engine was the little yard engine. They begged him to take the train over the mountain into the village and not disappoint all the children. Well, the little engine had never done anything like this before and said, "No, I can't do it, it is too far and too high a climb for me. I am only a little engine and I can't do it." All the animals begged the little engine, and finally he said, "Okay, I will try and climb the mountain." So off they went. The little engine hits the incline and can feel the strain of the heavy load.

The animals can hear the sound of his engine working overtime, and it sounds like: "I think I can, I think I can, I think I can." He climbs up the incline and the sound gets louder: "I think I can, I think I can, I think I can."

With tremendous effort, the little engine reaches the top and starts downhill, and you can hear this sound: "I knew I could, I knew I could, I knew I could." The self-fulfilling prophecy is everywhere in children's literature. The little engine thought he could and it created the energy needed to accomplish the task. This is a powerful force in our lives and it all depends on how we choose to use it. "Yes I can or no I can't." The choice is yours. This story illustrates the power available to all of us if we just believe we can. We can accomplish amazing results through the power of positive thinking. The little engine was using self-talk to build confidence and the self-fulfilling prophecy came into play to allow him to complete the task. We can complete our tasks with the same approach to self-talk and allowing the self-fulfilling prophecy to work in our favour. Setting a goal works magic to produce results.

There is an interesting motivational story you can find all over the Internet on the power of the self-fulfilling prophecy:

There once was a bunch of tiny frogs who arranged a competition. The goal was to reach the top of a very high tower. A big crowd had gathered around the tower to see the race and cheer on the contestants.

The race began. No one in the crowd really believed that the tiny frogs would reach the top of the tower. The crowd was saying: "This way too difficult!" and "They will never make it to the top." The tiny frogs began collapsing. The crowd continued to yell, "It is too difficult! No one will make it!" More tiny frogs got tired and gave up.

But one tiny frog continued higher and higher. This one wouldn't give up! He was the only one who reached the top! All of the other tiny frogs naturally wanted to know how this one frog managed to do it. A contestant asked the tiny frog how he had found the strength to succeed and reach the goal.

It turned out that the winner was *deaf!*

The wisdom of this story is a life lesson for all of us. Never listen to other people's negative comments about your attitudes or dreams for success. They take your most powerful dream and wishes away from you—the ones you have in your heart.

Always think of the power words have. Everything you hear and read will affect your actions! *Be positive!* And above all, do not listen when people tell you that you cannot fulfill your dreams. Always think: "I can do this!"

The winning frog was not influenced by negative words from the spectators. He could not hear what others heard about the task being impossible. The negative vibes influenced the other frogs to give up on the task, but the winner listened to his own voice, which said, "Yes, I can." When we think we can, we do.

Postive Self-Talk

"No one can make you feel inferior without your consent."
—Eleanor Roosevelt.

The following is an interesting poem about life. This poem describes the self-fulfilling prophecy. You can if you think you can, and conversely, you will fail if you think you will. Your thoughts generate activities that support what your mind is saying.

"The Man Who Thinks He Can"

If you think you are beaten, you are;
If you think you dare not, you don't.
If you'd like to win, but think you can't,
It's almost a cinch you won't.
If you think you'll lose, you're lost,
For out in the world we find
Success begins with a fellow's will;
It's all in the state of mind.

If you think you're outclassed, you are;
You've got to think high to rise.
You've got to be sure of yourself before
You can ever win a prize.
Life's battles don't always go
To the stronger or faster man;
But soon or late the man who wins
Is the man who thinks he can.

—Walter D. Wintle

This poem should be a wake-up call for all of us who underestimate the power of thought. You can choose to be positive or negative. The positive thoughts will always win the sale and win the day. Unleash this power within you and you will reap the rewards.

We have all heard the childhood phrase "sticks and stones may break my bones, but words will never hurt me." The problem is that words do in fact hurt us if we let them. We choose to let the words of others or our own little voice in our head have an impact on our ability to function. This is why it is important to keep your positive self-talk louder and more meaningful than what others might say. We can choose not to be hurt by others words. Remember, no one can hurt your feelings without your consent. You decide; put yourself in control.

You can decide that your own voice in your head will take precedence over the voices of others, and you can use the self-fulfilling prophecy for positive results or you can choose to let the prophecy have a negative impact on your behaviour. What a powerful tool your mind can be in changing behaviour and changing results.

Positive self-talk is simply the ability to tell yourself that anything positive is possible. Take command of your own attitude and tell your self again and again that "if it's to be, it's up to me." Only you can decide what you can accomplish, and you must tell your self of this goal constantly. This will build confidence in your abilities, making anything possible.

The way you think can and does affect your entire life. This can be positive or it can be negative. You can go through life thinking the glass is either half empty or half full. If you are less successful than you think you should be, it is likely because you have limited your thinking and your thoughts. Are you putting your mind into a positive position through self-talk, or are you letting your self-talk create doubt? Do you expect to win more often than you expect to lose? It's your choice.

If you have been expecting to lose more than win, it is time for you to take command of your thoughts and choose the self-talk that will open opportunities, and today is the day to begin that process. Try saying this into a mirror at least four or five times every day: "Yes, I can." This will influence your thoughts and move them into a more positive perspective of yourself.

This exercise might be difficult and seem foolish at first, but don't let that stop you—be persistent. You can change your habits. Success won't happen on the first day, but if you practice and stick to the exercise, you will take charge of your thoughts, expect to win, and your chances of success will be greatly improved. Furthermore, you will feel a lot better about yourself, which is a beneficial side effect.

Give it a try. You have nothing to lose but so much to gain with a simple little exercise in self-affirmation. When negative vibes come your way, be ready to overcome them with your own powerful positive thoughts. When your own little voice speaks up about the impossibility of this task, just remember it is only trying to protect you from failure and embarrassment or from feeling uncomfortable. Don't let that little voice prevent you from accomplishing your dreams and fulfilling your desires. Take the initiative, be persistent, and be assertive with your self-talk. This is within reach for all of us if we want it and go for it.

Rhonda Byrne's *The Secret* is a recent smash best-selling book. In a nutshell, "The Secret" is the self-fulfilling prophecy. It states that whatever you want, you can have. If you want it bad enough and focus on it, then you will get it. The book indicates that "The Secret" has existed throughout the ages and was used by a number of exceptional men and women who have gone on to become known as some of the greatest people who ever lived. The book states that Plato, Leonardo da Vinci, Galileo Galilei, Napoleon Bonaparte, Abraham Lincoln, and Albert Einstein were among the many who knew and implemented "The Secret."

You can easily implement "The Secret" today. Write down a personal goal and put it on the fridge. Look at it every morning and evening and once before you go to bed. Do this every day for as long as it takes. You will be surprised how this simple objective over time will change your behaviour and you will slowly start to see results that will move you towards this goal.

Many self-help books use similar techniques that are actually quite effective. Napoleon Hill's *Think and Grow Rich* was written in 1937 and has sold more than 60 million copies worldwide. Hill presented what he called "the secret of achievement." He presented the idea of a "definite major purpose" as a challenge to his readers to make them ask of themselves "in what do [they] truly believe." According to Hill, 98% of people have no firm beliefs, putting true success firmly out of reach. Simply stated, most of us don't know what we want and we therefore have no chance of getting what we want. Hill believed that thoughts are things, and this allows success-oriented individuals to attract like-minded people in order to accomplish anything.

Several passages of Hill's clarify the similarity between *The Secret, Think and Grow Rich*, and the self-fulfilling prophecy:

"Whatever the mind of man can conceive and believe, it can achieve."

"Desire is the starting point of all achievement, not a hope, not a wish, but a keen pulsating desire which transcends everything."

"A goal is a dream with a deadline."

"What you think, so you will become."

Napoleon Hill was a firm believer in the power of the mind in attracting the right energy to achieve results. Thinking and believing will lead to commitment, and commitment leads to results. You can if you think you can.

Hill also believed that people who don't succeed have one specific trait in common. The failures always know the reasons for their failures and are quick to point out the reasons to anyone who will listen. They have excuses ready to explain their performance. Here is a short sample from the list of the fifty-five famous alibis detailed in Hill's book:

"If I had a good education...."

"If only I had time...."

"If I could live my life over again...."

"If I had been given a chance...."

"If I could just get a break...."

These examples are simply negative self-talk that will continue to hold the speaker back from success. Eliminate the "if," and all of a sudden possibilities appear. "If only I had time" becomes "I have the time." What a difference in motivation and focus when self-talk leads to possibilities rather than obstacles.

It all boils down to you and the way you think. It isn't really a secret, as all of us really know. It's in our hearts, but we simply don't hold onto it long enough for it to work its magic. The main reason companies establish goals and objectives is to create a vision so everyone knows the desired outcome. Personal goals work the same way. Many years ago, Peter Drucker introduced Management by Objectives (MBO) into the field of professional management. MBO teaches that establishing objectives results in the objectives being attained more often simply because they were stated. The psychology behind this tactic is the commitment and consistency principle. Once we make a commitment, we all want to act consistently with that commitment. We will explore how to be more influential using this principle later in the book.

Earl Nightingale said, "You become what you think about." How does this apply to the context of your own life? Take a moment to jot down some of the strengths that make you the unique individual you are and list three specific goals you have for yourself. If everything were possible, what would you be doing with your life? Ask your family these same questions. It's interesting to observe how people automatically go to the negative. They say things like, "Well, that won't happen, so what's the point?" or they will say that they simply don't know. We should all know! If you're reading this book, then you know, so write it down right now!

Gary: Five years ago, I wrote down the title of this book on a whiteboard in my office— *Life Is Sales*. I wasn't thinking about a book at that time, but I liked the philosophy and it kept me focused on how powerful influence techniques were in getting what I wanted. Five years later, I have a publisher and I have a book that I hope you are enjoying. I certainly enjoyed writing it, and my goal of delivering the philosophy of "Life Is Sales" to a large audience has come to fruition. I hope it doesn't take you five years to achieve your goal, but if it does, it will be well worth the wait.

Chapter 2
I Like You, You Like Me

All things being equal in the value proposition between competing products or services, people will always choose to buy from people they like. It is interesting to note that even when things are unequal in the value proposition, people will generally still choose to buy from people they like. This is certainly not new to the experienced salesperson, but the various techniques used in relation to the liking principle might be.

The liking principle is a powerful tool for influencing and persuading others to move in our chosen direction. We will look into the various aspects of why people like others and what activities we can engage in to get people to like us quickly. People enjoy being with people they like and prefer to deal with people they like.

Who Do You Like?

Who do you like better, Oprah Winfrey or Donald Trump? Both are celebrities, both are extremely influential, both are wealthy, and both have qualities we admire. We think it's fair to say that the majority of people would admit they like Oprah better. Why is it that most people would say they like Oprah better than Donald Trump, and what impact does this likeability factor have on Oprah's ability to influence the average person? If Oprah puts her seal of approval on a book, it is virtually guaranteed to be a best seller. We like and trust

Oprah. When she makes a recommendation, we believe her and believe the book is worth purchasing and reading. That is influence of a high level from someone we have never even met.

Why would so many people be influenced by what Oprah Winfrey likes and dislikes? A true test of her influence can be assessed in the 2008 presidential election. For the first time in her career, Oprah Winfrey has decided to openly support a presidential candidate. She is on the hustings with presidential candidate Barack Obama.

Donald Trump, on the other hand, is not as likeable because he appears too opinionated, and perhaps we believe he might have alterior motives in his recommendations. He remains interesting and we love to hear The Donald rant about issues; however, he might be perceived as self-serving, while Oprah is seen as serving a wide community.

Former president of the United States Bill Clinton is a classic example of the principle of liking overpowering facts, as it allowed him to remain in the presidency and continue to be influential even during an impeachment. If Bill Clinton were able to run for president again, many believe he would win based on the fact that people simply like him. Why would so many people set aside Clinton's many peccadilloes and continue to like him? What is it about him that seems to draw people in?

The likeability factor might be one of the most powerful tools of influence we have and yet we rarely use it to our advantage to help build relationships. Have a look at your friends. Why are they friends? You will find that you share certain similarities. You have common interests. There is a sense of co-operation between friends. We like people who work with us in a co-operative way. We also like people who like us back and tell us so.

We are more easily persuaded by those we like. Why would this be? Why wouldn't we simply rely on the facts of the situations we're in rather than be influenced by those who have managed to make us like them? It all goes back to our original statement about honesty. People trust those who they perceive as honest and therefore believe what they say. People we like are perceived as being more honest and trustworthy than those we don't know and certainly more than those we don't like. It's human nature, and this tactic is being used on all of us on a daily basis by marketing companies, salespeople, and virtually everyone who wishes to influence our behaviour.

Home Sales Parties

The Tupperware party is a classic example of using many of the influence principles in this book. Many companies have now implemented the home party approach, where the hostess invites friends to their home to showcase the products. These parties range from kitchenware all the way to sex toys and lingerie, but the basic idea is always the same.

The hostess is provided with a percentage of the revenues as a commission for making the sales. Sometimes the salesperson is the actual hostess but often a professional presenter arrives to showcase the wares. Either way, the same persuasive techniques are at play.

The real power in these transactions comes from the hostess. The guests are influenced to think they are buying from a friend and have an obligation to actually purchase something from their friend who has invited them into her home. If you have never been to one of these parties, we suggest you attend one and observe the techniques involved and how you feel as the requests for sales are being made. We guarantee you will feel a real obligation to make a purchase.

Consumer researchers have investigated the impact of home sales parties and have confirmed the effectiveness of this approach. The social bond created by inviting friends is twice as likely to determine product sales than are the features and benefits of the product itself. People are more influenced by their friendship and liking of the hostess than by the product. These companies know this and it is interesting to note that the guests know this as well. Gary's wife has decided that she won't attend anymore of these parties, as she invariably buys something she doesn't need because of the obligation to buy something. But when a friend calls to invite her to a party, she struggles with the obligation to attend. She is torn between wanting to please her friend and knowing she will be obliged to buy something. Pleasing the friend usually wins the day and she has Christmas gifts for the children for the next three years.

These companies know all about the psychology of liking and influence and it is a billion-dollar business every month.

Referrals

We all seem susceptible to the influence of people we know and like. The power of the referral to family and friends is well known in sales circles and is related to the power of liking. Charitable organizations now regularly recruit volunteers who live in the neighbourhood to be canvassed and give each volunteer a small number of homes to visit in their immediate neighbourhood. The assumption being that people will be more likely to contribute to someone they know rather than a stranger. It works! We do contribute more to those we know.

The referral of a friend is the mainstay of the insurance business and door-to-door sales. A salesperson's first objective is to sell you something. If they fail, their second objective becomes getting a referral by name. The more names they get, the more likely it will be that a sale will occur eventually. This is called a warm lead in the business, as you actually have a name and can refer to the person who gave you the name as a friend.

Gary: The approach is simple and is usually done as a demonstration in your home. Once a customer admits to liking the product, which is usually quite easy, as the demonstrations are very effective, the sale is virtually assured. Recently, a vacuum salesperson attended our home with one of these water-filter high-speed vacuums with a glass collector. The sales rep just vacuumed our stairs and the dirt visible in the glass receptacle was embarrassing. We couldn't believe our house was that dirty and we therefore had to admit we were impressed with the machine.

We had just purchased another vacuum, so we weren't about to buy a second one. There was no sale to be made at our home. What came next, however, was the key to door-to-door sales. The salesperson said, "Clearly you can see the advantages of this machine over your own; I am sure you have friends in the area who would appreciate a demonstration of the quality of this vacuum." We had to answer yes to the fact the machine did an amazing job and yes we had friends. Next, he asked for some names and we foolishly provided some without hesitation. We felt guilty because we didn't buy anything, so we had to give him something in return. The power of reciprocity, which we talk about later in this book, just worked on us.

Now when this salesperson goes to my friend's house, he is now armed with both my friend's name as well as my own name and will say to my friend that I had recommended the demonstration of this vacuum in his home. Who would say no to a request that comes from a close friend? This is what the company counts on and it works most of the time. The power of a referral from a friend cannot be overestimated.

In the banking business, using the power of referrals to garner new business has become a regular practice. The banking business is one of the most competitive industries. They all have basically the same products with basically the same pricing and are located on the same street corners. So how do they get new customers?

They ask for referrals from existing customers who are happy with the service. Their customer surveys even ask this question: How likely are you to refer a family member or friend to our bank? A rating of extremely likely is the only answer that they measure performance on. They know that if a friend or family member recommends a bank, that person will be more likely to open an account, apply for a mortgage, or make an investment than if the bank just calls that person up without a reference. The liking principle is a powerful tool that more and more sales professionals are using. We will discuss some of the best practices later in this chapter.

As an influential professional, both socially and at work, it is important for you to know the factors that cause people to like one another. Why do you like some people and not others? Why do you like some people almost right away and others take time to get you to like them? There has been significant research over the past twenty years on this very subject, and we will investigate how we can use this research in our everyday lives to become more influential and successful.

First Impressions

Let's take a closer look at some of the factors that influence our propensity to like someone immediately. This has been called the first impression or the moment of truth. First impressions have an enormous influence over our perceptions. As soon as we meet someone for the first time, we all have a tendency to draw a conclusion about that person and then we spend the rest of the conversation looking for things that reinforce what we thought about that individual in the first place. It is a natural occurrence and almost impossible to curtail. The first impression is therefore a critical element in whether a person will like us and whether we can influence them.

It's not just first impressions on people either, it's first impressions on every aspect of life that come into play. If you walk into a restroom in a restaurant and it's dirty, where does your mind go next? If they can't keep the bathroom clean, what does the kitchen look like? Now the food will taste a little off—that is if you even stay at the restaurant to order something.

Gary: As I was preparing to fly back from a presentation I had made in Arizona, I sat down in my seat and noticed a napkin stuck in the little pouch on the back of the seat in front of me. Being curious, I reached in and pulled it out. Well, much to my surprise, I discovered a small piece of pizza wrapped up in the napkin. You know, those little pizzas they sell on airlines for five dollars each now that they don't serve meals any longer. What do you think happened next in my impressionable mind?

I thought to myself, well if the airline can't even clean the inside of the plane, I wonder what the engine maintenance is like. Is the pilot experienced enough? Do they have enough fuel for the trip? Just as these thoughts were going through my mind, I heard a different noise coming out of the engine as the plane started to move. I looked out my window and could see the wing and engine and noticed that several of the bolts looked loose. I poked the passenger beside me and said, "Did you hear that noise? It seemed unusual to me."

He just looked over and said, "No, that's normal."

I looked out the window again and the noise even seemed louder. As I stared at the engine, I noticed that several bolts holding the engine on the wing seem to be moving. I poked the guy beside me again and said, "Look out the window, those bolts on the engine look loose."

He simply said, "Look, everything is fine, there is nothing wrong with this plane, and don't poke me anymore."

I was in a state of panic. I don't like to fly all that much in the first place, and now the engine was making strange noises, bolts were loose, and the wing even seemed to wobble.

The entire flight was horrible for me. I kept hearing unusual noises. Every time the seat-belt sign came on, I figured we were out of fuel and going down in a farmer's field somewhere. Even the seats felt lumpy. All this happened because my first impression was influenced by a napkin with a piece of pizza in it. I then looked for ways to justify my first impression that the airline was sloppy and I was creative in what I used to justify it. My first impression was that this airline was careless in the little things and therefore must be careless about the really important things too. It wasn't until the plane touched down on the airfield that I felt better. A bad flight was made much worse because of a missed piece of garbage. First impressions count.

Appearance: Do You Look Good?

Does a person's appearance have an impact on that moment of truth? It is generally acknowledged that good-looking people have an advantage in a social setting. It is also recognized that this advantage goes far beyond a mere social setting. We immediately draw conclusions about people based on their appearance. These conclusions occur immediately and inform our perceptions of them. Generally speaking, good-looking people are immediately assigned positive qualities such as honesty, intelligence, kindness, and talent. We immediately like these people and have a desire to be around them. We believe they have more fun, more money, and more exciting careers. Most of us would deny that we make this automatic judgment but might believe that others will. Research has shown that good-looking people do have an advantage in life and we give it to them unknowingly. It seems we try to please people we like and find attractive.

Do blondes really have more fun? In August 2007, *Psychology Today* magazine published an article by Alan S. Miller and Satoshi Kanazawa entitled "Ten Politically Incorrect Truths about Human Nature." Long before blondes were immortalized in movies, women were dying their hair blonde. As early as the fifteenth century, women were dying their hair blonde to be more appealing, and apparently it worked. Blonde hair evokes a sense of youth and vigour, making blondes appear more attractive. This first impression is one of likeability. We immediately like someone for their blonde hair. The number of blondes we see indicates this preference, as many of the blondes are not actually blonde at all. We as observers know this, but it doesn't change our immediate reaction to blonde hair. Check this out yourself. The next time you see two women walking away from you and one is blonde and the other a brunette, notice which one your eyes linger on a little longer. It's human nature, and we are ruled by this even though we might try to refute any preference for blondes or for good-looking people.

It would appear the effects of attractiveness are found in all aspects of life. Hollywood and TV might be the best example. Few actors make it big unless they are good-looking. Attractive people tend to get opportunities first, though talent sometimes shines through either way. Many actors both male and female are successful because they are attractive rather than their acting skills. Will Brad Pitt ever win an Oscar? Many women certainly like his appearance though. He is paid handsomely for looking good because his audiences want to see him.

The judicial system might be an even better example, as the outcome of trials is supposed to be based upon the evidence of each case as reviewed by an unbiased jury. In one study, researchers rated the attractiveness of seventy-four male defendants at the start of their criminal trials. Later, the researchers reviewed the court records for the decisions in these cases. They found that the handsome men received significantly lighter sentences and were actually twice as likely to avoid jail time altogether. The same study also revealed that fines were twice as high when the victim was better-looking than the defendant.[6]

The Halo Effect

The aspect of psychology based on appearance has been called the halo effect. Basically, it occurs when one positive attribute affects other people's perception of an individual. The good quality becomes so powerful that it overcomes all other attributes and the perception of that individual becomes much more positive. Many HR professionals know how this works when managers provide performance reviews. If the manager likes an employee, the review is always more positive than if the manager has a neutral feeling towards them. Through the halo effect, a good-looking person appears to be smarter, a more effective performer, and more knowledgeable. In the judicial system, the halo effect results in lighter fines and lighter sentences.

Resesarchers M. G. Efran and E. W. J. Patterson conducted a study of the Canadian federal election in 1976. They found a clear correlation between attractive candidates and votes. The attractive candidates received more than two and half times as many votes as unattractive candidates. Follow-up research demonstrated that voters did not realize this evidence of favouritism towards good-looking candidates. Of the Canadian voters surveyed, 73% denied demonstrating any favouritism based on appearance. Only 14% would admit that it might have been a possibility.

D. Mack and D. Rainey published an article in the *Journal of Social Behaviour and Personality* entitled "Female applicants' grooming and personnel selection." As most HR professionals and managers already know, good-looking people get jobs quicker and get better jobs. Mack and Rainey studied the grooming in hiring situations. In a simulated interview, the candidates with good grooming accounted for more favourable hiring decisions than did actual job qualifications. The interviewers, as in the election study above, claimed that appearance played a very small role in their decision-making process.

This might explain why good-looking women are featured in car ads and why trade shows always have good-looking people at their booths. It would appear that attractive women can persuade men more easily than unattractive women, and by the same token, ladies, it would appear that attractive men can persuade women more easily than unattractive men. The halo effect comes into play, and just because people are good-looking, we automatically attribute unassociated skills and traits to them and we automatically like them better too. If we like them better, we are more susceptible to being influenced by them. Turn it around: If you become more appealing in appearance, you will be liked quickly and enhance your ability to influence and persuade those around you. Below are the best practices to think about when preparing to meet clients for the first or second time. The objective is to make a positive first impression and enhance the opportunity to be liked immediately. You want your clients to find reinforcement for your strengths rather than looking for those weaknesses that we all have. We have both strengths and weakness—the challenge is to showcase our strengths in that all-important first twenty seconds of meeting a client.

Best Practices: Greeting

Consider implementing these best practices around the greeting phase of any interaction, be it business, social, or personal.

1. Comb that hair, dress up rather than down, put on a little makeup to enhance your natural beauty. You only get a single opportunity to make a good first impression.

2. Each of us is equipped with one of the best influence tools available. This tool significantly enhances that first impression immediately. It's your teeth. People like people with teeth. That's right; a smile is the first thing people will notice when they see you. Think of going into a bank, a store, or going to the checkout at the grocery store and the person there has no teeth visible. What is your impression of that individual? What are your impressions of that store and the management of the people and even the products they sell? Take a moment right now and look in a mirror and close your mouth without a hint of a smile. Take a good look. Now smile and show some of those lovely teeth. What a difference. People who smile are automatically more receptive, they are seen as open and welcoming, and even more trustworthy.

As someone wanting to be more influential, your simple ability to smile is an invaluable tool. Be observant in the marketplace and social settings—the people who smile tend to have more people around them.

3. Before meeting clients, look in the mirror—check the hair, the clothes, and smile a big smile with lots of teeth. This does two things: It allows you to check the teeth for any foreign material that might have been lodged there by mistake and it shows you how good a smile can be. You will notice that you feel better instantly.

4. Use self-talk to say a few positive words about yourself and to clarify what your objective will be for this meeting. Pump yourself up. Sales are full of rejection. Self-talk will rebuild your confidence so you look good and sound good.

5. Establish an objective that can be attained. Maybe it's as simple as getting another appointment. If you establish an objective of closing the sale on the first attempt, you will face rejection all day long. Focus on building the relationship first, and business will follow. People buy from those they know and like. This is your objective.

6.   Now for the actual greeting. Do all the usual pleasantries you read in any book or magazine, such as smile, make eye contact, have a firm handshake, but don't be aggressive. Don't use the Donald Trump technique of turning the handshake into a power struggle by moving your hand so that yours is on top. This is not about power at this stage of the meeting; we will discuss the power of authority later in the book.

7.   Many salespeople use the business card as a wrap-up device after the discussion or presentation. They might thank the client for their time and give them a business card. We suggest you consider handing out the business card when you first meet a client. Why is this so important? Well, what does the client do right away when you hand them your card? That's right, they look at it. It's human nature to do so with something new. You have spoken your name and the client has not only heard your name but has also looked at the business card and read your name. Two stimuli to help the client remember your name is far better than one. It assists with the liking component because now they know your name. This is a simple technique, but it's surprising how many professionals still don't appreciate the power of the card being presented first.

8.   The client's name is very important to them. We suggest you practice using their name twice in the first sixty seconds. Not five times—that makes it too obvious and appears manipulative. Twice to show respect and that a bonding is occurring. People respond well to their names. Besides, it also helps you remember names. There is nothing worse than building rapport with a new client only to forget their name.

9.   Scripting is an integral part of any sales success. You should be very comfortable with what you will say when greeting a client for the first time. If you go to a furniture store, the salesperson will almost always ask, "May I help you?" We as customers usually say, "No, thanks, I am just looking around today." We may well be look-

ing for something, but we prefer to do our looking without the pressure of a salesperson. The only time this changes is when we really do have a specific purchase in mind and we want to buy it and get out quickly. Consumers generally like to shop around and touch the merchandise.

Knowing this situation always occurs at retail stores, what could a salesperson say instead? This is what scripting is all about. You know the question and you know the usual response, but you really haven't worked out a good way to ask the question so that the client will want your help and advice. Being with the client is what closes sales, not waiting for the client to make up their own mind or, worse, go to a competitor to shop. The greeting at the entrance to a store is your moment of truth—your moment to make a positive first impression. The positive first impression will result in more sales and more referrals. We know looking good and smiling makes a difference—what you say makes a difference too.

Here are some examples being used in the market that might be of interest to you: "How may I help you today?" is much more effective than the closed-ended question "May I help you?" *How* is open-ended and requires an answer more than "yes" or "no." "Hello, my name is John—here is my card. I would be happy to show you around our showroom today." This usually gets a name from the client, which is an excellent first step.

"Hello, I'm John—here is my card. Let me show you some of our special features we have available this week." This approach is a little more forceful, but not pushy.

The key to this exercise is that you need to know how people respond to your current approach. If they don't stay with you, practice other approaches. Listen to others in your business and see what they do. Go to competitors and see how they handle the introduction. You can't really get great lines from a book; they must come from your heart to be believable, and you need to practice them until they come from the heart. People want to buy, so give them a chance to like you and they will buy from you.

10. Practice, practice, practice. Practice the greeting, be comfortable with the approach, and observe the reaction of your clients. If they smile, you are well on your way to building a relationship and a win/win sale. If not, keep practicing—persistence is another key to your success.

What's Your Name?

Students at the University of Western Ontario in London, Ontario, have developed a new dating strategy called "Hey, Ashley." Our friend Sandra Thompson of London has a son Chris, who recently told her he was going down to the local bar to play "Hey, Ashley." Sandra had never heard of this game before, so she asked what it was all about. It appears that young men looking to pick up girls at local bars have discovered one of the principles of influence and turned this scientific principle into a game to get dates.

The rules of the game are simple. A group of young men go to the bar and wait until a group of young girls come in or congregate in an area close by. One of the young men will yell, "Hey, Ashley!" in the direction of the girls. If one of the girls' names is Ashley, she will immediately turn in their direction with a quizzical look. Most of the time, Ashley will come over to the boys to see how they know her and a conversation ensues, telephone numbers are exchanged, drinks are purchased, and before long, the other girls join the boys and the game is won.

The boys are using the fact that people respond favourably to those who use their name. This game, while simple, is based on the psychological imperative that people respond when they hear their name. They immediately like the person who knows their name. The boys are using influence and persuasive techniques in a fun way to meet new people. According to Sandra, it works like a charm.

Now, why does this simple strategy work? First, the boys are playing the odds. They usually choose a name that was quite popular eighteen to twenty years ago for newborn babies so they have a higher likelihood that one of the girls will have it. Apparently,

Ashley is a popular name among students in the London area. It could just as easily be Jennifer or Sarah, but the boys increase their odds of success with a popular name, and it's the odds of success that they are interested in.

If by chance there is no girl in that group named Ashley, they have two choices. They could use another name to gain someone's attention or move about the room and locate another group of students. To maintain the integrity of the game, it appears the boys will stick with Ashley until they find one. Bets are placed on how many times they try the technique before success and also on the success of the strategy in getting Ashley and her friends to come over. No luck? Well, there is always another bar just down the street in every university town.

The power of a name suggests that one of the boys knows Ashley and that Ashley knows one of the boys. This leads to an immediate liking and recognition by Ashley and she is driven to come over and investigate further. This is all the opportunity the boys need. Once Ashley comes over, introductions are made and the ritual dance of liking begins in earnest. This creates the opportunity to meet someone and is much more effective than many icebreakers boys use to get girls to notice them. Girls are fully aware of the many feeble attempts boys try to win girls over in the bar scene.

Another interesting aspect of this game is that it is completely safe from rejection. Boys fear rejection by girls on a daily basis. They lose face; they lose prestige and self-confidence when a young girl says no. This technique overcomes the problem of asking and uses influence to get the target to approach. It's an ingenious strategy to increase the odds of getting dates, and it's apparently lots of fun as well. Thank you, Sandra, for sharing this delightful story about your son.

Similarity

People like people who are similar to them. Look at your personal friends, and sure enough, one of the reasons you like these friends is that they are similar to you in some way. It could be a similarity of opinions, personality traits, background, culture, hobbies, or even proximity.

Many studies have shown that we have a tendency to like those people who are like us, and we can therefore relate to them in a more positive way. People-watching is a marvellous pastime many of us engage in, and it is interesting to note that people at a party or business function will gravitate towards people who seem to be similar to them in some way. Men in business suits will be gathered together, while those in business casual will be ensconced in another corner. The artistic types will be gathered in another corner. We attend a lot of business functions that are basically a social event for networking, and circulating is part of the job of a networker. We often find that conversations are short and superficial until we find someone with a common interest, and all of sudden, we like them immediately. It might be fishing, children, job similarity, or shared cultural background. The words flow much easier now, as a bond has been created simply through the act of finding a similarity.

There are now experts at selecting jurors for trials, and part of their agenda is to choose jurors who share similarities with the accused. If jurors can empathize with the accused, they will be more likely to associate with that individual and even begin to like them. This is rooted in our subconsciousness, but it is powerfully persuasive in giving the accused a much better chance of being acquitted or at least receiving a reduced sentence.

An Unethical Sale

Gary: Unethical salespeople use this similarity technique to persuade you to purchase their products over others that might be more suitable. A perfect example happened to me at a local stereo retail franchise. The salespeople are on commission, but I knew this already and so was prepared for some hard-style selling approaches. I was looking for a DVD player/recorder for my home. Over the years, I had videotaped my children growing up and had a library of six VHS videotapes of our family from over the past twenty years. My objective was to purchase a DVD recorder so I could edit the VHS down from the unwieldy twelve hours to a more respectable four or five quality hours and also edit the video for our friends and supply them with a DVD of just their family over the years.

I am not gifted in the technology department and so was looking for an extremely simple machine to operate that would accommodate my needs. I don't like reading manuals, so the simpler, the better. I entered the store and was greeted by a nice young man named George, who immediately discovered my name was Gary, as I knew he would, and used it several times early in our conversation. I explained my needs and my requirement for a simple device. Well, he had just the machine for me, and it was on sale. He proceeded to explain to me that his father had purchased one of these exact same units two months ago and had transferred all his VHS family movies onto DVD and it was a piece of cake for him. The unit had a hard drive so you could download the VHS and make it very simple to edit and burn a new DVD with just the material you wanted. He showed how easy it was to operate notwithstanding the fact the converter had about twenty-four different buttons on it. The player would also tape TV shows and movies and easily transfer them to DVD.

This salesman was using the similarity principle on me very effectively. He had a father who had the same challenge as me. The father bought the unit and loved it, making me feel more comfortable in purchasing the unit. I liked this young man and I believed him because he had personal experience with this same DVD recorder. Needless to say, I bought the DVD recorder.

When I got it home, I noticed that the manual was 100 pages long and so I set that aside. I set it all up and plugged it all into where it was supposed to go. I tried a DVD and could actually watch it on the TV. Well, that worked fine. I tried to tape a TV show, but to no avail. Apparently, it was more complicated to hook up the cable than what I was told. I then plugged the VHS unit into the player and could see the VHS on my TV but was totally incapable of recording it onto the hard drive. It was then that I pulled out the manual and attempted to learn how to use it—to no avail.

I still have the DVD recorder and use it to watch DVDs. I have never been able to tape a TV show or edit my VHS tapes. I later discovered that this unit was on sale because it was discontinued by the manufacturer due to an overly complicated process to operate it. I finally took my VHS tapes to a professional and simply had them copied in their entirety onto a series of DVDs. I will find a way to properly edit the material one day.

This salesperson used the principles of liking and similarity to persuade me to purchase this particular unit. I can only surmise that the commission on this unit was significantly higher given the fact the DVD recorder was discontinued and they wanted to clear the shelves. I was duped by an unscrupulous salesperson using similarity as a tool to gain my confidence, and it worked. The power of similarity is best used when it is legitimate.

Both the salesperson and the store have received bad reviews from me for over a year now. A quick sale rather than a win/win relationship resulted in some bad word-of-mouth advertising. I will never buy from this store again and all my friends have been warned as well. What is the value of one quick sale compared to all the future business I would provide? This approach is quite short sighted, yet it remains common in the field of sales. The legitimate use of similarity will build better long-term bonds, and the clients will like the company and salesperson better and provide positive word-of-mouth advertising. Why do some choose the short-term win?

Finding similarities is also considered building rapport, the exercise of finding that common ground and discovering those similarities. It makes sense that we trust a person we like. I liked the young salesman and I trusted his advice.

Look at cliques in high school. Each clique has a similar dress code. There are preppies who don't associate with the rappers, who don't associate with the athletes, who don't associate with the skateboarders. These groups are easily identifiable by their clothes. It is rare to see boys with the crotch of their pants down to their knees mixing with the girls all dressed in black with black dyed hair, black lipstick, black finger nails, and black stockings. Each is making a statement about who they are, and they associate with people who are similar to them.

> Liking is an important influence tool, and similarity enhances liking. If we want to be more persuasive, we need to find the similarities that exist between people.

Best Practices: Similarity

1. Ask new contacts open-ended questions to learn as much as you can when building rapport with them. Finding a real similarity will significantly enhance the relationship almost immediately.

2. When visiting clients, try to match the clients in dress as much as possible. If customers wear a suit, it is advisable to wear a suit as well. It is always better to be a little overdressed than underdressed.

3. Look around the environment for clues that might lead you to guess an interest. If you see four bowling trophies on the credenza, odds are this person is a good bowler. So what do you say? Some would comment on the trophies and ask about bowling. This shows interest but not similarity. It might be more effective to forego mentioning the trophies and instead mention that you yourself are planning on taking the family bowling. The response from the client will be immediate and positive. Now this does work best if it's the truth, but a little exaggeration doesn't hurt. An outright lie, of course, kills the relationship.

4. Find out where the client lives or went to school and find a similarity there. "My spouse attended that university back in the early eighties." A new bond is created.

5. Have you had people say, "Oh, you worked for XY company, do you know George from Toledo?" Many people use it to try and find a similarity in people they know. It often works, espe-

cially when they discover they do know the same people. A long conversation ensues, and the friendship and liking start to build.

6. Meet over lunch. People are always more receptive to influence over lunch than elsewhere. It's hard not to chat amiably and share personal information over lunch. An astute observer will look for similarities with which to build the relationship.

7. In his book *How to Win Friends and Influence People,* Dale Carnegie says that by becoming interested in other people, you will get them to like you faster than if you spent all day trying to get them interested in you.

8. Find a similarity at all costs. This is a critical stage in the selling process and winning the relationship.

9. Target clients who are more like you either culturally or ethnically and you will have more immediate success.

I Like You

When someone says they like you, you will find it almost impossible not to like that person in return. Think back to grade school or junior high when boys and girls first started getting interested in each other. The boys were shy to make the first move in fear of being rejected, and the girls were shy for fear of not being pursued. Can you remember when one of your friends would come over to you and whisper, "You know Johnny really likes you a lot"? You would glance over at Johnny, and all of a sudden, he got a lot better looking and a little taller. You couldn't help yourself—you started to see nice qualities about him and you started to like him better. In fact, you started to put into play your own strategies to get closer to Johnny, and so the wooing would begin. This approach is used quite successfully by preteens and it maintains its power over us from then on. It still works on all of us no matter our age. Had we all known this secret as youths, we would have been much more successful with relationships.

Why does this simple little technique work? Why would someone you already know become more attractive simply because you are told they like you? A young person is easily influenced by a few words to appreciate another person more than they did mere minutes before. Can influence and persuasion be this simple? It would appear that in the realm of liking, telling someone you like them affects their feelings toward you immediately.

Researcher Aronson E. Wilson tested this theory by pairing college students together.[7] One group of paired students was told their partners liked them, and the other group of pairs was told that their partners didn't like them. The "liked" group was much friendlier with each other, argued less, and co-operated more than the groups who were told their partners disliked them. It seems obvious that we would work better with someone who likes us. If this is the case, why wouldn't we all simply tell those we work with that we like them? It is a mystery, as the evidence is quite clear: People are more influenced by those who like them and who tell them that they like them.

Gary: A number of years ago, I was flying back from a conference, and I was sitting on the plane with an older rather distinguished-looking gentleman. I was busy reading a magazine and so didn't socialize with this man that much other than a perfunctory hello and a comment on how the seats weren't all that comfortable. I wasn't looking to influence at that stage of the flight.

As I was reading my magazine, I noticed an article on the ability to read foreheads. Well, this intrigued me, so I read it. When I was finished, I turned to the man beside me and said, "Listen to this, this magazine says people can read foreheads." The look on his face indicated that he thought I was one of those people into parapsychology and other off-the-wall philosophies.

Undeterred by the look, I proceeded to read part of the article. I said, "It says here that written on everyone's forehead are the words *I want to feel important*. What do you make of that?"

His face again registered incredulity, and he said, "There is no way that those words are written on everyone's forehead. Where are you getting your information?"

"The information was coming from a well-regarded publication on psychology, and it was well-researched. Here, have a look yourself," I said.

He took the magazine and glanced at the article, and then said, "Sorry, but this is completely incorrect."

"What makes you so sure? This is a very credible magazine with international circulation."

"Listen, I am a double Ph.D. and I can tell you that the words *I want to feel important* are not on everyone's forehead."

I was a little taken aback by his credentials, so I said, "So, Doctor, Doctor, what do you think this is all about then?"

"The words on the forehead are not *I want to feel important*, they are *I need to feel important*. It is a basic human need to be appreciated, and as we get older, especially with men, the letters get larger and easier to read as the forehead expands."

What this really means is we are all searching for validation. We do *need* to feel important; we need to feel we are making a contribution; we need to be appreciated. We also like people who appreciate us and tell us so. This is why a compliment is such a powerful tool in building a liking relationship.

Compliments

Keep in mind that people buy from people they like, are influenced by people they like, trust people they like, and that compliments get people to like you quickly. Most of us are suckers for flattery. The message is written on everyone's forehead. Have a look in the mirror, and sure enough, there it is: *I* need *to feel important*. Anyone wishing to be influential should look at everyone's forehead and pay attention to those words. They are telling you how best to influence people.

Are compliments more effective if they are the truth? Apparently, it doesn't matter much, unless they are so over the top that you feel manipulated; otherwise, any reasonable compliment, whether it's true or not, is quite effective.

The *Journal of Experimental Social Psychology* published an article by D. Drachman, A. DeCarufel, and C. A. Inkso called "The extra credit effect in interpersonal attraction." The article outlines their experiment that indicates the effects of praise on men in North Carolina. The men were given comments about themselves from another person who needed a favour. Some of the men received only negative comments, and others received only positive comments, while the rest received both positive and negative comments.

The results were quite interesting from an influence perspective. The individual who provided only positive comments and praise was liked the best by the participants, even when the men knew that the person providing the praise had something to gain from their liking him. It didn't matter; they liked him anyway. The positive praise didn't even have to be true to be effective in getting the men to like the person providing the praise. The positive comments produced just as much liking from the praise when they were untrue as when they were true.

How do we explain this interesting aspect of human behaviour?

Even when we know a compliment is false, we still like the person who provided the praise and are much more susceptible to be influenced by that individual. It goes back to what's written on our foreheads. We all *need* to feel important, and receiving praise, whether true or false, seems to satisfy that need.

Generally speaking, most of us feel that we are above average. Various studies have been conducted using secret ballots in groups that ask this simple question: Are you above average or are you below average compared to the people in this room? The studies discovered that over 95% of people believe they are above average, which is curious because it is statistically impossible. It does show, however, that false compliments could be just as effective as true ones. Many of us have a bit higher opinion of ourselves than reality might dictate. That is good for self-esteem and good for the influencial professional.

A compliment on someone's clothing is always safe—since they are wearing the outfit, they must like it. It doesn't matter if you like it as much as they do. A compliment on the lovely new shirt, blouse, or suit is quite appropriate and will enhance that individual's perception of you almost immediately. If you visit a client at their home, feel free to compliment the house, the yard, the children, even the dog because they like these things and will believe compliments about them.

You will get people you don't know well to like you faster if you provide a compliment early in the conversation. If you already know them well, the relationship will grow further if you provide compliments. The old saying "If you have nothing nice to say, don't say anything at all" should be replaced with "If you have nothing nice to say, find something nice to say."

Men and Women

Marriage is an interesting social practice that provides significant data on how people get along. Current statistics indicate that 50% of all marriages will end in divorce. That is a scary statistic for those young people who are madly in love and looking forward to a blissful romantic life together for the long term. What happens to these young lovers after marriage?

On June 25, 2007, the *Men's Health* blog *The Mysteries of the Sexes Explained* by David Zinczenko stated that 70% of men wish they received more regular compliments from their partner. It was always felt that men needed to compliment their partners more often, but it would appear men need a little cuddle time too. Some of the suggestions for compliments might surprise you.

"Your arms are definitely looking bigger." Men like to look good too. It seems 90% of men have at least one body part they would like to improve, and noticing an improvement is quite important to guys.

"Ha ha ha ha ha ha." Men think they are funny. In high school and at work, men have always tried to make people laugh. A good, hearty, gut-level laugh is about as flattering as it gets because men really do value their sense of humour.

"Wow." It doesn't matter where it comes from, but this short little word has awesome power and it is best used in a whisper. This could be the ultimate ego booster for a man.

So, ladies, these are just a few short suggestions on how a compliment can affect your persuasive powers on the homefront. Use these sparingly but wisely.

Communication

A lack of communication is often considered the number one culprit in marriage breakdowns, but there is another component that has received very little study: the words *I love you*. This is the most powerful likeability tool in our vocabulary. On a recent talk radio program, they were discussing the merits of couples telling that they loved one another. The host was of the opinion that actions speak louder than words—that the words were ineffective in maintaining the relationship, but actions ruled the day. Many listeners disagreed with this approach and for good reason. In management circles, actions do speak louder than words because employees watch the bosses' actions for clues on how to behave and clues on what is really going on. Words are just speeches in many instances, so people rely on observation to confirm their assumptions. This works because employees don't live with their bosses, they only work for them and don't generally converse on a daily basis with the executives of a company.

Marriage is different. We live together, we eat together, we holiday together, and we even sleep together. We believe that in every marriage, there is doubt about the love the other holds for their partner. We sometimes forget that our partner is in fact in love, and we need positive reinforcement on a daily basis on this particular matter. It is simply not enough to show your partner you love them— you must verbalize this. It seems that men in particular have a difficult time understanding this simple aspect of marriage. If you do love your partner, why wouldn't you want to tell them and tell them often? They love to hear it and they actually love you more when you tell them. It's the liking compliment system at work in your own home.

Reciprocal Liking

Reciprocal liking is described in psychological terms as an effect whereby a person who is liked by another person will have a tendency to return that liking. We have described this aspect of human behaviour earlier in this chapter. The reason why this works is simple: People enjoy being in the company of people who make them feel good. We all like to be with people whose company we enjoy. It is interesting that we seem to enjoy their company more if they like us and say so.

B. F. Skinner was the researcher who studied and documented reinforcement and its impact on behaviour. Animals are trained with food by using this method of reinforcing positive or desired behaviour. In humans, our needs are a little more sophisticated, but the basic principle applies. People will repeat behaviour if it is positively recognized and rewarded. A manager who thanks an employee for being creative and showing initiative will be more likely to see that employee repeat that behaviour in the future. A compliment after an action will cause that action to be repeated more often than if it's not reinforced. This is an oversimplification of Skinner's work, but the basic principle of behaviourism is that behaviour can be modified using reinforcement. Reciprocal liking falls into this category. This is a powerful tool for anyone wishing to build strong relationships and should not be overlooked while planning sales strategies. It can be used to influence family or friends or fellow employees on a work team. People like people who like them first.

Exposure Effect

The more you see a client, the more likely you are to gain their business. Mortgage brokers or lenders attempting to gain business from realtors are well aware of this exposure effect. This effect is well known to advertisers as well. The more familiar we are with a product or brand, the more we express a liking for it. The term *exposure principle* is used to characterize this phenomenon.

The more we see someone, the more we tend to like them. This kind of exposure is compounded by the propinquity effect, where there is a tendency for people to form friendships with those whom they encounter frequently. It would appear that familiarity breeds liking rather than contempt. Things we are exposed to start to grow on us and we develop a taste for them. When we make choices, we usually choose the familiar. "Better the devil you know than the devil you don't know" has been a hiring credo among HR professionals for years.

If you ride the subway, you can appreciate the propinquity effect. Those commuters who travel long distances on the train usually try to sit in the same seat every day, and over time, they become aware of others on the train who are doing exactly the same thing. Before long, a bond and friendship might grow amongst these commuters, as they usually board the train at the same station at the same time every day.

Researchers L. Festinger, S. Schachter, and K. Back followed friendships in a small apartment building and published their findings in an article entitled "The Spatial Ecology of Group Formation." They discovered that neighbours on the same floor were most likely to be friends, and those on other floors were least likely to be their friends. The exceptions were those in apartments near the staircase and mailboxes, as they had friends on both floors.

We talked about divorce earlier, and it is interesting that many divorces are the result of one of the partners falling in love with their partner's best friend. Why does this happen? Well, the exposure effect says we like those who we see often and it would appear we *really* like those who we see really often. A word to the wise for those in marital trouble: Beware of the best friend because that's where they might turn to for solace, and the more they see each other...well, you know the rest.

We have friends who have talked about this a great deal in the past few years, as we observed some of our friends going through divorce. It was interesting to note that many of the extramarital relationships were with the spouse's best friend. We have no scientific data on this unusual effect, just anecdotal evidence. But we can guess that what is behind this occurrence is based on the exposure effect. Best friends obviously see a lot of each other, and the more they see each other, the more they like each other. Similarities come to the surface on a regular basis, and if the marriage is facing some difficulty, which many do, then a spouse's best friend begins to look better and better.

Gentle and innocent flirting is the first stage, as both feel out the other's level of liking. The flirting itself is a powerful message that reinforces the level of liking. Soon, secrets are shared and a confession of marital discord results in an even closer bonding. In many cases, this leads to the next inevitable level of liking: intimacy. Suddenly, all the rules have changed. Excitement, risk, and passion reinforce the level of intimacy, and the current partner just can't compete with the excitement provided by the new partner. This is a sad story, but with marriage breakdown pushing 50%, it is easy to see how this could happen to all of us.

It all starts with liking and the exposure effect. We are all susceptible to these influences. We can be masters or targets of these techniques; it all depends on your knowledge of their impact on people and how you wish to implement certain strategies in your life and business.

The message for anyone in sales should be clear: If you want more business, be in your clients face more often. Cement those relationships with exposure, and when the time comes for a referral or a sale, they will want to deal with you. Maintain close contact with your key suppliers of business and your best clients. If you make them your friends, you will prosper.

Law of Attraction

The more we have similar attitudes to other people the more we are attracted to them. Opposites don't often attract, but birds of a feather do flock together. This is why we are all trying to find a similar attitude or similar interest during the rapport building section of the introduction. When we do, the liking begins and you have moved closer to becoming much more persuasive. People say yes to those they know and to those they like. Like-minded people do attract each other.

Cooperation

We all like people who cooperate with us. Teams produce better results when they cooperate. Cooperation is simply the practice of a group of individuals working together to reach a common goal instead of working independently in a competitive environment. The success of the objective is attained through the success of all the individuals. Generally speaking, people will say yes to a request from those with whom they are cooperating.

Gary: A few years ago, I received a sizable cheque from a business associate I had loaned money to. The loan was repaid and he gave me a personal cheque for $42,000. I took the cheque and went to my local bank branch to deposit it. I had been a customer of this bank branch for twelve years and liked the staff and the service. The branch was close to my home, so it was easy for me to do my personal banking there. They had great hours, which I found convenient, given my schedule at work. They were even open on Saturday.

I took my cheque to the bank one morning and stood dutifully in line while the tellers at the wickets handled the various customers in front of me. One of the tellers beckoned me to come over and said, "Good morning, how may I help you today?"

She wore a name tag that read "Julie," so I said, "Good morning, Julie, I have a cheque to deposit into my account today."

I used the name technique to enhance the liking aspect between Julie and I. It seemed to work, as a big smile came across her face and she said, "I would be happy to take care of that here for you, please swipe your access card."

I swiped the card and entered my PIN, and all of my personal banking information popped up on her computer screen. She could now see my name and all the business I had with the bank and that branch. She said, "Okay, Mr. Ford, what account would you like to deposit your cheque into?"

I signed the back of the cheque and wrote my account number on it as well. I handed it to her and told her the account number. She took my cheque and typed in the account number and then turned the cheque over. As soon as she saw the amount, a cloud seemed to have passed over her face, as her smile disappeared and was replaced with a frown of concern. Wrinkles appeared in her forehead as she studied the cheque. I wasn't sure what was happening, but I knew that it wasn't good.

I said, "Anything wrong? I just want to deposit the entire amount into my account."

"Excuse me for a moment I will have to see my supervisor," she replied.

With that, she walked away from her workstation and went over to another woman in the branch sitting at a desk. She handed my cheque to the woman and seemed to whisper something to her. The supervisor took the cheque and looked at, turned it over once or twice, and then glanced up at me with that same furrowed brow I had just seen on Julie. She looked back down at the cheque and again glanced in my direction.

This looked like trouble, and I was wondering what was going on. I had never had a cheque referred to another person in the branch in my twelve years with that bank. I had always been served in the finest fashion. I was starting to get a little nervous. Had something happened to my account? Had someone stolen money from it? Had I inadvertently bounced a cheque? Did they think I was a crook? All these thoughts ripped through my mind in a matter of seconds.

The supervisor took one more look at me and then appeared to sign the cheque herself. I assumed this was some type of approval process—now that she signed the cheque, all would be resolved and I could go about my business.

Julie came back to her station with a look of concern on her face; I knew then that this wasn't over. Something was wrong with the cheque or with me or with the bank and I was getting a little agitated by now, as I didn't have a lot of time to waste.

Julie returned and said, "I'm sorry, Mr. Ford, but we will have to put a ten-day hold on your cheque until it clears the bank."

"What do you mean a ten-day hold?" I said.

"We will deposit your cheque today into your account, but we will be holding the funds for ten days to ensure the funds clear and this cheque is paid."

"Are you insinuating that this cheque is not good and that I am not good for the money?"

"No, Mr. Ford, not at all, it is our company policy to hold all large personal cheques for ten days."

"But what if I need that money right away? Are you saying I can't get at my own money in your bank? I have been with this bank for twelve years and have been a good customer and have substantial investments here."

"I'm sorry, Mr. Ford, but that is our company policy."

"Well, this is ridiculous. I can't believe I can't access my own money because of one of your stupid company policies. Just deposit the cheque and I will move it out today."

"I'm sorry, Mr. Ford, but you won't be able to access the money for ten days."

Well, I was getting angry now. I have never responded well to anyone citing company policy as a reason for lack of service. I had been at this bank for twelve years, and most of the staff knew who I was, and yet they wouldn't let me have my own money. This seemed unacceptable to me.

I then said, "Listen, I have been here for twelve years and most of the staff know me, so what's the problem with depositing my cheque? It's a good cheque; you don't have to worry about that. It is a repayment for a loan I made to a friend."

It didn't seem to matter, as she looked at me with a sober face and shook her head back and forth and pursed her lips in a sign of resolution.

Well, this was the last straw for me. "Okay, give me back my cheque and close out my account and give me a draft for the balance. I can't deal at a bank that doesn't trust me. I trust you to look after my money, but you don't trust me. I would like my balance right now please."

Julie handed me back the cheque and proceeded to close my account and prepare a draft for the balance. She handed me the draft, and I stormed out of the branch feeling indignant.

As I slipped behind the wheel of my car, I calmed down a bit and realized what had just happened. Here I was in my car with two cheques now, not just one, and no bank account anymore. How could this have happened? All I really wanted to do was deposit the cheque and purchase a thirty-day certificate of deposit with the $42,000 cheque until I decided what to do with the money, and now I was sitting in my car with two uncashed cheques and no bank account.

I reviewed what had just happened in my mind and suddenly realized that I had failed miserably in influencing Julie to do what I wanted, and she had failed miserably in influencing me to do what she wanted. We really had the same objective. She wanted me to deposit the cheque and keep my accounts open. I too wanted to deposit the cheque and keep my accounts open.

I didn't use my own techniques of influence that were available. I didn't notice the opportunity to use cooperation to get what I wanted, and Julie didn't use the principle of cooperation to get what she wanted.

As I looked back on the situation, I asked myself what should have happened. If Julie had asked when I needed the money, I would have said I wanted to buy a CD from the bank and the hold-fund situation would not have been an issue. We could have cooperated on how to handle the ten-day delay in gaining access to the money. I didn't even need the money for at least thirty days. On the other hand, I could have asked what alternatives were available for this money so it can earn interest right away. If I didn't need the money for at least thirty days, she could have informed me of the various investment options.

An even better solution would have been for Julie to take the initiative to suggest I see a financial planner to discuss investment opportunities for this deposit. I would have felt more important and would have resolved our issues to the benefit of both. A win/win situation. The challenge was for Julie to get over the company policy issue and for me to get over my ego about the fact this is my money and I have a solid reputation at that branch.

This is how easy it can be to turn a simple situation into an ugly one when we don't think of how to cooperate and instead think of how to protect ourselves. Cooperation is a powerful tool for getting what you want. Once cooperation begins, it feeds upon itself and both parties work hard toward a resolution. If cooperation is not part of the conversation, as in my banking experience, a satisfactory resolution might never be attained. We had created a lose/lose situation, and at the time, I was the bigger loser. Two cheques and no bank account, and now I had to go through all the trouble of starting over at a new bank or swallowing my pride and going back into the branch and apologizing for not working cooperatively with Julie to solve a simple problem.

I swallowed my pride and went back into the branch, apologized to Julie, and explained what I wanted all along. She too apologized for not asking further questions about the deposit, and together we laughed at our own foolishness and I proceeded to explain to both of us the power of cooperation. I now have my old account number back, the cheque was invested for thirty days, and I am still banking at that same branch. Julie was promoted to supervisor, and we still share a knowing smile about this incident when I go into my branch.

This is a simple little story about how cooperation can get what you want. At first, I didn't use this skill, but I should have known better.

Who Do You Like?

In the realm of influence and persuasion, is it more important for you to like your client or that your client like you? Take a moment to think this question over. Write your answer down on a piece of paper. It does have ramifications in how we decide to proceed with the liking principle when we want to be influential and persuasive.

We have presented this question to thousands of salespeople over the years and the usual response is that it is better if the client likes you. They reason that if the client likes you, they will want to deal with you. At first blush, it might appear that a client liking you will give you a better chance to be influential. After all, since they like you, they therefore want to please you.

A small percentage of the people will think about the question a little deeper and present the option that it is better if the client knows you like them. What is the difference here really?

If a customer likes you, it doesn't naturally follow that you like them as much. However, if the client feels you like them, it suggests a deeper bond has been created and the friendship will mean that you will take care of them. You will provide meaningful advice and not steer them wrong. They trust you to protect them and cover their backside. It is therefore better for the influence practitioner to genuinely like their customers and tell them so. This creates a much stronger bond than if they simply like you.

Joe Girard, one of the most famous car salesmen of all time, is recognized in *Guinness World Records* as the "World's Greatest Salesman." For twelve years straight, he won the title as the number one salesman. He was selling Chevrolets and sold on average six automobiles a day.

How could he be so consistent for so long? He had two simple rules: 1) offer the car at a fair price, and 2) let them buy from someone they liked. "And that's it," he is quoted as saying, "finding the salesman they like, plus the price. Put them together, and you get a deal."

What was Joe's secret to liking? He simply told people he liked them. After a client purchased a car, Joe would add that name to his database, and every month that client would receive a card in the mail that had a simple message. That message was "I like you." It soon became a family tradition to buy a car from Joe. Family members all bought cars from Joe. They liked and trusted him. They felt that he liked them and they therefore were going to get a good deal at a fair price. Liking influenced the honesty and integrity components. In car sales, this is quite an edge to have over your competition. The loyalty to Joe was legendary, and it all started with his two simple rules.

Notice that Joe is not offering the car at the best price but a fair price. Remember, all things being equal, people will buy from those they like. It's also true that all things being unequal, people will still buy from those they like. Joe Girard knew this and believed this and became the number one salesman in the world.

You now know this as well, and it's up to you to decide what to do with this knowledge. Take the "I like you" principle along with the other principles in this book and success will find you.

Chapter 3
Reciprocity: It's Better to Give Than to Receive

Connie: The day after we moved into our country home, a neighbour knocked on our door. Kathy refused to step into the disarray. From the porch, she welcomed us to the area and insisted we come over to her house for coffee when we were ready to take a break. We accepted her invitation and enjoyed our first visit with our new neighbours. Kathy and Gord told stories about the masons who put up our beautiful stonework, about the eighteen foot snowdrifts, mice, and houseflies. By the end of our visit, the differences between country and suburban living were growing apparent. We were most appreciative of their hospitality and their lessons in country living. As we turned to leave, I was compelled to reciprocate, as though some spirit moved into my body and took over my mouth. There was absolutely no choice in the matter; it just spilled from my lips: "Will you come over to our house next?" The need to repay Kathy and Gord for their kindness was overpowering me.

That need to repay weighed heavily until we were finally ready to have Gord and Kathy to our home for a visit. Why did I feel so compelled to repay an invitation to an almost complete stranger? Have you ever found yourself in a similar position? Maybe it was the time you arrived at the entrance of a department store at the same time as another shopper. The shopper opened the door and gestured for you to go in. You smiled, bowed your head in thanks, and stepped in quickly. You automatically opened the second door and gestured with your hand and a smile for him to proceed this time. And you felt relieved when he did, as your brief debt was repaid. The stranger's first kind gesture was repaid all in the matter of seconds with your similar gesture. Why do we do this?

If I were to invite you to dinner at my house, you would probably invite me to dinner at your house next. If a friend buys you a coffee on break today, would you buy him one on break tomorrow? What is this feeling we have that makes us respond this way?

In our quest to get what we want, we will come across the rule of reciprocity. In his book *Influence: The Psychology of Persuasion*, Robert Cialdini goes as far as to say that this human phenomenon is a "universal principle." This principle applies every day and everywhere in life. In fact, humans have been automatically responding this way for thousands of years.

The rule of reciprocity states that we are obligated to give back to others the form of behaviour that was first given to us. When someone does something for us or gives us something, we feel obligated to do something for that person in return. Most of us try to be fair and equitable in our lives. We have this instinct that drives us to repay those who have given to us. As you grow aware of this automatic human response, you will learn to create it in others intentionally so they will feel compelled to help you. In the context of obligation, people will say yes to those they owe. It is automatic. People will say yes to your requests more often and you will get more of what you want out of your life. After all, life is sales!

In this chapter, you will learn how to create and recognize priceless moments of opportunity. You will learn how to optimize these openings, know what to put into them, and learn how to better capitalize on what is already yours. You will learn how to make powerful requests and improve your results.

Reciprocity in Action

Our fundamental need to repay others for the gifts they have given is pretty simple to understand. If someone you know sends you a birthday card, you will probably want to send them one. Giving creates a sense of obligation in the receiver. This obligation is what makes us want to repay others for the gifts they have given. A university professor in California decided one Christmas season to send Christmas cards to a sample of perfect strangers from around the country.[8] He went to phone books and picked out a random sample of people in various cities across the United States and sent these people Christmas cards. He anticipated some kind of response from these cards but was not prepared for the avalanche of cards he received from these absolute strangers. It seemed that people received a card from this professor and simply sent a card back without question. It was an automatic response to repay in kind for the gift they had just received. It is this automatic response that we are most interested in when it comes to being more persuasive and influential.

In his DVD *The Power of Persuasion,* Robert Cialdini takes this Christmas card story even further. Apparently, Cialdini told the story to his classes at the University of Arizona. One day, a student came up to him after class to talk about it. She was a mature student who had already raised her family and had decided to return to school. She told Cialdini that he had just solved a decade-long mystery in her home. Apparently, she had received a Christmas card about ten years ago from the Harrisons in California, and she did not know any Harrisons. She had asked her husband, but he did not know any Harrisons, and her kids were too young at the time. With a great deal of effort, she resisted sending them a card that year because she thought it was a mistake. But the following year, they received another card from the Harrisons, so she sent them a card. They were now in the tenth year of exchanging cards with these people and she still didn't know who they were.

This is an amazing story about the power of obligation when we receive a gift or a favour. Ten years later, this woman was still exchanging cards with a perfect stranger. The key to this story is that the sense of obligation created is predictable. What do you do if you get a card from someone you didn't send a card to? As a master of influence, when a response is predictable, we can be better prepared to capitalize on it. A gift or favour creates a sense of obligation. When that feeling of obligation is upon the receiver, we have a moment of opportunity. We give a gift or favour that creates a sense of obligation and a moment of opportunity. The true power of this moment lies in the fact that people tend to say yes to those they owe.

As we look more closely at the rule of reciprocity, you will discover how most people squander these moments of opportunity. Moments of opportunity happen every day and yet go unnoticed and untapped. And then we wonder why we aren't getting the results we want.

Where It All Began

Reciprocity has been around since ancient times. It is in our basic makeup and is what makes us uniquely human. All human societies train their members in the rule of reciprocity. It really lays the groundwork for social and commercial interaction between people. It has established the framework for the exchange of products and services. The simple rule is: If you give us something, we will repay you for that item.

Imagine the life and times of prehistoric societies. How did they survive? Every day was a struggle to stay alive in harsh environments. Hunters and gatherers needed to procure food to eat. Some days, the hunt was successful, while others weren't. When the hunt was unproductive, the tribe had other means of procurement. Our ancestors learned to band together and share food and skills. It was a necessity of life.

Reciprocity was a basic human skill within prehistoric societies if they were to survive in those harsh early days. According to archaeologist Richard Leakey, it is the "essence of what makes us human." The rule of reciprocity was then and is today critical to our survival.

The reciprocity skill we have makes us a unique species. It literally is an automatic human response. We are wired for it. In *The Origin of Virtue,* Matt Ridley claims this "unique mechanism of human being allowed for the division of labour and exchange of goods and services, and this creation of interdependencies is what binds us together into highly effective units." When we receive a good or service, our sense of obligation to repay is born and gives rise to our need to reciprocate. People who have learned to master this human response have the magic to survive and prosper. Survival of the fittest dictates that the societies who mastered the art of cooperation and practiced reciprocity were the societies who prospered. This principle of reciprocal exchange was the basis for their success and was ingrained in their culture.

The rule of reciprocity is sometimes referred to as "the principle of exchange." Our ancestors set the groundwork as they exchanged services and commodities. Barter was the system of trade; if someone gave a product away, it was assumed that it would be repaid at a later time. Fast forward to the twenty-first century. What do we do today? In many impersonal transactions, we use money as a means for valuing our exchange of goods and services. If we pick up a loaf of bread at the store, we have an obligation to pay for that loaf of bread. Barter systems and referral networks are commonplace, with their roots based in the rule of reciprocity.

The rule even applies to life on the playground, where we often teach Luke 6:31, "Do unto others as you would have them do unto you." Imagine sitting on a park bench, breathing in the fresh air and feeling the sunshine warm your bones. The children are playing in the sandbox. Cyclists ride by on the bike path, and all is right with the world. Suddenly, you hear a screech and your perfect moment comes to an abrupt halt.

"I want that shovel! Gimme that shovel; it's mine!" You listen and watch as little Janie runs over and grabs the shovel out of little Tommy's hand. Janie pushes Tommy over into the sand. Tommy retaliates and pushes Janie back. A game of tug of war erupts over the shovel. Janie screams bloody murder. You decide this confrontation has gone on long enough and requires you to referee.

You take Tommy aside and ask him, "Why did you push Janie?"

You know his response even before it comes out of his mouth: "Because she pushed me." Even at the age of four years young, we feel obligated to repay others for the behaviour they have given us.

A more apt quotation in this situation might be Matthew 5:38, "An eye for an eye, a tooth for a tooth." Revenge is the dark side of reciprocity. Cultural clashes around the world have been going on for centuries and are based on revenge. If someone in one village kills someone in another village, the other village will want to retaliate by killing someone in the first village. The carnage continues for centuries and the original wrong is often forgotten in the desire to get revenge. Violence begets violence. Much of the international strife in the world today is based on this aspect of human nature. For our purposes, we will focus on the positive aspects of reciprocity, where a good deed will be repaid in kind. However, don't forget that a bad deed can also be repaid in kind.

"Be sure to give in return for what you have taken"; "Please share—you'll feel bad if you don't"; "Say thank you when someone gives you something." These are all things we say to our children early in their development. That sense of obligation has formed the basis of our cultural heritage, and we start teaching it to our children at a very young age.

In 1992, researcher Peggy A. de Cooke studied children and how they feel a sense of indebtedness.[9] A hypothetical exchange between two friends or two acquaintances was described. In her findings, she discovered younger children feel a greater need to reciprocate the favour regardless of the cost or size. As the child gets older, the larger favours increase the child's obligation to repay. Another key finding in her study showed children are even more inclined to repay the favour for an acquaintance than for a friend. Even from a very young age, children have this automatic response, this need to repay others for the gifts they have received.

We have an even greater propensity to repay the favours given to us by acquaintances. What a tremendous finding, reinforcing how precious it is to practice the rule of reciprocity in business, where we have many acquaintances. Consider working out your reciprocity muscles in business as you would work out your other muscles in the health club. The more you exercise them, the stronger they get.

Reciprocity As Manipulation

It is not in our best interests to manipulate people for unethical reasons. We need to be sincere in our actions with those we wish to influence. The Hare Krishna society had been collecting money around airports for years. In the '60s, the robed devotees noticed travellers were simply not donating as much as they used to. They needed a new approach, so they decided to give out flowers. Travellers would often try to return the flowers, but the devotees would refuse, bow down, and ask for donations instead. Travellers reluctantly gave them. Once they got down the hall, the travellers might throw the flowers into the trash. The devotees would pick the flowers out of the trash and hand them out again.

It was clear to the devotees: If they gave a gift of a flower to the traveller, the traveller would feel a sense of obligation and give a donation. They were right. Their donations increased with the use of a token gift. However, the real beauty was they could reduce their costs by recycling the flowers that previous recipients tossed away. Travellers eventually caught onto the exploitation and the Hare Krishna society was asked to leave the airports.

What the Hare Krishna society was practicing could be referred to as manipulation. For most, the word *manipulation* has a negative connotation. Manipulation implies being misled. The devotees gave something away that had no value to the receiver, and yet in return, they received something of value. This was a one-sided equation and is certainly not our focus when using the rule of reciprocity.

Find a sincere and ethical way to practice the rule of reciprocity. Our goal is to lead others to a place where they will be genuinely satisfied and they will feel obligated to give something back to us for what we have given to them. When they do give back to us, that obligation will shift to our shoulders and a mutually beneficial relationship born. These win/win exchanges provide for long-term and fulfilling relationships.

There is a powerful, methodical, and ethical way we can get what we want out of life. The ability is in all of us. The rule of reciprocity is a proven means for getting what you want. It is scientific and predictable. What you really want is for someone to say yes to your requests wholeheartedly. With this awareness of human nature, how do you set the stage for people to say yes to your requests and to thank you? How do you make people feel obligated to do as you ask or return a favour in kind? We will look at these questions in more detail and discover how we can create win/win situations for all involved.

Do you want to associate with people who do not repay their debts? These people are aptly named sharks, welchers, leachers, or deadbeats. Think of an always-needy friend or family member. We bet you can come up with a name or two to add to this list. Some professions are stereotyped as these kinds of manipulators, such as those in the used-car industry and commission-based electronics stores. We do not want to associate long with people who do not understand the mutually beneficial aspect of the rule of reciprocity. These folks fail to understand it is not just about today's sale but also about tomorrow's sale and future client referrals. You have a choice to make. You can either manipulate clients short-term or create win/win situations for long-term relationships. Success and satisfaction come from mutually beneficial partnerships. All good salespeople are in the business of long-term repeat sales.

Where Is Reciprocity?

Have you ever attended a Tupperware, PartyLite, or Botox party? A neighbour invites you to share in some camaraderie and a mere couple of hours to hear about the latest gadgets or cosmetic procedures. "You don't have to buy anything, just show up," your neighbour tells you. You like your neighbour and feel compelled to attend. After all, she has done a lot for you. She volunteers to collect your mail and water your plants whenever you are away on vacation. She lets out your dogs and even babysits in a pinch. You feel you owe her. You accept her invitation and attend her party.

At the party, you do not feel a need to purchase anything, but you do feel pressure to show support for your hostess. What is this feeling you have? The rule of reciprocity is at work. What you feel is a sense of obligation. You purchase a fifty-dollar item and the pressure falls away. The home party organizations know the power of this rule.

Home party organizations have also mastered the "liking principle," as discussed earlier in the book. It is hard to say no to people you know and like. If you are that likeable neighbour, what did you do to get people to like you? Knowing you have this likeability, what do you want your neighbours to say yes to? In this scenario, your neighbour first gave to you by helping while you were away. When she extended an invitation to her home party, you felt obligated to say yes. While at the party, you felt obligated to repay her for the unspoken debt you owe her. You spent a few dollars at her home party and your sense of obligation was relieved. This is the rule of reciprocity at work: a win/win situation and the exchange is complete.

Imagine you are working on a big project in the office and need help in order to meet the deadline. You sheepishly ask for help from a colleague. Much to your surprise, this colleague is delighted to help you. In fact, he is relieved you have finally given him a chance to repay you; after all, you have supported him in the past. You had forgotten you had stayed late with him for a couple of nights to sort out a systems problem critical to the operation of his department. Since that time, he has carried around this burden of obligation. He has been waiting for a chance to repay you for your kindness. This is the rule of reciprocity at work.

In 1985, a nation provided financial aid to Mexico after it had experienced a severe 8.0 magnitude earthquake. We feel compelled to give to those in desperate need, especially in times of natural disasters. However, the money in this instance came from Ethiopia, a poor Third World country whose people suffer horribly from disease and starvation. This didn't make sense! Shouldn't the money have gone from Mexico to Ethiopia? Ethiopia was appealing to the world for food and support for their own people, and here they were giving aid to Mexico! Even though Ethiopia had a desperate need for food, shelter, and clothing for their own population, the Ethiopian Red Cross sent $5,000 to Mexico City.

When asked why a nation in such a desolate state would feel compelled to give to another, the Ethiopian Red Cross said they sent the money to Mexico because in 1935, when Italy invaded Ethiopia, Mexico helped them. This was repayment for a long past debt. Fifty years later, the sense of obligation remained strong. Catastrophic suffering from dire conditions of disease, famine, and cultural differences did not dissuade Ethiopia to give back to Mexico. Once Ethiopia was aware of an opportunity to repay their obligation to the country that gave them such a wondrous gift fifty years earlier, they did so and proudly. Large favours are remembered for a long time. This is the rule of reciprocity at work in the world.

These acts of reciprocity occur every day in our lives, in the world, in our communities, at work, and at home. Yet we seldom stop to think about why this is happening, nor do we recognize the special opportunity before us. Reciprocity is an automatic human response. When someone gives us a gift or does us a favour, we thank them, and a sense of obligation is born. It is this sense of obligation that makes us want to repay, and we do. How do we now take this automatic human response and develop it further?

Thank You

Connie:　In Canada, a lawyer is required to close the purchase of a real estate transaction. Occasionally, a lender will call their First Canadian Title account manager, looking for a reputable real estate lawyer for their homebuyers. As an account manager excited to have my first referral opportunity, I went to one of my top lawyers and asked if he would take care of these clients. He was pleased with the offer of an introduction but also a little reserved. He later confessed he had mixed emotions. He wondered why I was bringing these clients to him and what I wanted back from him. Yet the only audible words that came from his mouth were, "Why did you choose me?" I said that I value his business. His reputation is impeccable, and I was certain I could count on him to take good care of my clients' needs. In fact, I was delighted to have an opportunity to support him in his business.

Some people might be naturally suspicious of a gift. They might be slow to realize you are truly in service to them and have their interests at heart. With the rule of reciprocity in mind, we now know one way a sense of obligation is created. It is by giving someone a gift, a material item, a compliment, your time, knowledge, or encouragement.

As you leave a client's office, what is it you want them to be thinking about you now and in the future? "There goes the pen lady" or "He's a great drinking buddy" or, better yet, "Wow, that guy cares about my business and brings me value even beyond his product. He is welcome here anytime! In fact, I need to find a way to help him in his business like he does mine." Are your actions and words consistent with the image you want to leave in your wake?

Connie: When we give someone a compliment, gift or favour, what do they say? Thank you, of course, and they are left with that feeling of wanting to repay you. When we are acutely aware of that feeling of obligation, we are eager to repay. On the drive to a dear friend's family wedding this summer, I was running early, so I stopped for a coffee. I parked the car in the Tim Hortons parking lot and walked slowly, waiting for a car to pass from the drive-through lane. The car stopped suddenly. The driver opened her window and the man in the passenger seat called out past her, "Hey!" I stopped, and was anticipating a request for directions in a neighbourhood I knew nothing about. The passenger spoke, "Nice legs!" I blushed, nodded thanks, and smiled broadly as I went in to Tim's to get my coffee. Hey, at forty-four years young, I still have it! I thought to myself.

When I left the store minutes later, the couple had parked next to my car. It seemed a little odd. As I approached my car, a man came by on foot and asked for a spare dollar so he could take the bus. I reached into my purse, pulled out several dollars, and gave it to this stranger. I watched as he headed towards the bus stop, aware of the couple in the car watching me. Was I more apt to cooperate with this stranger's request because someone had given me a compliment just minutes earlier? Was I more apt to be generous because someone who had complimented me was watching? You bet I was. I felt good and was very happy to give this man a few spare dollars. I couldn't help but wonder if it was a setup for a psychology study. When that sense of obligation weighs on us, we are much more likely to say yes to a request, even to a stranger.

Let's look back a little at the examples at the start of this chapter. Someone held open the shopping mall door for you, and you felt obligated to return the favour in kind. A stranger gave you something first and it caused you to thank them and feel obligated to repay the debt, and it all happened in a nanosecond. That sense of obligation is born once we feel someone has done something of value for us. A gift is given, and a sense of obligation to repay comes with it. I send you a birthday card and you send me one. If I invite you out to lunch, will you invite me?

A Gift Improves Results

In his article "Effects of a favour and liking on compliance" published in the *Journal of Experimental Psychology,* psychologist Dennis Regan of Cornell University outlined his classic study of reciprocity.[10] He had subjects work in pairs in a fake art appreciation study. One of the subjects was an actor, and during a short recess, the actor would leave the group. For one set of groups, he would return with a Coke for his partner, and in the other groups, he would return with no gift at all. In both situations, the actor would ask his partner for a favour. He was selling raffle tickets for his high school back home and would receive a prize if he sold the most raffle tickets. Were the participants willing to buy one of his raffle tickets? The results were surprising. The actor sold almost twice as many tickets to the people who had received the free Coke.

It would appear that the participants had a sense of obligation to repay the actor for the free Coke, and when he asked them to buy something, they were more likely to say yes to that request. The actor had created the context for increasing his sales by the use of reciprocity.

In another part of the study, Regan varied the likeability of the actor. He wanted to determine if people are more willing to do favours for people they like. In this case, the actor had to answer the phone and was extremely rude to a customer on the other end for half the groups to see. The other half witnessed the actor as being quite polite on the phone.

The results, as expected, were that the actor sold more of his raffle tickets when he was pleasant and polite on the phone. However, the importance of the likeability factor was no match for the unsolicited bottle of free Coke. The free Coke almost doubled the sales compared to only a 20% reduction in sales when he acted rude on the phone. The interesting aspect was that the free Coke had as much effect on ticket sales when he was rude as when he was polite. The free Coke trumped the likeability factor, so it didn't matter if they liked him or not. It was far more important that they had a sense of owing the actor something, so they bought more raffle tickets.

We should all pay attention to the power of reciprocity. If used properly, it will have a huge impact on your results and significantly increase the chances of your clients saying yes to your requests.

The Road to Obligation Is Filled with Gifts

In *Man and Superman,* George Bernard Shaw gives us something to think about with regards to gift giving. He writes, "Do not do unto others as you would that they should do unto you. Their tastes may not be the same." Sometimes we all fall into the trap of thinking people are all the same or others think just like us.

Connie: As a newlywed, I thought I knew what my husband would like for his birthday. I purchased a gift I liked, and I looked forward to his reaction when he unwrapped his present. His birthday came and I proudly presented the gift. Much to my surprise, his reaction was not a favourable one. I disappointedly returned the purchase I liked. I have since taken a lesson from Karl Popper, who says, "The Golden Rule [do unto others as you would have done unto you] is a good standard which is further improved by doing unto others, wherever possible, as they want to be done by."

As you go about giving gifts to those you wish to influence, consider their unique wants and likes. Do your best to give them what they want. Ensure your gift is well thought out, special, personal, and a surprise to them.

Receiving Thanks

In our workshops, we present a scenario to participants that goes something like this: You are a professional mortgage broker, realtor, insurance salesperson, or financial planner. You provided some great advice to a client. They took your advice, and now, two weeks later, they come back to see you and say, "I just wanted to come back to tell you how delighted we are with the service and advice you provided to us. My family could not be happier and I feel my financial affairs are finally in order. I just wanted to thank you for taking the time to really set us up right for our future."

We then ask the participants to write out a quick two-sentence response to the client who has just come into your office and expressed their heartfelt thanks.

We have done this exercise thousands of times and it is surprising how many people are simply unprepared to respond to this acknowledgement in a meaningful way. We hear many good responses and many typical ones. What do most people say when someone says, "Thank you"? They say, "No problem." It is almost a national epidemic. We all want to say "no problem" when someone thanks us wholeheartedly for a job well done.

What does "no problem" really mean to your client? With tongue in cheek, we explain—we rant, actually—"Well, it was no problem. It's just part of my job. I would have done it for anyone. Actually, you are not even all that special. It's why they pay me the big bucks, so I can do this for you. It was no big deal. Anyone in the world could have done it. No need to thank me. It was nothing!" Wow!

How does your client feel now after they just told you how much they appreciate your extra effort and you respond back with "I didn't really do anything"? Does this response leave your client with a positive lasting impression? No, it doesn't. You have just fumbled away one of the most powerful opportunities in the sales conversation.

The moment after a thank you is the opportunity you want to use to reinforce the fact you did do a favour for this client. Therefore, when you ask the client for something later, they will be more apt to say yes to your request because they feel obligated to repay you. Most salespeople do not even recognize this powerful opportunity and few seem to know what to put into that moment to increase their sales results and referrals.

Why do we say "no problem"? Whose feelings are you really with when you say "no problem" after receiving a sincere thank you? You are with your own shy feelings. You have turned inward and brushed off the compliment with a "no problem." Many of us are humble people and we really don't want to accept accolades openly, so we downplay our personal involvement in the results. As a professional, whose feelings should you be with to leave a lasting impression? What do you want to leave the client with before they walk out of your office? Step out of your own feelings of awkwardness and back into the office with the client. You want to be sure you end your interaction powerfully. You need to acknowledge that you did do something special and that your work is worthy of praise.

As a master at reciprocity, you need to know what to say. You want to enhance that sense of obligation tastefully. This moment distinguishes the masters from the amateurs. A master sales professional will have scripted their words and practiced their response for this moment of opportunity.

Connie: I was visiting family in California recently and noticed a trend of "uh-huhs." My sister Betty and I were out shopping, and when I said thank you to a store clerk, she said, "Uh-huh." I said, "Pardon me?" Betty explained that is what people say here after someone thanks them. They say "uh-huh." "Eh?" I said in Canadian, wondering what "uh-huh" meant in American.

     After a lovely restaurant meal with my sister, I thanked our waiter for his great service, and he said, "Uh-huh." There it was again—that ambiguous response sounding like a grunt of some sort. I ribbed him. I said, "What do you mean by 'uh-huh'? I'm Canadian and I don't understand American. Does this mean, 'Yeah, I know you're thankful—thankful for all this great service I've given to you for the last hour and a half, you moron'?" The poor boy stood shocked. "No, Miss. That certainly is not what I meant. I don't really know what I mean by 'uh-huh.' We just all seem to say that here." The waiter concluded, "What I really meant to say was, 'You're welcome.'" And he bowed away.

Let me share with you the encouragement we give our workshop participants. When a client says a heartfelt thank you for a big job well done, stand tall with your hands at your side and really let it in. Let their kind words right into your heart. You work hard for your clients and they know it. You absolutely deserve the compliments they are paying to you.

I will never forget one of our participants who said, "No one ever thanks me!" All I could think of was Rodney Dangerfield's "I get no respect." The room was silent—dead silent—until a woman spoke. She was his fellow co-worker in the cubicle next to him. She went on to say, "That's not true. The staff thanks you all the time for the help you give them. I hear people each and every day thanking you." This man was stunned. He was so uncomfortable being acknowledged that he could not even remember hearing his co-workers' words of appreciation.

This is not uncommon. Many people simply don't know how to accept a sincere acknowledgement or appreciation graciously. Take a moment and ask yourself how you typically respond when a client thanks or acknowledges you. Do you experience this moment of awkwardness? Are you willing to train yourself and turn this into a moment of opportunity?

Let's practice just for a moment. Stand up—yes, stand up. Place your arms at your sides, take a deep breath, and relax. Read every word, but try to hear them spoken to you out loud: "I thank you for all the hard work you do for us. You pay special attention to all the details and it means a lot. I appreciate having you here. Thank you very much for taking care of my business!" Good work! You can sit down now. Nice job! You did it. You took it all in. How did that feel? It is not easy being open to hearing the compliments and really letting them in. Practice receiving words of acknowledgement graciously. Stand tall, shoulders back, chest out, stomach in and let the love in.

When I was a twentysomething, my sister coached me on receiving compliments. When Betty complimented me, I would point out how I could have done it even better. Betty scrunched up her face. It was the first time I understood the impact my response had on those who gave me compliments. Betty coached, "Conn, just say thank you."

Learn how to accept a compliment, as though a sweet little old woman were giving you a box of chocolates for Christmas. You can do it! By graciously accepting a compliment, you honour those who compliment you, and you are left with a moment of opportunity!

What Should You Say?

So, what exactly should you say to those who thank or compliment you? Well, you shouldn't say, "Great! Now you owe me something in return." Some of our participants go right for the throat after an expression of thanks. This does not build the relationship. It might get you one referral, but no more. They create a one-off transaction rather than build a mutually beneficial partnership.

We are big believers in scripting. It is the key to every sales-person's success. Script what you will say after a client thanks you. Once you have received a client's words of gratitude, it is your chance to let them know you've accepted their thanks and to nurture your relationship for the future. Try something like, "You're welcome. I enjoyed working with you. I want you to know I am committed to helping you. Can I count on you to come back to me with your future financial needs?" As the client agrees, invite them back for the secondary need you have identified or ask for a referral. Script it. Practice it. Eventually, your script will come naturally and your business will improve. Script, script, script! It might feel uncomfortable initially, but step out of your comfort zone and practice. It will become second nature.

What can we say to create a long-term win/win situation? How can we enhance that natural sense of obligation tastefully so people will realize they have received a big favour from you and you want the favour returned in the future? We suggest you script two responses: Script one for a small favour and another for a big favour.

Here are a few lines you might want to make your own: "You are most welcome. You are one of my best clients and I am glad I was able to provide advice. It wasn't easy, but we did it. I want you to know that the next time you need financial assistance, you can count on me to be here for you. Since we determined your next financial goal is your retirement savings, let's meet in two weeks to set this up. Is a morning or afternoon appointment better for you?"

Depending on the situation, some might say, "I know if the situation were ever reversed, you would do the same for me." What do these words really mean? They are saying, "I just did you a favour and I know you will do one in return," but in a nice way. It clarifies that a favour occurred and there is an obligation to repay. Now the stage is set for you to ask for the business or a referral and your client will be ready to say yes to that request.

If you are working with a business partner and looking for referrals, consider this: "It was my pleasure to provide this level of service to you. This is what good business partners do for each other." Two things happened here: First, you told the client you liked working with them, and second, you stated that they are your business partner. What do business partners do for each other? They reciprocate business!

"You're very welcome. My business is based on referrals, and one of the best ways you can thank me is to refer me to one of your friends or family members." These are just a sample of the kinds of powerful responses you can make after a client thanks you. You will be amazed at your results if you replace "no problem" with something more constructive and professional.

Saying "you're welcome" lets the client know you've received their thanks. You will use your own scripted words. Let the client know what they mean to you—how much you value their business and what they can count on from you in the future. Paint a picture of your future partnership in your response. And remember, script it! Do it now while the ideas are fresh in your head and make it your own. Consider writing them in the back cover of this book.

Gift Giving Ideas

A gift creates a sense of obligation, leading the recipient to want to repay you, so what should you give them? Your budget only goes so far. How can you provide value with a limited expense account? It's not just about the money! Look beyond the dollars. Figure out whom you truly want to influence and what would really benefit them. Here are some ideas colleagues and clients have shared over the years.

Many clients have what we call a gatekeeper, which could be a receptionist or an assistant, but they generally protect the decision maker from people like us. A simple technique is to offer the gate-keeper a pen the next time you are in the office and see what happens. We guarantee that if you do the delivery well, it is a decent pen, and you throw in a compliment, you will gain access to the decision maker faster than any other technique. The gatekeeper is often underpaid, unrecognized for the value they bring, and generally treated poorly. You can win them over quickly to support your efforts to gain access to the decision makers. This works in the offices of lawyers, realtors, accountants, lenders, brokers, and many more. The pen is mightier than the sword. This simple gift creates that sense of obligation, and the gatekeeper now wants to repay you by allowing access.

Consider the emotional exchanges we make in day-to-day life. Reciprocity is not limited to just exchanges of commodities, services, and cash. Your child smiles at you and you smile back. Someone compliments you on a lovely outfit, and you compliment them for having such good taste. Your boss acknowledges your efforts on a project, and you thank him by saying you could not have done it without his support.

The gift of acknowledgement is an incredibly powerful one and is rated among the top motivating factors for employee performance. When someone appreciates us and tells us so, all is right with the world. Thanking someone and recognizing the action they took to accomplish a result is an emotional exchange—this is the rule of reciprocity at work.

The larger favours, like Mexico's helping Ethiopia, have a longer-lasting impact than small favours do. We can recall big gifts and favours given to us more so than the small ones. In addition, we tend to better remember the gifts given by an acquaintance more than the ones from those we know well. What does this mean to you in your life or at work?

We learned in chapter 2 that people need and not just want to feel important. So let us give them what they need. A compliment about an outfit, behaviour, or a meaningful conversation about their dreams and goals are all lovely gifts, and they're free! Catch someone doing something nice and tell them! Timing is everything. Give compliments freely right after you witness the behaviour or action. When you walk into a new client's office, look for something to like and tell them!

A gift can take the form of being a friend with a shoulder to cry on or being a good listener. Encouragement is priceless. A smile, a hug, an offer of assistance even though it has nothing to do with your product or service is appreciated and notably generous. Don't you want to hang out with people in your life who encourage and support you? Of course you do, and so do your clients. What can you do to demonstrate your sincere interest in their success? Ice cream on a hot day, Easter eggs, Halloween treats, chocolate any day, lunch delivered to their office on their busiest day of the year, or a donation to their favourite charity in their honour are gift ideas.

With small businesses being the driving force behind our economy, the sharing of industry information and community happenings will be helpful to the entrepreneurs who are busy with their day-to-day operations. You might be a refreshing link to the business world by sharing economic forecasts and trends that will help them stay connected. Stay informed in their area of expertise and discuss key changes in their industry. This might have nothing to do with your product or service but it sure portrays you in a caring light and makes you a valued resource to their business.

A client's favourite gift could be an introduction to a prospect or centre of influence. Invite your client to a meeting where they can have such an introduction. Look for ways to cross-pollinate your network of contacts. Coffee is nice, but give a client what they really want: more clients and more business. This will create a powerful long-term reciprocal relationship.

The gift of a greeting, birthday, or condolence card from an unexpected business client is a nice touch. When Connie was a new account manager on the road for the first time, one of her clients mentioned he was celebrating his birthday on December 31st. She made a note and mailed a birthday greeting to him. He was touched. Up until that point, Connie was just another field representative. Years later, they are still in touch. He is more than just her client; he is a good friend who encourages her in both business and life endeavours, as she does his.

Introduce key clients to an executive in your company. Invite one of your executives, product people, or head office types to join you on the road to meet clients face to face. You know how great it is to put a face to a name or a face to a voice on the telephone. The benefits go back to head office too. People who know and like each other work better together. Hearing a client's concerns first-hand has a much greater impact. Cooperation between departments is enhanced as you come to realize the challenges you each face in making your company profitable.

Hockey games, golf matches, lunches, and all these things are great for bonding and create a context for reciprocity. The real power comes when you can do something unusual for the client. Something for the family is always a winner, as parents never seem to spend enough time with their kids, so a mother/father–son/daughter event is effective. Sometimes sending them to a game is better than you attending with them.

Very few sales and service people sincerely thank clients for their time and business. In our workshops, participants are asked what feelings they want their client to walk out of their office with. Being appreciated and being there for them in the future are the top two favourites. Yet, so many people end with a mere "thank you" or "you're welcome." These common pleasantries don't leave clients with the feelings you wish to instill. They don't leave that lasting impression you want. Tell your clients they're important.

Becoming a trusted partner in building the success of a client's business is a great feeling. Sharing tips, feedback, or coaching might also provide tremendous value if your client is open to receiving them. First ask their permission before sharing your observations and suggestions.

What feelings do you have when a virtual stranger offers you a gift? Are you happy? Are you thankful? Are you suspicious? A prospect or client could have mixed feelings about your gift. Many of us have a natural inclination to be suspicious of a stranger bearing gifts. As a sales professional, you need to be prepared for their reaction and ready with your words of thanks and encouragement for the future. Most interactions are quite predictable and you need to be prepared with professional responses to influence your results.

Clients and co-workers thank us on a daily basis, and yet we brush them off as unimportant courteous exchanges between people. A simple "thank you" can be a huge moment of opportunity for you to significantly enhance your ability to be more influential and persuasive. There is money, opportunity, and sales in every "thank you" you receive.

Why Go First?

Now that you know someone you want to influence, how will you proceed? If you want to be a master of influence, you need to take control of the influence situation. How will you accomplish this?

Connie: Here is a story that illustrates setting the tone for the relationship you want to foster. Several years ago, Sherry and Fred, a highly energetic couple, invited me and my husband, Greg, and four other couples over to their home for drinks. We were sharing wine and cheese and getting to know each other a little better.

We all sat down with Sherry and Fred as they shared their idea of creating a dinner club. They had a vision of adult dinner parties scheduled over the next year. Every other month, a dinner party would take place. Each couple agreed they would be responsible to host the "Dinner Club." Fred proposed that each dinner should have a theme. The hosts would provide all the food for the night. The guests were not to bring any potluck dishes or hors d'oeuvres. Sherry emphasized that when a guest asks, "What can we bring?" the answer was to be, "Absolutely nothing—just bring yourselves." Being humble thirsty guests, we could never arrive at the door empty-handed, so we were allowed to bring an alcoholic beverage to offer up at the door as our admission ticket to the Dinner Club. At each meeting, the visiting couples were going to experience a gourmet dinner.

We set out the schedule for the next year. Sherry insisted no changing of dates! The Dinner Club Saturday nights were now cast in stone. She conceded births, deaths, and weddings would be the only cause to reschedule. Sherry and Fred, being masters at influence, took the initiative to invite everyone over to their house to enroll them in their Dinner Club idea. To set the tone for the coming year, they hosted the first party.

Sherry and Fred's invitation arrived in the mail. This was during the olden days when people still sent invitations by Canada Post rather than email. We were to bring towels and swimsuits, which seemed very odd, as Sherry and Fred didn't have a pool and it was January. The invitation was to a hot tub party, which was still perplexing, since Sherry and Fred didn't have a hot tub either.

I watched what I ate for the next few weeks, hoping to drop four sizes to fit in my swimsuit without being self-conscious, all in vain. We scheduled the best babysitters we knew—the in-laws—and looked forward to getting out. Some of the other Dinner Club members also had young children. Somehow, after the kids came, we seemed to have drifted away from adult-only evenings, so this was such a welcome opportunity to get out as couples again.

The day arrived! We fed the kids and in-laws, and reminded them of the bedtime rituals. We put on our coats and began the designated driver dance, negotiating who would be driving home later that night. I admitted that I would be happy with just one glass of wine for the night and would still be sober enough to drive home. We arrived quickly, as we were both starving, and knocked on Sherry and Fred's door at the scheduled time with our towels, swimsuits, and a favourite bottle of wine in hand.

The couples gathered and became reacquainted. The noise level rose as we tried to uncover why we brought our swimsuits and towels. In their outrageous manner, the hosts served a gourmet meal: melt-in-your-mouth roast beef, roasted potatoes, gravy, perfectly prepared vegetables, and horseradish. The alcoholic beverages were in abundance. With bellies full and bloated, Sherry and Fred invited us to don our swimwear, finally letting us in on their secret. A portable hot tub was in the backyard just a frosty six feet from the sliding glass door. Cigars and digestifs were served at the hot tub.

It was a decadent night, with a gourmet meal, a soak in the tub, no kids, and great conversation with some new friends. At their inaugural party, Sherry and Fred set the tone for the Dinner Club. It was a delightful year, and so was the next one. Since Sherry and Fred went first and set the tone, the guests were all indebted to them. With the bar set high, the guests had a lot of fun and worked hard to repay them.

Okay, so it is up to you to go first. Don't wait for someone else to set the tone for the relationship you want to have. At our workshops, we always say *give first, give first, give first*. A thoughtful gift will get that "thank you" you're after so you can jump into that moment of opportunity with both feet.

Weekends at Costco is another familiar environment for putting the rule of reciprocity to work. Tasty samples of food are given away for free at the end of every other aisle! When you try the store sample, don't you feel just a little guilty if you don't buy the product, especially if you liked it? Maybe you fake taking the product and return it to the shelf later or offer a compliment in exchange for the sample. Gary would tell you Costco is where he lunches on Saturdays—boy, you can sure fill up on free samples!

Every society trains its people this way. The organizations that play by the rule of reciprocity have an enormous advantage. Therefore, it is up to *you* to go first. You need to take the first step if you truly want to influence. It is up to *you* to set the tone for the relationship *you* want to have. Take initiative!

How We Can Put Reciprocity to Work

Gary's son Michael was a waiter at a restaurant while he was in university, and Gary coached him on the rule of reciprocity. Michael was a charismatic waiter. He had fun serving his clients and did a terrific job promoting the menu choices that would suit their palates. He welcomed people warmly with his million-dollar smile. He would share his personal favourites from the menu. He would even go so far as to let his patrons know if a dish was not a top-notch selection. They trusted him. He recommended wines that would compliment the food, and was very attentive to removing the finished plates. When it came time to present the bill to his patrons, Michael would lay the bill down and thank his patrons for choosing his restaurant. His tips were average.

Gary made a few suggestions as to how Michael might increase his tips. Taking his dad's advice and applying the rule of reciprocity at this moment of opportunity, Michael would thank his patrons and his patrons would return the thanks. Michael began presenting the bill with a candy for each diner. His tips increased.

Michael enhanced his position further. He fine-tuned his actions at the final presentation of the bill. Michael now set down the bill with two candies for each patron. This simple technique increased his tips yet again.

In an attempt to increase the tips even further, he tried another approach. He would deliver one candy for each patron along with the bill, and then he would turn and start to walk away. Two steps out, he would stop in his tracks, count to three, then dramatically turn and return to the table. He would smile, lay down a handful more of candies, and express how he enjoyed serving them—a closing smile and away he went.

What do you think Michael's results were? His tips nearly doubled! With the unexpected extra candies, and a "liking" statement, Michael had created a strong sense of obligation in his patrons and had been amply rewarded for his efforts. So, what happened here? How would you feel if you received Michael's great service, advice, charm, and, at the end of the meal, his unexpected extra gifts? You would feel full and pretty darn special, and you would be compelled to generously write up the tip. The three ingredients to this successful gift were that it was personal, a surprise, and timely. Michael would later admit that it was all about the turn. If the turn was done with a little flair, as though he just remembered to give them additional candies because they were so nice, the patrons would dig deeper into their wallets. This is the rule of reciprocity at work. The sense of obligation weighed heavily upon the patrons just at the time they paid out their generous tips to him.

Why Do We Resist Help?

Connie: When we offer assistance to those who need it, they sometimes decline it—silly people. What would have them decline our helping capable hands? Maybe we are someone they never want to be indebted to, or maybe it's something else.

I recently was travelling to Nassau and spied my last opportunity for a Tim Hortons coffee and bagel before leaving the country. The line was long, but I felt it was well worth the wait even if I was risking not boarding on time. A university student travelling home to Winnipeg was in line ahead of me. As we approached the cashier, he suddenly realized Tim Hortons is a cash-only operation: no debit cards, no credit cards. He lowered his head and was moving out of the line. I asked if I could buy him breakfast. "No, no," he responded. "I can't let you do that."

Why did he respond this way? Was he not hungry? His automatic sense of "I will never be able to repay you" kicked in. I said, "I would hate to see you go home hungry, so please, let me give this small gift to you." He smiled and finally agreed. We chatted in line until it was our turn to order. As he was about to place his order, he suddenly said, "I feel guilty letting you buy me breakfast—I can't." Never having the chance to repay the favour was weighing heavily on him.

I said, "Please don't feel guilty. How about this? The next time you have an opportunity to take care of somebody else, repay this small favour forward. Will you?" He smiled and agreed. He ordered his bagel, and I mine, and off we went our separate ways, bagels in hand.

Would you not agree we were both better off for the experience? The need to repay debts in kind can be overpowering for some and understandingly implied for others. We have to paint an explicit picture for others on how to repay.

Networking

In business, we are all out in the marketplace, looking for more clients and more opportunities. We attend networking functions, meet with groups of clients and potential clients, and go to social events in the hope of finding new clients. The normal approach to networking is to attend these functions with this intent of finding new business. We enter the room and look around, trying to find people who might be able to do something for our business.

Taking a closer look at the rule of reciprocity, we might need to reconsider our approach in networking. There are three rules to networking that are of value to anyone who networks for business. The three rules are *give first, give first,* and *give first.* Why, you may ask, give first? If we give first, the prospective client will say "thank you" and that will be our moment to shine. We will fill that moment with the power of the rule of reciprocity.

What happens when you walk into a room and find an opportunity to help someone, especially in a business scene? The rule of reciprocity kicks in. That person will feel obliged to help you in your business as well. If you want to start a relationship, it is your responsibility to initiate it. You must be the first one to give.

When you move into a new neighbourhood and want to make friends, what do you do? Well, you don't sit in the backyard with a couple of beers and wait for someone to come to you. No, you act first. You take the initiative and invite a neighbour to your home. When they arrive, they will feel obligated to invite you back, and a new friendship begins.

You need to act first to grow your business. Networking opportunities take on various forms. Customer appreciation events, chambers of commerce, Rotary, business networking groups, associations, Christmas parties, and trade shows are all opportunities to network. These are professional work environments and we should treat them as such.

Connie: Many years ago, I did home shows with my husband. We were new to the duct cleaning industry and we initially thought it was important just to attend. We thought just having a booth would do the trick. I don't know what our exact thoughts

were, but it might have been the "consensus principle" at work: Other duct cleaners were doing it,
so it must be the right thing to do. We will talk
more on the consensus principle later.

After many hours over a seemingly endless
weekend, it was hard to tell if this was money and
time well spent. The following year, we got a little smarter. We offered a home show special to
people who would book appointments by calling
our office. That helped to put some dollars and
"sense" to attending the show. The year after
that, we got even smarter and brought our schedule and booked appointments right there. In the
following years, we set a target for the number of
jobs we wanted to book at the home show. Year
after year, we would try to beat our previous
record-breaking results.

Why is *networking* today's buzzword? When we are invited to a
client event, what do many of us do? We step into the room as
though we were a debutante at her sixteen-year-old coming-out
party. If we don't see someone we know, we shrink off to the bar.
With newfound courage in hand, we look again for someone we
know, preferably from our own company, so we can commiserate
together. After all, here we are away from our families and obligations at some networking work function, just making an appearance, to make our company look good. Just "being at" an event
does not count as networking.

Others create these soirees as a business card exchange. You receive cards that say a bunch of people were there, and in the spirit
of reciprocity, you give yours in return, and then you move on to the
next person and swap cards. At the end of the night, you have a
pocket full of business cards but made no meaningful connections.
Having a pocket full of cards does not count as networking.

Networking is meant to be a powerful activity. It is the actions
one takes to make meaningful connections with others. So, what

can we do to ease our social awkwardness and spend our time effectively and meaningfully at those business events?

The purpose of attending a social gathering of professionals or community members is to build relationships. After all, people want to do business with and set up referrals for people they know, like, and trust. Every gathering is a chance to connect and practice the rule of reciprocity. You might be new at it, so set realistic goals for this event.

In *Endless Referrals,* Bob Burg writes, "It isn't just what you know and it isn't just who you know. It's actually who you know, who knows you, and what you do for a living." By working these events, you are out to influence people and to also have them influence their own circle regarding you and what you do for a living. Attend these functions with a clear purpose: to influence people and expand your network of contacts.

Set a goal for your participation in the networking event. What should it be? (a) To get three sales? Nope! (b) To make an appearance, and then sneak out early? Nope! It's (c) To meet one new person and strike up a meaningful conversation where you discover what this person does and needs. You will ask this person questions to discover how you can be of service to them and their network. You will look for an opportunity to provide them with a gift first, either now or in the near future, thereby creating a moment of opportunity. As a master of the rule of reciprocity, you will know what to say to create a mutually beneficial relationship. Good work! Your goal is to meet someone and create a meaningful relationship.

Test time! When you walk into the event and look around, you say to yourself, "Where's the bar?" *Wrong!* You instead look around the room and say, "I'm going to find someone to help." Look for that person standing alone. Find out something about them and their business. If this is someone you really want to influence in the future, find a way to give first. This is not about you. It's not about begging for business or selling your wares. Find out what makes this person tick and practice flexing your reciprocity muscles. Deliver a gift to this person. Maybe you can introduce them to someone else in the room. We hold a warm spot in our hearts for some-one who has taken care of us in our social discomfort. In the fu-ture, deliver yet another gift to them. A pertinent article, a phone call, an introduction of a client to their business, which shows it is all about them. Find a way to do it again and again. Remember, the number one rule for networking is *give first, give first, give first*. If you want to set the tone for the relationship, you are the one who must take that first step to initiate the gift. In return, you will have created that sense of obligation. This person will want to look for a way to repay you.

Connie: I recall the developing relationship of one of my favourite lawyer clients. After several occasions of having given first, he finally turned to me and asked, "Why are you doing this for me?"

It was a very easy question to answer. I said, "I know I can count on you to provide top notch service to my clients and I know you would do the same for me should you ever have a chance to refer business back to me." Over the next few months, he sought out several opportunities to re-ciprocate. Moreover, we have been terrific part-ners ever since. In our relationship today, we cannot keep track of who owes whom—it just doesn't matter anymore. I want his business to prosper as much as he wants mine to.

My favourite place to golf is at a charity event on the practice putting green. I am a social golfer, not a real golfer. You know my type. Instead of golfing with the same three people all day long, I love to meet almost every golfer as the host of the putting competition. This is one of the few places on earth where people don't mind parting with $5 of their hard-earned cash for charity. It's inevitable: One of the foursome pulls out a $20 bill and loudly says he is paying for his group. With the rule of reciprocity in action, this brilliant guy gets to drink for free for the rest of the tournament as his group repays him for this kind gesture on the putting green.

Today's way of doing business is win/win, not win/lose. Win/win relationships rule the world of selling. What do you sell first? You sell yourself, of course. As stated in chapter 2, people must know, like, and trust you in order to want to do business with you in addition to your having the product or service they need.

What Are Some Give Firsts in Business or Personal Life?

How do people feel when they move to a new neighbourhood? They might feel very out of sorts, as they are not familiar with the basic amenities. Where is the local convenience store, pizza place, or supermarket? Who is a good dog groomer, or a dependable heating contractor to service the furnace? We were most impressed to see a realtor share a list of local service providers they recommended in the community to a new homeowner and offer up their assistance in their new neighbourhood.

How do people feel when they consider moving their bank accounts? It's just too much work, and what if something goes wrong? Will paycheques be switched into the new account on time to cover the monthly hydro, telephone, and mortgage payments? If the account balance is miscalculated, will the new bank honour cheques like the credit union did? Connie recently experienced the bank account transfer process and her new account manager reassured her she would keep an eye on her money to ensure it would all move over without a glitch. And it did! Whom do you think she phones now when she has a financial need? She calls her account manager, who looks out for her finances.

You are on a first date. What is the tone you want to set? Do you bring flowers or a small gift to impress your potential boyfriend or girlfriend? Or do you bring nothing at all?

Give first if you have someone you truly want to influence in your life. What might you say or do first to set the tone while building the relationship you want? Intentionally create that moment of opportunity after the recipient thanks you, and now you will be ready.

Gift vs. Reward

Which is more effective at getting your client or prospect to do as you wish, a gift or a reward? Do incentives work better than gifts?

This is an interesting question in sales, as many corporations spend millions of dollars on trinkets emblazoned with their company name and logo to give to their clients. We all like freebies, but are they really free? Do these gifts come with strings attached? Does the company logo on the picture frame sitting on your desk remind you to use this company for your business transactions? Although we think we are powerful in making choices and not easily manipulated or influenced, we often show preference to the companies we see most often. Have you noticed the strategic placements of brand name products in movies? Advertisers know we skip through commercials, so they are always looking for new ways to ensure brand exposure so we will recognize them when we're shopping. Have you noticed the drinking glasses in front of the judges on *American Idol*?

But which is more effective in getting what you ask for, a gift or a reward? We attended a workshop where Robert Cialdini discussed a survey where the two options were employed. One group of professionals was gifted a $20 cheque and were later asked to complete a lengthy survey. The second group of professionals were promised a $20 cheque if they completed the lengthy survey. Sixty-six percent of the professionals responded to the survey with the promise of a cheque as a reward for their time. Seventy-eight percent of professionals completed the survey when they were given a gift of $20 in advance of the lengthy survey request. A mere 1%

of the professionals cashed the gift cheque and did not return the completed survey. The results show what we have learned: A gift offered before a request gets a noticeable improvement in response rates.

The auto industry is famous for offering cash incentives for buying a new car. How effective are these incentives? The American auto companies have been using this approach for years, while Toyota and Honda have not. In recent years, GM, Ford, and Chrysler have lost market share while Toyota and Honda have gained share. The incentives merely indicate that the American companies are selling on price while the Japanese companies are selling on value. Value almost always wins out over price, and yet we never seem to learn this lesson. Short-term gain is for long-term pain.

Charities employ the gift technique when they make an appeal to prospects and ask for donations. When you receive a gift of an identifying tag for your key chain to have it returned in the event of loss, are you compelled to make a donation? In addition, are you not even more compelled after you have lost your keys and successfully had them returned? When you receive holiday gift tags, are you compelled to make a donation? Charities have seen a significant response to charitable donations from the give first strategy in asking for donations.

Best Practices
1. Decide whom you want to influence.
2. Decide on a thoughtful gift or favour to give them.
3. Find a way to help your prospect in a business sense.
4. Carefully script what you will say after the recipient says thank you.
5. Give first, give first, give first, and create a moment of opportunity.
6. Practice flexing your reciprocity muscles.
7. Make your response to "thank you" come from the heart.
8. Smile and look the client in the eye when you deliver your re-

sponse.

9. Pause for a few seconds after your response to let the sense of obligation sink in, and then ask them for what you want.
10. You are the initiator in building the relationship to a new level.

Chapter 4
Powerful Requests: Get What You Want

In this chapter, we will build on what we learned in the previous chapter on the rule of reciprocity. We learned that there is a moment of opportunity after someone says "thank you" and it reinforces that sense of obligation a client has to repay you. Now that we have created the right context, it's time to talk about how we want to phrase our request. Remember, people are more likely to say yes to those they owe.

When that moment of opportunity is before you, what will you do? Will you perform well and hope to be justly rewarded for your efforts? Will you hint at what you want or will you make a powerful request? It would appear that many of us are rather humble people and we would prefer to hint at the business rather than ask for it. You might discover that you *don't* ask for what you want. You might already be a success, but was it because you asked for what you wanted or because satisfied clients guessed and brought you what you needed? Other times you might feel frustrated at your results and wonder why your actions are not as effective as you would like. You will discover more about your personal style and we will help you to grow your business by getting more yeses from your clients in those moments of opportunity.

Let's face it, most of us don't really know what we want. "Sure I know what I want," your little voice says. "I want lots of money, good health, a family, and a lovely home." Drill down deeper. What exactly does that look like? What is "lots" of money? Is it $5,000 in your chequing account, or a million-dollar real estate portfolio? Is your lovely home a downtown rental or a five-bedroom estate in the country? You will discover a method to determine specifically what it is you want.

Connie: In our workshops, we discover time and time again that we are all humble people. We often feel that if we do things right then good things will happen to us. People should just know what it is we need and they should bring it. Being humble costs us dearly. I attribute the failure of my first marriage to this strange belief. I truly thought that if my husband loved me enough, he would know—automatically—what I needed without my asking. We don't like to ask for what we want. We would much rather hint at it. This applies to both business and our personal lives. You will discover how to empower yourself and calm that little humble voice in your head.

Those who do make powerful requests always outsell those who hint at the business. You will learn how to make powerful requests during moments of opportunity. If you practice these simple approaches to enhancing your ability—know what you want, create an empowering context for yourself, and ask for what you want—you will reap significant rewards in your professional and personal life.

Decide What You Want

One of the first rules to asking for the business is to know what you want. Many of us think we know what we want, when instead we are uncertain. With a specific goal in mind, we will know whether an appointment has been a success. As you prepare for a client meeting, take a few minutes to plan it out and think about the results you want.

We know certain predictable things will happen in every appointment, as you will read in chapter 10 on the various stages of the sales conversation. When these certain predictable things occur, we need to be ready. We need to know exactly what to say, especially during the moments of opportunity we intentionally create. Scripting is a powerful tool for successful sales professionals.

Here is a brief overview of the sales conversation. We need to be ready for the appointment. We need to welcome the client, ask why they are here, restate, and ask clarifying questions. Then help the client with their needs and thank them for their time and business. The following are some questions you might ask yourself as you prepare:

1. Why is the client coming to meet me? What is their primary need?
2. What additional needs do I foresee that they might not?
3. Review the information I have about my client. What more do I need?
4. What do I really want out of this meeting? What else?
5. What questions do I have for my client? List them.
6. When the client thanks me, what will I say?

A sales professional will script out specifically what they will say, but that little voice in your head speaks up: "I'll wing it since every client is different. Who knows what they will say? I have to respond in the moment." There is some truth to that argument; however, here is where we separate the ordinary from the extraordinary.

A successful professional will foresee how the meeting is going to go even before it starts. Create your desired outcome and you are more likely to accomplish it. Be intentional. After all, you will find what you look for. In *The 7 Habits of Highly Effective People,* Stephen Covey puts it this way: "Begin with the end in mind." So create a powerful appointment with specific goals. With planning and practice, you will be growing your business more than you thought was possible.

So, what do you want from this appointment? Let's ask it this way: In your wildest dreams, what is the absolute best outcome you can think of for your meeting? How will you get that result? What will you say?

Thank you—Thank You Very Much

After a client expresses their heartfelt thanks, we know we have a moment of opportunity. Take a minute right now to write down what you might say in response. Imagine a situation in your past where a client praised you highly for your extraordinary work. How did you reply? Write down a sentence or two right now. We will come back to what you have written in a moment.

When your client thanks you, they want to repay you for your efforts. It is your job now to help the client understand how to repay you. What did you decide you truly wanted from this appointment?

After the response to "thank you," most of the participants in our programs move to ask for a referral or for more business. How we make this request is a critical component to the sales process. Here is a good question to consider when making a proposal to a client:

If you have two options to present to a client, which do you present first, the larger request or the smaller request?

In business, we often have more than one option to present to a client that will meet their needs. Assuming that both options meet their needs, the question is, which do you present first?

We have experienced many different answers to this question in our workshops. Participants will say they want to provide the lowest cost option first to gain the client's trust and then add on features and benefits to demonstrate the added value with the increased cost. This is called the up-sell technique and is used by many in the sales business. McDonald's even uses this technique when they ask if you want to supersize your meal, and we often say yes to those extra fries.

Other participants disagree, and indicate they would present the higher cost option first because the client just might say yes and the sale is complete. If necessary, these participants feel that they could retreat if the client says no. We call this the down-sell technique, which is also used by many in the industry. We start high and take away features and benefits to reduce the cost.

Before we answer the question, we wish to present some interesting research. A group of researchers conducted a study that clearly highlights how concessions can have an influence on getting people to say yes to a request that few people would agree to.[11] They posed as representatives from the county juvenile detention centre and approached students walking by on campus to ask if they would be willing to chaperone a group of delinquents on a day trip to the zoo. This was to be a volunteer program, and as the researchers expected, only 17% of those asked agreed to do it.

However, another group of students were asked a different question first—a much larger request: Would you volunteer to be a big brother or big sister to one of the kids down at the centre, which would require two hours of your time every week for the next two years? Well, as you can imagine, the students were stunned by this large and time-consuming request. Most of the students refused the large request.

The researchers then made a concession. If they refused the large request, the students were asked if they would chaperone a group of delinquents on a day trip to the zoo. Under these circumstances, three times as many students agreed to the concession compared to those who were only asked to chaperone. It was the same request, but when they made a large request first, the students were more receptive to the second request. Why did this happen? It's the power of making a concession.

A concession is the act of conceding. By conceding something, such as a point previously declared in an argument or debate, we are admitting to or acknowledging that the other party is right. When you make a concession, you are giving something up. If we follow the rule of reciprocity, the person you are dealing with will be obliged to give up something in return.

It's the art of negotiation. You could start high and make a concession, and the other person negotiating will feel obligated to make a concession in return. We see this in our everyday lives when we negotiate. The example above is an extreme one, but it clearly points out the impact that making a concession can have on us all. When someone gives us a gift, the predictable rule of reciprocity kicks in. We want to repay in kind. If we concede to you, you will feel compelled to concede to us and say yes to our second request.

Lunch Bag Lady

Connie: I was asked to be a member of the "Lunch Bag Ladies" organization—the mothers committed to providing nutritious lunches to the kids in elementary school. Volunteer "Bags" would be required to collect orders from each classroom, make shopping lists, and collect money each week. They would shop, put meals together, and deliver the freshly made lunches to each classroom. This would take hours each week. As a full-time career woman, wife, mother, housekeeper, and chief bottle washer, I just couldn't figure out how to add this "membership" to my already overpacked life. I wanted to say yes and felt guilty for not contributing to such a great cause; I sheepishly said no.

The president of the Lunch Bag Ladies said, "Well, if you won't do that, will you be a server at our quarterly hot dog day?" I immediately said yes, and the guilt was lifted from my shoulders. What just happened in this conversation? Could the rule of reciprocity also be at play when someone makes a concession to us? Was the rule of reciprocity at work on me here?

When someone turns down a request and the asker immediately follows through with a second smaller request, there is a sense of obligation to repay the asker with a concession. This is exactly what the Lunch Bag president did. She asked if I would be a full-fledged Lunch Bag Lady and I declined. I felt guilty saying no and she knew it. She immediately made a concession, asking for a less onerous commitment. I felt obligated to concede. My position of "no" changed to a guilt-free "yes," and I happily dished out wieners on hot dog day.

Our question again is: If you have two options to present to a client, which option do you present first, the most expensive or the least expensive? The research indicates that you should start with the most expensive option first, and if the client agrees, the sale is over and everyone is happy. However, if the client says no, then you have a chance to retreat. If you then make a concession, the client will feel obliged to concede with a yes to the second request.

The client will often accept your first recommendation. No need to keep selling. The client might ask a question to clarify before accepting your first proposal. The client also might reject it and offer up a reason for declining. At this point, you are prepared to concede to their point and offer up your second recommendation.

What happens to us when someone says no? We shrink like a wilted flower. We feel rejected. We might even take it as personal rejection. Unconsciously, we might say the client doesn't like us and we back away from the situation, trying to escape from their company as quickly as possible. Most salespeople are afraid of "no" because they really don't know what to do.

Moment of Opportunity
Remember that "thank you" is a moment of opportunity for you.

The word *no* is also a moment of opportunity. It might be a word you try to avoid at all costs, but in the context of concessions, *no* is a word that presents an opportunity. That is the power in the moment of opportunity after someone says no. The key is to be ready with a concession to capitalize on it.

Service Charges

Who buys more of the most expensive service charge packages at banks, people who choose them online or those who go into a branch and discuss them with the staff? Most of the participants in our workshops will always respond that the branch staff will sell more of the most expensive service charge packages because that's what they sell. They are the salespeople after all and know how to sell. These are usually the participants who suggest offering the most expensive option first from the previous question.

From our research at most banks as of mid-2007, the Internet outsells the branches on the most expensive service charge package by a ratio of four to one. Why does this happen?

When you log onto online banking and search for service charge packages, they list the most expensive first. Once clients see the cost, features, and benefits, it creates the context for what they want and they were sold. For those who thought it was too expensive, they moved down to the second on the list and would buy that. By simply putting the most expensive service charge package first, the banks increased sales of their top three packages. The websites make powerful requests, and the clients respond by buying.

In contrast, branch sales professionals reviewed the service charge packages for best fit, and decided to offer the less expensive package or the most frequently sold package in that marketplace. They would censure themselves! They even had trouble seeing the value of the most expensive package and were afraid clients might say no, so they would offer the least expensive packages that would meet clients' needs. Even when a higher priced option was the best fit, they would present a less expensive option based on their personal judgment. Then, they really hoped the client would agree with their suggestion. What often happened was that the client would take the less expensive package and end up paying extra fees because the package didn't meet all their needs and they would come back to the branch to complain. The branch would refund the extra service charge and sometimes move the client to a more expensive package. All this extra work simply because they didn't give the client a chance to say yes to a more powerful request.

With this evidence in hand, a bright regional leader declared a new best practice in his region. The top service charge package was to be offered uncensored to clients. Service charge revenues sky-rocketed! The staff felt better too. They were relieved to have plan B or a slightly less expensive option in their pocket should plan A fail. They were shocked by their results. They assessed their clients' true needs and presented the appropriate package; meanwhile, service charge revenues increased significantly, and, more important, these clients never had a service charge issue or complaint after the sale.

Refrigerators

Have you purchased a refrigerator from a major retail chain lately? Go into the store and have a look at how they have the refrigerators laid out on the floor. They are all in a row with the most expensive stainless steel beauty first in line. You can't help it; you must stop at this fridge and open the doors and see all the movable shelves and the size. Wow, this is quite a fridge. This first refrigerator you see creates the context for what you want in a refrigerator. The stores know this and it is why they are set up in that order. It wasn't always so. A number of years ago, the refrigerators were set up with the stoves as a package in appearance. They soon discovered that by placing the most expensive item first in a row, people would buy more of the expensive refrigerators. They didn't sell any more refrigerators, but their revenues went way up.

So if you want to buy a refrigerator at one of these stores, what should you do? Cover your eyes and run to the back of the store and start looking there. You will save money and be just as happy with your purchase. It won't happen, however, as that stainless steel beauty is calling your name as you walk by. The power of concessions is at work even with refrigerators.

Referrals

People have great difficulty in asking for a referral. Most salespeople want referrals and will make attempts but not powerful requests. They might say, "If you have any friends or family, I hope you'll give them my business card," or, "If you were happy with my service, I sure hope you'll refer me." The one we hear most often is mentioned in chapter one: "If you have any family or friends who would be interested in our service, could you give them one of my cards?" When we restate this one with a pause after "friends," they usually get the message about hinting at the business rather than asking for it. It is such a simple matter to change the request to: "Will you please hand out my cards to your family and friends who would be interested in our service?" A few simple word changes and the impact on a client is significant. It is now a meaningful request. The initial statements are minor requests, which is certainly not what you really want from clients. Satisfied clients are dying to help you but don't know how. Imagine what would happen to your results if you made powerful requests at these moments of opportunity—when clients thank you.

Remember, we are humble people and we don't want to appear too bold, and we are afraid that people will say no to us. When we only hint at the business, we will get what we deserve. Asking for the business is where success lies.

Put yourself in the client's shoes. Your client has just delivered a heartfelt message of thanks and wants to repay you, but you are busy being humble and deflecting their thanks. This leaves the client feeling uncomfortable. The sense of obligation weighs heavily upon their shoulders. Since childhood, we have been well trained in reciprocity, to repay others for their kindness. Clients do not know how to repay you. This moment of opportunity ends up feeling awkward for both of you.

Imagine finding your boldness and letting go of your humbleness. Let's look at your words and scripting. Look back at what you wrote. What do you say after a client thanks you? Check to see if it validates the fact you have done the client a favour. Does it instill a sense of obligation for repayment? Do you paint a picture of the future in your relationship? Do you ask them for something? What do you ask for? Does your sentence or two include a question mark? Remember, asking requires a question!

In our workshops, many people discover that they make statements when they thought they were asking for referrals. "Thank you very much!" "I sure hope you'll come back" or "I hope you'll refer me to your friends and family." This is just the beginning; we really need to look at what we want from our clients. What is the best thing clients could do for us? Sales are all about powerful requests, and concessions, if necessary, to close the deal.

We always ask our participants about the best thing customers could do for them. They often state such things as, "Talk about me to their friends" or "Give me more business" or "Provide referrals." We ask them to be more specific. What is the best thing a customer could do? Some will suggest getting a name or having them move all their business to you. The second one is quite good, but when it come to referrals, what is the absolute best referral you could ever get? Someone will finally say, "Introduce me to a family member or friend who would want to deal with me." That's it. An introduction is the very best referral you will ever get. Our suggestion is to make a powerful request and ask for what you want. How will you ask for this introduction?

This is more difficult than it might seem, especially when you are face to face with a client. Just try it and see what happens. You could say, "I know you really appreciated the service I provided. Will you introduce me to a friend who would be interested in our service?" If the client says yes, you have done an exceptional job, but if the client says, "No, I'm not too comfortable with that. I don't really know anyone at this time," then this is your moment of opportunity. You can make a concession, and the client will be ready and willing to say yes to your second request. That second request could be, "Well, here are a few of my cards, will you hand them out to your family and friends who would be interested in talking to me?" The client will likely say yes to that request, and almost immediately.

Here is the difference. Under the first scenario, when you just asked them to hand out cards, they will take them home. Three days later, they might find the cards in a pocket and say, "Oh yeah, Susan did a great job for me. I will put this card away, and if I need more advice, I'll call her." No referrals to speak of.

Under the second scenario, they will find your cards three days later and say, "Oh yeah, I promised Susan I'd hand out a couple of her cards to my friends. John is coming over tonight; I'll give him one and tell him how great she is." That's the difference. The referral behaviour will be changed because the commitment to you is stronger after you made a concession. Try it on for size, and be sure to make those powerful requests.

Brokers and Realtors

Mortgage brokers often try to get more business referred to them through realtors. It is a tough competitive business—realtors have brokers chasing them all the time. The concession approach works exceptionally well with realtors as well. After you have done an amazing job for a realtor and he has thanked you, the usual approach is to ask for referrals. We ask these salespeople what they want from realtors. Many say more business; some say two good deals for a change. When we ask what they *really* want from a realtor, someone will finally say that they want all their business.

This is a powerful request, but what words will work best? We suggest they say, "We worked really well on this deal; I would like to partner with you and be your exclusive mortgage provider. Will you work with me?" That's a powerful request that few mortgage brokers would make. They are nervous about being so bold but we have had many try it and they have been amazed at the response. They find that this is exactly what the realtor has been looking for so they can reliably secure their clients' financing and close the sale.

If the realtor says, "No thanks, I already have three people I use on a regular basis," what can you do? That's right, this is a moment of opportunity for you to make a concession. "Well, if you can't do that, will you let me quote on all your deals?" They might still say no, but this is another moment for you to make a further concession. You could say, "Well, if we can't do that, are you working on a deal right now that I can pre-approve?" We will almost guarantee that the realtor will be ready to say yes. The weight of the obligation is heavy on their shoulders and they want to repay the debt they owe. This gives you another opportunity to prove your worth, and when you do, you repeat the entire exercise all over again. Within a few months, the realtor will be ready to say yes to that exclusive partnership.

Would You Like Dessert?

Have you noticed that most restaurant servers want you to order dessert after your meal? This makes perfectly good sense to the restaurateur; there is a large margin of profit on desserts, and when the server increases the total bill, this means a higher tip. After a nice dinner and perhaps some wine, the server will usually ask if you would like to see the dessert menu. If they don't have a dessert menu, they will simply ask if you would like dessert. Most of us are quite happy to say "no thanks" to this request, as we are often concerned about calories. The restaurant doesn't sell many desserts with this technique.

Thinking in terms of reciprocity and making a powerful request, what could a server say to a patron after the meal? The statement "Would you like dessert?" doesn't work well because it's easy for us all to say no. Restaurants that sell more desserts simply have their staff make more powerful requests. They say, "How was everything today?" We respond with, "Everything was wonderful, thank you." A moment of opportunity occurs after "thank you."

"That's great, I am delighted you enjoyed yourselves this evening. Now, to top off your meal, we have some amazing desserts; today, we have our chocolate mousse cheesecake drizzled with fresh raspberry sauce, our chocolate pecan pie with ice cream…" and they go on to list several other delectable desserts, describing them in great detail. They then say, "Which one of our desserts would you like today?"

We now have a choice of desserts, which sound amazing, rather than just a yes-or-no question about having dessert that we don't know about. This is the difference between knowing what you want and making a powerful request and being humble and making a weak request. The results in dessert sales speak for themselves. It is this simple to be persuasive and influence your client to do what they really want to do anyway. They just need some encouragement.

Now if the client says "no thanks" to the desserts, our server can now retreat to offering an exotic coffee and will usually win the order. If not, retreats to coffee or tea work as well. Pay attention to your servers' sales approaches. You are their source of income, and the tips will make or break their night at work.

Up-Selling

In the financial services industry, advisors want all of a customer's business. Most customers, on the other hand, want to spread their money around. It seems they feel better about having investments in several locations. As an advisor, let's say you just put together a great plan for a client's money invested with you. The client is delighted and thanks you a great deal for the extra work you put into this program. The moment of opportunity is to clarify the sense of obligation with your response to their thank you. The request you want to make is for the transfer of all their other assets to your institution. What do you say?

Many will be humble and make a small or a weak request. We have heard such questions as, "Would you perhaps consider moving more of your assets over to our company?" Is this a powerful request? No. It's a humble request that is already anticipating the rejection about to be delivered.

Make that powerful request by highlighting what you have done and recommend they transfer the rest of their assets under one roof. You could provide some additional reasoning behind this request, but the request must be for all their business. If they say yes, you can rejoice. If they say no, it is a moment for a concession, where you could request they move all their RRSPs to you. You will get them to say yes to this second request much often using the concession technique than if you were to just ask for RRSPs first. Be more comfortable making powerful requests, and be prepared with a well scripted concession.

Powerful Requests

Connie: At the age of sixteen, I had a job as a part-time teller with a national trust company. It was a fabulous job for a kid in school. I made a fortune. When I finished school, I joined the company full time and enjoyed the work. Actually, it didn't feel like work at all. It felt more like I was destined to be there to make a contribution to this company and their clients. In the eighteen years with this organization, I was promoted twelve times. I went from retail banking, to corporate lending, to pension trust, to the securities industry, and back out to finish my career in retail banking. I loved this company. If you asked for my name, I would shake your hand and tell you my name along with the company name. It was automatic. I was the company. I finished school, dated, married, and bought my first two houses while I worked there. I had my two children while employed by this company. I grew up in this organization.

Then one day, I was fired. I didn't see it coming, especially since my review a couple weeks earlier showed that all was fine. Nevertheless, the company was very generous in my termination. They provided career counselling and a severance package, and when I went back to ask for more, they gave it to me. However, what I needed most, they couldn't give me: my identity. I didn't know who I was without working for this trust company. I was devastated.

My sister Betty suggested I do a course on inner child and family of origin work. Betty and our younger sister, Linda, had both done this amazing work. I flew to California and spent three long days in this course. Something was brewing in my soul. At the end, I was unleashed into the world. I went home to practice my new skills for in the real world for two weeks. I then went back to California for five days to complete the course. The work was cathartic. I got to know who I was, where I came from, and why I was here on this planet. I saw incredible things about myself and the world around me.

As the course came to a close, we were asked to invite loved ones to the graduation. Betty and her husband, Michael, would be there. Everyone else was in Canada. My husband, Greg, was home taking care of our kids, the house, the dog, and his business. I really wanted to share this with him. I wanted to have him there. I called him on the phone and left this message: "I am finishing this amazing course. On Sunday night, I complete the course and I really wish you could be there." Click. I hung up the phone. One of the participants in the course asked if my husband was coming to the graduation. I told her that I didn't know. When asked why, I explained that I was only able to leave a message a couple of days ago and still hadn't heard back. She asked what I said in my message. I told her. She asked, "What else?"

"That was it."

"Connie, you never asked him to come!"

Oh no! I only hinted. I never asked for what I wanted. When I got back on the phone and got that darn answering machine again, this time I said, "Greg, I'm doing this life-changing course and I really wish you could be here Sunday night to join me at my graduation. Will you please come?" Click.

I never heard back from Greg. The graduation celebration was about to start. The ten graduates were joined arm-in-arm in a love circle, with their heads bowed down and their eyes closed. The facilitators were in the middle of the circle and ran down the list of the graduates' incredible accomplishments. As they read, the door to the room opened and the guests tip-toed in. I felt all my anxiety wash away. I rationalized that it didn't matter whether Greg were here. He would see the benefits of my work when I got home.

The facilitators finished their summary and said, "Now, open your eyes, turn around, and embrace the world and your family." And who was standing right behind me when I opened my eyes? You guessed it! My husband was standing there, arms wide open for an embrace. I cried from the bottom of my heart. It was an amazing gift to share with my husband. Not only did he make arrangements for the kids and the business, he flew down in a terrible snowstorm. Also close by were Linda, Betty, and Michael. It was truly a magical night for us all. Even more so because I had made a powerful request!

From that point forward, I practice making powerful requests. I learned that when I hint at the business, I am disappointed by the results. Powerful requests include a clear question, and they make things happen! We promise you too will be rewarded if you apply this lesson. Make powerful requests!

Negotiating

Many people say they absolutely hate negotiating! When it comes time to ask for the price on a big-ticket item, these people will ask the price and willingly pay it or just walk away to avoid any further discomfort.

On the other hand, some people just love to negotiate. Where do you find these hard-nosed negotiators? You find them at garage sales, of course. People negotiate at garage sales all the time. We ask $5 for a lamp, you offer $3, and we settle on $4. It's a game. The unwritten rule at garage sales says the price is always negotiable.

Start at the top of your range as you begin your negotiation. The prospect should not be surprised at where you start. When the prospect pushes back, you drop your price a little, but not to the bottom of where you could potentially go. Make small concessions, little by little, otherwise you leave the prospect with a mixed message. The client is trying to figure out how low you will go. If you retreat to your rock-bottom price immediately, they will not believe you are truly at your bottom and the negotiation will be over. As you near your bottom price, make the concessions smaller and less willingly. Maybe there is a reciprocal concession you can ask for in repayment for the concessions you have already made.

Connie: I used to be one of those people who hates to ne-
          gotiate, but it is an area in my life I decided to
          transform. Being a powerful negotiator in sales is
          definitely a good quality to have!

          I shared my dislike for negotiating with my
          mentor. After numerous chats—"What does ne-
          gotiating mean to you? What is it you don't like
          about it?"—we got to the root of my problem. It
          was my belief that negotiating meant someone
          had to win and someone had to lose. I love to be
          of service to people, to make a real difference in
          their lives, and to create win/win situations. To
          me, the word *negotiating* had a negative conno-
          tation implying win/lose.

          We created a new context for negotiating.
          Negotiating became a discussion about a client's
          needs and wants and a sharing of my objective
          for the client. It has become a dance of win/win
          so no one walks away feeling like they have to
          give away the farm to close the deal. Coming
          from this new context of negotiating is how we
          honour each other to create win/win solutions; I
          have much more freedom and pleasure in these
          discussions today.

          To have meaningful long-term relationships,
          we need to create mutually beneficial win/win sit-
          uations. In my role as an account manager, I take
          great pleasure in introducing my lawyer clients to
          my lender clients. In the end, my lenders receive
          value from my lawyers, and my lawyers receive
          value from my lenders. I make two people happy
          and gain more business in my line of work. Even
          better yet, my company pays me to do it.

Creating Empowering Contexts

Imagine you have been called in to your boss' office for a meeting this afternoon. Where does your mind immediately go? Do you say to yourself, "What am I getting into trouble for now? I wonder what she wants?"

What happens if you dwell in that "Am I in trouble?" mindset? How does the rest of your morning go? How does that forthcoming meeting affect your mood?

Stop right there! You could go down that dirt road of suffering and misery or you could create an empowering place to stand. Which one will you choose? The choice is yours.

Connie: When I was working for a trust company many years ago, I met an influential man. His shirt was usually untucked and had spills of past meals on it. His hair was dirty and uncombed. He walked with a gait. Every morning, he headed to the free coffee and cookies in my branch. I judged him harshly, and maybe you would too. I thought this man was probably homeless and having his breakfast almost every morning in my branch. This man taught me, then a branch manager, a life lesson I will never forget.

He was indeed living on a shoestring budget when it came to his clothing and appearance. Weeks later, the receptionist told me I had an appointment with a highly valued client. I looked out into the waiting area and did not see a highly valued client. I saw that dirty, uncombed, poorly dressed man walking towards me with a handful of scrunched up papers. He sat down in my office. I held my breath; he smelled like he looked. He said he wanted a discount if he were to renew his mortgages with my company. I found it hard to believe the man across from me owned a bar of soap, let alone a house. I asked him for his renewal notice, and much to my surprise, he did have a house—six houses and six mortgages up for renewal, to be exact. I was shocked. This dishevelled man was a landlord. His clothing budget was minimal, but his net worth wasn't. I made the mistake of judging a book by its cover. It's human nature. Lessons in influence can come from some of the strangest messengers we meet.

We sometimes judge wrongly, and we take actions based on these misjudgments. In our workshops, we teach our customer service officers (CSOs) not to judge a book by its cover. When a CSO opens a bank account, they judge the client and offer the lowest priced option to the client first.

When we ask why, CSOs often respond with, "Well, I wouldn't want to pay that much to do my banking."

"But, you have done your homework. You know how the client likes to spend their money. You know the best choice for them. Why do you still offer a lower priced option?" We finish the rant and softly say, "Why would you not give clients what they really need and want?"

We often let our own personal feelings and judgments get in the way and risk falling into the trap of thinking that all people are just like us. Even when CSOs have gathered information and do what the bank pays them to do, they still go with their personal judgments first.

When we discover why we do things, we begin to see how ridiculous it is to treat others based on our own judgments. Think how powerful it would be to offer people what they want based on what they told us they need.

When you do your homework and give an informed professional recommendation, present your higher priced option with your compelling reasons. Then wait. Timing is important.

The Powerful Pause

We all know the sound of nothingness, anticipation, tension, angst, and the sound of the brain mulling things over, trying to figure out what to say. The sound of silence in a pause screams at you. A pause of five seconds seems like five minutes to you, but a pause of five seconds to a client seems like two seconds.

Salespeople generally don't like pauses. We love to fill in the silence with the sound of our own voices. We want to keep selling and talking away, much to the detriment of the sale. We offer option A, and before a client even has a chance to speak, we offer option B. This talks them out of option A before we even know if they were going to accept that proposal. We haven't given them a chance to consider option A in the first place.

Make your recommendation, make your request, and then wait for the client's thoughts and comments. The client needs a chance to digest what you have just presented. Maybe you've presented this same recommendation five hundred times before, but this client—in this moment—needs a chance to think. It's difficult to do so if you keep on filling that silent think space with your words. The client needs to understand and figure out in their own mind. Let them! Don't succumb to the screaming silence. Wait patiently. If you cannot do it patiently, at least do it silently.

When a lender successfully sells creditor insurance, it's often sold at a package price. The lender might say, "Your loan, disability, and life insurance payment is four hundred dollars a month. How does that sound versus your twelve credit cards at twenty-eight percent?" Pause. Wait.

Give the client a chance to say yes. Use the power of a pause. If their answer is no, be prepared with a concession in the moment of opportunity and your chances of getting a yes are significantly higher than if you waited for another day to come back with your concession.

Making Concessions and Big-Ticket Items

Let's look at big-ticket items, the rule of reciprocity, and the principle of concessions in a retail situation. Who are the salespeople who come to mind as masters at sales, masters of negotiating, masters of making concessions?

Connie: My husband and I were recently looking to purchase a new car. We had combed through the consumer guides for the past year, as well as the automotive section of the newspaper. We had narrowed down our search for the new family/business vehicle to two models, a Subaru and a Hyundai.

Being a keen observer of people—salespeople in particular—my antenna was up the moment we entered the lot of the car dealership. As we walked through the door into the sales centre, I watched for the initial welcome. I am one of those people who judge the quality of a restaurant by how clean the bathroom is. It's all the little details that make the biggest of difference in my customer experience, which determines whether I want to deal with you.

We drive a lot in our family, so simply taking a new vehicle for a test drive is not enough. The service experience is equally important to us. At the dealership, I check out the service department, a place where I had hoped not to spend too much time. I noticed the faces of those waiting for their cars to be repaired. I sat down, picked up a magazine, and in the chit-chat with the person next to me, I found out their experience with this service centre. I love the windows that look into the service garage. I could see the mechanics working away, greasy handed and with enough care to place seat covers into the cars before sitting in them. I like the signs over the windows that read, "The reason we work at ABC dealership: for our customers and their families." I wanted the mechanics to be able to see our anxious faces as we waited for the diagnosis of any automobile problems.

The two car options were within a few thousand dollars of each other. We sat in the first vehicle and checked out the storage space beyond the seating, the kilometres per litre rating, and the warrantees. We had taken the first model out for a test drive, but it didn't have quite the feel we wanted, so off we go to test drive the alternate choice.

This is where the fun began, as my service radar is finely tuned. We stepped through the door and were met with a warm beautiful smile. "How can we help you today?"

We explain what we are looking for. The receptionist came around the counter to shake our hands and take us to the resident expert in the field of crossover vehicles. We shake hands and pleasantries are exchanged. The salesperson took us over to the car we were here to see. We sat in it, and it passed the sit test. We opened the doors, pushed down and pulled up the folding seats, checked out the spaciousness, and then looked to each other and nodded. This is looking good so far.

"Do you want to test drive the vehicle?" the salesperson offered.

We did, but I had just noticed the sticker price on the window and said, "This car is more expensive than the competition's version we just drove."

The salesperson went on to describe the features and benefits of the model before us.

"I understand," I said, "but I'm still not convinced it warrants the higher price."

"The price is not negotiable, but I will check with my manager while you take it out for a test drive."

We returned from the drive. We liked this vehicle, but we didn't want to show all our cards just yet; this is a big-ticket item and we wanted to negotiate. We wanted a concession on the price. The salesperson returned and said, "How was the ride?"

"Not too bad," we responded, trying to hide how much we liked this vehicle.

"It's highly unusual, but the manager has offered to reduce the price of the car by three hundred dollars, but please keep it quiet."

Our eyebrows rose a little, and we started to like the car a little better now that a concession had been made. We walked around it, stepped aside to chat privately, and then agreed we wanted more. "We really like this car, does it come with the car mats or do we have to buy them on top of the price?"

"I noticed from your driver's license that it's your birthday next week. The mats will be my personal gift to you if you buy the car today. Happy birthday!" he replied. I was beginning to like this guy; how thoughtful he would notice my birthday! He asked us about our hobbies and discovered that skiing is one of our pastimes. The conversation went downhill from there—downhill skiing, that is.

"Where do you ski? Have you skied anywhere else in the world?" he asked as he suggested an add-on package we should consider adding to the car purchase. He went on to describe how easy it is to mount skis onto this high performance roof rack.

After a long day of skiing, you want it to be easy to get the car packed up and go home. I was thinking about how I push myself to do that last run and enjoy the full day, and how exhausted I usually am, wishing someone would just carry me home. Never mind getting my ski boots and ski suit off and packing up the car. "Good point!" I responded.

The rack package was $750. We had to have it. The transaction was no longer about the car—it was about the options. At that moment, the salesperson knew he had the sale.

So what can we take away from this car shopping experience? What can we learn from it to practice in our own jobs?

The person started out by offering the highest priced option first, and he made it seem as though the price were non-negotiable. When we didn't budge, he went to the boss—the authority figure—and grudgingly made a concession. We stayed in the game. We asked for a further concession and he made a personal one by offering the car mats as a birthday gift out of his own pocket. The rule of reciprocity is in high gear with a personal gift. We expected the concession made by the boss, but when the salesperson offered up a personal concession of his own, we felt the obligation weighing heavily on us and made a concession of our own. We accepted the "needed" roof rack option and therefore accepted the car with the rack.

When you have two options to present to a prospect, offer the higher priced option first. If the prospect takes it, you are done selling. If not, present your concession and the prospect will likely respond with a concession of their own: an acceptance of your second request. It is predictable. It is human nature.

Another big-ticket item we all hope to purchase once or twice in our lifetime is a home. Let us take a look at the buying and selling process and how concessions come in to play in the real estate industry.

Let's say you have found a house you like and are ready to make an offer, but you aren't prepared to pay the full asking price. Do you offer the absolute top price you are prepared to pay right off the bat? What do you expect will happen when your agent presents the offer? How will the vendor's agent respond? What might the vendor think if you decided to save everyone time and offered your biggest and final concession right off the top?

Despite going straight to your top offer right at the beginning, what do you think the vendor would expect? You got it, further concessions. The vendor expects that the purchaser has more to offer. The vendor pushes for more without realizing that this is your top offer and the deal dies.

When you present a small concession first, the vendor feels obligated to respond with a concession. You then ask for another small concession, getting closer to your top bid, and the vendor comes back with another concession. Now you are close to an agreed price. When negotiating for high-valued items or contracts, be very careful not to offer all of your potential concessions in just one shot. Our advice to you is to break it down and present each concession.

Review of Concessions

Most of us are humble people and are afraid to make powerful requests. You will be more successful if you know what you want and then ask for it. If the client says no to your first request, you can use the rejection as a moment of opportunity to make a concession and the client will be more likely to say yes to your second request than if you made that request alone. Always ask for the most expensive first and be prepared to make a concession when you have options to present to a client.

It is not always the question itself that wins the day but instead the context in which the question is placed. In the context of concessions, people tend to say yes to those they owe.

Best Practices

1. "Thank you" is a moment of opportunity. It creates the context for you to ask for the business or a referral.
2. Decide on your goal for your client interaction.
3. Decide what kind of relationship you want: a client or referral source.
4. Ask for what you want, don't hint at it.
5. Powerful requests are questions, not statements.
6. When you have two options to present to a client, always present the largest or most expensive request first.
7. Give your client the opportunity to say yes.
8. If they say no, be prepared to make a concession.
9. "No" is a moment of opportunity. It creates the context for you to make a concession.
10. People are more committed once they have agreed to a concession.
11. Script out your powerful requests.
12. Practice making powerful requests with your co-workers.

Chapter 5
Do As I Say: The Power of Authority

We have a regrettable tendency to be unduly influenced by authority. An authority figure such as a doctor has credibility and influence simply by the designation of their title. We seem to set aside our normal rational thought processes and blindly believe someone in authority and often do as they request without question. These authority figures are assumed to have more knowledge or expertise in certain areas and we therefore tend to trust them and do as they say. In many instances, such as in the case of a doctor, they do have expertise in areas we don't and it makes perfectly good sense to trust them and do as they recommend.

The use of authority in a sales environment is a powerful influence tool, and there are various ways to enhance one's authority and credibility. The most effective authority figure is a credible authority—one who is both knowledgeable and trustworthy.

Weaknesses

Here is a simple sales-related question that many of you face when dealing with a presentation to a customer, a group of customers, or a direct sales conversation: If you have a weakness in your product or service offering to a client, when should you mention this weakness? Early in the conversation, in the middle of the conversation, at the end of the conversation, or never? Remember that most products or services have some type of weakness associated with them; however, for this question, we will not include the items that must have full disclosure to a client by law. Let's assume for this question that it is a small weakness.

The Question

You have a weakness in your product or service. When during the sales conversation would you mention this weakness, early, late, in the middle, or never? Now write your answer down on a piece of paper so you can refer back to it.

We have asked this question of over four thousand salespeople in our research, and the answers always indicate a great variety of responses. We usually present to groups of salespeople in the same role in the same company, and we are surprised at the disagreement that occurs when we discuss the answers.

It seems there is no specific training around this question of when to present a weakness. Many suggest in the middle—we call this the "toasted sandwich technique." You slide the weakness in between the cheese and lettuce and hope the client won't notice the weakness at all. It's sandwiched between the features and the benefits.

Others suggest mentioning the weakness at the end. These salespeople believe that since they have laid out such a successful sales pitch, the client is already sold, making the weakness mentioned at the end an afterthought with little impact on results. We call this the "carpet sales technique." Imagine the client standing on a carpet, and when you're finished the presentation, you reach down and pull the carpet out from under the client, using the weakness. If the client is still standing, you have a sale.

Some have suggested they would never mention a weakness unless the customer asks about it, since it might not be a weakness at all. There's no sense in raising an issue that might not even be an issue.

Finally, some say to mention the weakness at the beginning to get it out of the way and so it can be overcome by the features and benefits. It would appear that many salespeople think the client will forget about the weakness as they proceed with the features and benefits. Perhaps these salespeople believe clients have short-term memory problems.

The Answer

What is the correct answer? Most people we have interviewed focus on the product rather than look at what the customer really wants. We believe the customer really wants to buy from someone who is knowledgeable and trustworthy. Salespeople often forget that what they are really selling is themselves. The client wants affirmation early in the conversation that the salesperson is someone they can trust and who knows what they're talking about.

Outlining the weakness early in the conversation tells the client that you are both knowledgeable about your product or service and honest enough to explain the pros and the cons. The client will often say to themselves, "Wow, this person really knows their stuff and they are even honest enough to showcase the good with the not-so-good to really give me a clear picture of what I'm buying." This shows the client that you are an authority on the subject and honest enough to give the straight goods.

Everything you say after this impression of knowledge and honesty is ingrained in your client's mind will have much more impact. The client will be much more willing to buy from you. Consumers want to buy from people they trust. Would you buy a house or invest your retirement funds with someone you didn't trust? None of us would. We all want to deal with people we trust. This simple action will enhance a feeling of trust between you and your client. The client will have a more positive relationship with you, because they will trust what you say next.

Weakness First

Marketing companies use this tactic quiet effectively. Before they added a variety of flavours, Listerine would say, "The taste you hate twice a day." Buckley's is a classic case of using the weakness strategy to persuade you that their product works. They are quite upfront in telling consumers that the product tastes awful but works. What would happen if they didn't tell you about the taste in the marketing ads? You buy the product, take it home, pour some of the liquid onto a spoon, and take a sip. *Wow,* this stuff tastes terrible. The next thing you do is check the best before date to see if the product has expired, because no product should taste this bad. You discover that the date is fine and you assume the product must have gone bad, so you throw out the entire bottle. If this were the case, the company didn't inform the prospective client of the product's weakness to its detriment.

Instead, Buckley's openly tells consumers that the product tastes awful. You buy the product, take a sip, and say, "They were right—it's awful; therefore, it must work." Having Buckley's tell you it tastes bad creates a sense of credibility in the company. It gives their product promise equal if not more credibility. Buckley's amazingly effective marketing strategy works again and again on all of us, and they have created a huge brand around awful taste. This is a great example of positioning product weakness first to build trust and persuade clients to buy a product.

Realtors

Real estate agents are required by law to tell clients of any large weaknesses in the properties they sell. If an agent is aware of a giant leak in the basement of a house, they must divulge this information. But many other weaknesses in the house don't have to be mentioned, and many agents refuse to use this weakness technique. We think this approach should be reconsidered. Consider that a purchaser is spending a huge amount of money on a home and are usually inexperienced in buying something of this magnitude. They are looking for someone they can trust—someone with authority, knowledge, and honesty to assist with this purchase.

In our discussions with realtors, many have indicated that they will be honest in their approach with all their clients. They might go into the kitchen and say it's a little small, but that the dining room and family room are just awesome. If the weakness is obvious, it is always advisable to mention it first rather than have the client say, "This kitchen seems a little small." When the client says it, the weakness becomes a problem in purchasing the home, but when the realtor mentions the weakness, it has much less of an impact because it is always followed by a feature that overcomes it.

It's all about credibility. A good salesperson is in business for the long haul and not just one sale. Repeat business and referrals are provided to salespeople who are presenting themselves as honest, knowledgeable, and able to provide advice on the pros and cons of the potential purchase. Mentioning a weakness early in the conversation does just that.

Mortgage Brokers

In the mortgage business, clients always ask the mortgage rep or broker the same question almost immediately: "What's your best rate?" A good salesperson knows how to handle this question to build their credibility. A weakness first is a powerful tool in this instance as well. How do you respond to this question?

According to our own research, most people try to shift the client away from rate and talk about features and benefits, terms and conditions, and service options, but the client still has one thing on their mind: the rate. No matter what the broker says, the client still has "What's your best rate?" vibrating inside their head. With this rate noise going on in a client's head, it's hard to get through to them that a mortgage is something other than simply rate. Most clients shop for a mortgage and already know that the broker might not have the best rate in town. Try this response on for size: "We might not have the best rate on every term, every day, but no one really does, it is a very competitive market and it all depends on your selection of the various options. Let's go over some of our options to see what is available to you."

This is a definite weakness about rate, and it's mentioned upfront. The client immediately is at ease as they realize they are dealing with someone who is knowledgeable and honest enough to provide the pros and cons of their product. The client will pay more attention to the rest of the conversation and everything discussed will resonate more with the customer because it will be spoken with some authority. Even if the customer shops around for rates, they will be more likely to give you a second chance because they trust your advice. This approach might not be right for everyone, but it is surprising how effective mentioning a weakness early in the conversation can be in building trust and rapport with a new client.

Authority

Merriam-Webster defines *authority* as the power to influence thought, opinion, or behaviour and persons in command. Authority has an amazing power over all of us and it influences our daily lives. Authority has been the subject of study in a variety of settings, from the family (parental authority); small groups or teams (informal authority of leadership); organizations such as churches, schools, business, bureaucracies; and even nations.

Many religions around the world consider God as the supreme authority. God is believed to have the ultimate authority and wisdom, which far exceeds that of mere mortals. This divine being provides rules, regulations, and directions for all of us to follow. This authority is unquestioned by the devout and it rules their behaviour. Faith in the divine wisdom of God overrules individual decision making and provides guidelines for behaviour. The Ten Commandments clearly demonstrate the word of God and carry tremendous authority with Jews and Christians.

Religions have used this authority of the divine to influence behaviour since the beginning of time. Authority is a powerful tool of influence for all of us to consider when we want to be more influential. What are some of the aspects of authority that provide the power to influence?

The Milgram Experiment

Perhaps one of the most intriguing studies on authority and influence was conducted by Stanley Milgram, a Yale University psychologist. His findings are outlined in his book *Obedience to Authority: An Experimental View*.

Milgram began his experiments in July 1961 in response to the Adolf Eichmann trial for war crimes. At the time, many were questioning how the Holocaust could have happened and whether it was possible that Eichmann and the others responsible for the millions of deaths of Jews were just following orders. Needless to say, this question was debated by scholars and the media for years.

In 1974, Milgram summarized his findings in the article "The Perils of Obedience" published in *Harper's Magazine*:

> I set up a simple experiment at Yale University to test how much pain an ordinary citizen would inflict on another person simply because he was ordered to by an experimental scientist. Stark authority was pitted against the [participants'] strongest moral imperatives against hurting others, and, with the [participants'] ears ringing with the screams of the victims, authority won more often than not. The extreme willingness of adults to go to almost any lengths on the command of an authority constitutes the chief finding of the study and the fact most urgently demanding explanation.
>
> Ordinary people, simply doing their jobs, and without any particular hostility on their part, can become agents in a terrible destructive process. Moreover, even when the destructive effects of their work becomes patently clear, and they are asked to carry out actions incompatible with fundamental standards of morality, relatively few people have the resources needed to resist authority.[12]

The Experiment

The study was set up with actors playing certain roles. The experimenter was played by a man in a white lab coat with an austere and professional demeanor. The subject was another actor. The participant was unaware that this experiment was a setup. Both the participant and the subject were instructed that this study was designed to study memory and learning in different situations.

The participant and the subject were given slips of paper that indicated what role each would play. It was set up each time so the unaware participant was always given the slip of paper labelled "teacher" and the subject was given the slip labelled "learner." The teacher and learner were set into different rooms where they could communicate but not see each other. In the study, the experimenter told the teacher that the learner had a heart condition.

The teacher was then given a 45-volt electric shock as a demonstration of the shock that was supposedly going to be given to the learner. The teacher was given a list of word pairs to read to the learner. They were then to repeat the first word of each pair and provide four responses for the learner to choose from to test their memory. If the answer was incorrect, the teacher was instructed to hit a button to administer an electric shock to the learner. The voltage was increased with each incorrect response.

The teachers actually believed they were administering electric shocks to the learner. After a number of incorrect responses and ever-increasing voltage shocks, the learner would bang on the wall and complain of the pain and his heart condition. After several instances of these escalating complaints from the learner, all responses from the learner would cease, and they would no longer answer the questions.

At this point, many people indicated their desire to stop the experiment and check on the learner. Some subjects paused at 135 volts and began to question the purpose of the experiment. Most, however, continued after being assured by the professional in the lab coat that they would not be held responsible. Several participants began to laugh nervously or demonstrated signs of stress when they heard screams of pain coming from the learner.

If the participant wanted to halt the experiment, they were given verbal prods by the experimenter in this order:

1. Please continue.
2. The experiment requires that you continue.
3. It is absolutely essential that you continue.
4. You have no other choice; you must go on.

If the participant still wished to stop after all four prods, the experiment was halted. It was also halted after the participant had given the maximum 450-volt shock.

The Results

How many people do you think would actually deliver the maximum voltage? Milgram had polled his senior students and colleagues and no one expected more than 2% to actually deliver the maximum voltage.

In the first set of experiments, 65% of the participants administered the maximum voltage. Many were very uncomfortable with doing the experiment and wanted to stop several times but continued. No one stopped below the 300-volt level.

Milgram and other psychologists performed this experiment in other parts of the world with basically the same results. The overall results were that between 60% and 65% of the participants were willing to inflict fatal voltages to the learner on the instructions of the authority figure in the lab coat.

Implications

Milgram himself feels he knows why we could do such horrible things. He says it has to do with a deep-seated sense of duty to authority. The real culprit in the experiments was his subjects' inability to defy the wishes of the boss—the lab-coated researcher—who urged and, if necessary, directed the participant to perform their duties, despite the emotional and physical mayhem they were causing.

It would seem that we are more influenced by authority than we could possibly imagine. No one would expect that they could fall into this trap of blindly following orders to inflict pain, especially when the victim is screaming for relief, and yet we do. Obedience to authority is the basis of the military. Soldiers will follow and execute orders and commands from senior officers without question. They believe the responsibility for their actions rests with the commanding officers and not with themselves. They are merely instruments for carrying out the orders of others.

In his book *Learned Optimism,* Martin Seligman calls this response learned helplessness. When we feel powerless to control the outcome, we abdicate complete personal responsibility and simply comply with the requests.

Compliance

The more trappings of authority evident, the more compliant we become. A four-star general has more authority than a sergeant, and soldiers will more quickly and completely comply with the general's requests. The pomp and ceremony of certain religious groups add to the authority of the religion itself and increase the compliance of the faithful.

We admit it is a little frightening that we can be influenced so easily by someone in authority and subvert our own good moral standards to their requests. The message to those of us who want to be agents of change is to look at ways of enhancing our authority in a sales or management situation. We will look at several other studies that support this and then try to apply some of this knowledge to what we do in our everyday lives. Authority is a powerful tool to effect change and influence others.

Iraq

The war in Iraq has revealed the dark side of human nature and how authority and blind obedience can cause us to do irrational acts. In 2004, the media started to report accounts of abuse and torture of prisoners held in the Abu Ghraib prison in Iraq. On April 28, *60*

Minutes provided graphic images showing American personnel abusing prisoners in unimaginable ways. Investigation after investigation followed, and in 2007, director Rory Kennedy released the documentary *Ghosts of Abu Ghraib*. The film investigates the abuses and reaches the conclusion that the soldiers were following orders from their superiors—orders allegedly approved by the Secretary of Defense Donald Rumsfeld.

How could young American men and women treat other human beings with such disdain for humanity? Granted, this was a war, but the types of atrocities demonstrated and photographed were unbelievable to most Americans. We again go back to Milgram and the tendency for people to inflict pain on others simply because they are told to do so by an authority figure. The responsibilities for their actions have shifted to another and they simply become instruments of the authority figure with no free will whatsoever. Does this explain why good American boys and girls would behave in such horrendous ways? We leave this for you to decide.

History is littered with the bodies of soldiers who believed in the infallibility of their leaders, and the leaders themselves who believed in their invincibility. The blundered Charge of the Light Brigade during the Battle of Balaclava chronicles the death of 118 souls who blindly followed instructions and were caught unaware. Custer's Last Stand is another example of a leader convinced of his own wisdom and led his men to certain death. Authority has an awesome power over all of us.

Social psychologists have pondered this and agree that, as shown in the Milgram studies noted above, most people will obey an authority figure. They will go as far as harming someone if they feel they are being directed by who they feel is a legitimate authority. They comply with the authority even when they feel stress at performing acts they would normally not even consider doing. They shift the responsibility for their actions onto the authority figure. Moreover, when demands are gradual in their escalation, with each successive action, compliance increases. We will talk a bit more later in this book about consistency and commitment. With each successive task, people tend to be consistent with previous actions. They base their decisions to proceed more on what they had already done rather than an objective assessment on the act itself.

These were horrible incidents of the abuse of the power of authority on innocent victims, and yet they provide some insight into human behaviour that we should all be aware of. Scam artists are everywhere, and they will use whatever methods are available to them.

Enron

Enron: The Smartest Guys in the Room is a documentary film released in 2005. Most will remember Enron as one of the largest business scandals in American history. The principals of the company were charged and the trial was well publicized. The film features interviews with employees discussing the transfer of electricity from California to other states where there was a surplus. California had legislated the free market for energy, so Enron created a larger demand for their electricity by shifting power out of California to cause a series of blackouts. Naturally, the price of electricity leaped higher with the shortage, allowing Enron to supply that shortage at elevated prices. They made billions of dollars with this strategy. The employees knew exactly what they were doing—that transferring energy out of California would cause blackouts.

Profit was the sole focus at Enron, and employees were constantly told to break the law for the good of the company. Few Enron employees ever came forward to report this massive corruption within the company. Eventually, the ship started sinking, and many executives were selling their shares while encouraging employees to retain theirs. How could honest individuals be blinded by greed and authority to set aside their moral compass and simply do as they were told? We believe the Milgram studies on obedience and authority were at play at Enron as well. We simply are far too susceptible to authority for our own good. It would be prudent for us all to occasionally step back and check our moral compass to ensure we are taking responsibility for our actions.

These examples outline the dark side of authority. People can be cruel and unusual if they feel the authority providing the direction is strong enough. On the other hand, the authority principle can also be used to get people to move in your direction when the outcome will be positive. We are quite susceptible to the influence of those we see as an authority, whether positive or negative.

At a very young age, we are instructed to listen to our elders. They are more knowledgeable than we are, and taking their advice proved to be a wise thing to do. Their experience in life provided valuable advice. As we grew older, we found new mentors in teachers and bosses who also knew more than we did. We became conditioned to follow the dictates of those who we perceived as more knowledgeable or authoritative. This provided shortcuts to success and detours from many of the dangers lurking in the school of hard knocks. As we matured, this approach made so much sense that we often followed the authority figures when it made no sense at all.

Obedience to authority was rewarding in the early years and it becomes easy to simply follow it without thinking. Life has become so complicated and busy—and with the Internet so full of information—that we simply cannot research all the information we need, so we rely on figures of authority and knowledge to help us. This is part of the reason we all blindly respond to those in authority. It saves time and energy and soon becomes an automatic response. This makes us susceptible to the unscrupulous, but it also is a method of getting what you want—and quickly. We leave the ethics of these methods to you.

Tools of Authority
Quotations
Authors and speakers use a simple technique of quoting respected authorities. Readers and audiences are more likely to believe your positions if they are tied into the work of an authority figure. Quo-

tations of Aristotle or Socrates seem to add credence to any presentation. In the political arena, presidential hopefuls will quote John F. Kennedy or Lincoln to support their particular viewpoints. Religious figures will quote the Bible passage that suits their particular needs, and we in the audience transfer the reliability of the quotation to the speaker's points. It doesn't seem to matter to us that quotations from the Bible can also be used to refute the exact same points. Quotations are carefully selected to support the concepts being presented.

Referring to scientific research is another time-honoured technique used to influence our opinions. Although research is always subject to interpretation, refering to a specific study adds credibility to our position. Marketing companies will often indicate that six out of ten doctors recommend a specific brand of painkiller, and we are influenced by this information. If we hear that eight out of ten dentists recommend a specific brand of toothpaste, we are drawn to that specific brand as though it were the best. We trust those in authority to provide accurate and reliable information to help us make our daily decisions. We don't have the time or the expertise to conduct this research, so we rely on experts to inform us of their opinions.

This approach turns ridiculous when we also start to believe that movie stars or athletes are authorities on aftershave lotion or a specific skin cream. Even the "man in the street" interviews seem to sway us towards a product. These individuals aren't experts and have no visible authoritive credentials, yet we are influenced by these ads. It would appear that the simple fact of using a product can turn someone into an expert and therefore become more believable.

An argument or proposition using an appeal from an authority doesn't make the conclusion invalid, nor is it unreasonable to question whether it's true. A statement by an authority is not guaranteed to be true. We have a tendency to believe something is true if it's on the news. We believe it must be true because a journalist has ostensibly investigated the facts and is reporting accurately, even though we all know that even journalists have biases that affect their credibility. This whole aspect of authority and credibility is an interesting part of our psychological makeup. It happens automatically and most of the time we don't even realize how much we are being influenced by it.

The classic example of parental authority in action is the phrase "because I said so." Children are always asking questions and scrutinizing decisions. They use the word *why* thousands of times during their childhood, and as they get older, they shift to *why not*. Rather than make a logical explanation to the child, we as parents fall back on the authority principle and respond with "because I said so," and most of us actually believe this strategy will work. The parental authority is a time-saving tool for parents. Just saying it is so doesn't make the assertion true or false, but it certainly clarifies who has the authority in the relationship. There is no need for additional proof in this instance, as the simple statement holds credibility because of the authority held by parents. We expect obedience with this simple phrase. We don't always get it, but that is the beauty and challenge of parenting.

In the business world, we all want to be more influential. We want to convince others that our ideas are the best ones—we want to move people to our way of thinking and influence them to buy from us or do what we want them to do. Even in social settings, we want to influence our friends.

Gary: I was recently with some friends and we wanted to go to a movie. We had several choices and some disagreement on what movie to see. If you want to be more influential and get the group to go to the movie of your choice, what technique could you use? One of my friends tried the authority approach with one of the all time classic moves. He said, "They say this movie is one of the best this year." The word they seems to invoke some unknown authority indicating a good movie. How many times have you used the infamous they to support your argument? Who are they and why are they deemed a reliable source for information on movies, or anything for that matter?

I didn't like this choice and so decided to use my own authority method in the discussion. Roger Ebert, a well-known film critic, had given my choice a "thumbs up" designation and indicated it was one of the finest movies of the year. I used this credible source in the movie business and my friends said, "Oh, is that right? Well, then, it must be a good movie and we should go see that tonight."

Why would Roger Ebert's opinion influence the decision to see a movie? The same reason that books have lists of important people with positive "blurbs" on the cover. The same reason movies list all the positive reviews in their ads, in addition to any Academy Award nominations they've received. It is the principle of authority in action. If someone says so, it must be true. The more reliable the source seems, the more credible the statement and the more powerful its influence on us.

Many books and movies get rave reviews and end up making no money because they don't appeal to the masses, only to the reviewers' senses. Many movies and Broadway plays have bombed because of what the reviews have said about them. Negative reviews seem to have more of an impact on attendance than do positive reviews. If a reviewer didn't like a play, it must be a stinker, but if he liked the same play, we think it might be good, so we might go to see it. These same tools are available for all of us to use.

Authority by Proxy

Authority by proxy is another example of using authority figures to our advantage. You likely have met those who love to drop names of important people. They will be at a social function and casually mention that they met with the president of the company the other day or mention that they had discussed an idea with the senior VP. They are trying to invoke the authority of others to substantiate their own importance and authority. This rarely works, however, as most people see through this thin veil of bull and the authority of the speaker is usually diminished rather than elevated, and yet these name droppers continue with this technique.

The other method, which seems to be more effective, is the manager who indicates he was talking to his boss, who feels they should implement a specific plan. Rather than using their own authority or persuasive techniques, they rely on the authority of a more senior person to support their initiative. This is tougher to deal with, but after a few times it is easy to spot. Quite often the story is just that: a story. This person might have never mentioned this project to their boss, but they invoke the authority of the big boss anyway. These people are simply incapable of leading by themselves and require coaching to take more responsibility for the decisions.

Shifting responsibility upwards in an organization has been used by managers since the beginning of management. This is not a technique we would recommend, but it's one that you should be aware of and spot when it is being used. This is not dissimilar to the parental technique of "wait until your father gets home." Rather than deal with the issue, it is being delegated to someone who seems to have more authority and are therefore more likely to get the task accomplished. The child then spends the day in fearful anticipation of the arrival of the father, and over time, this can and does negatively affect the relationship the child has with both parents.

We all take responsibility for what is in front of us and the results will over time surprise you. We all have the power to be in charge of our lives.

Titles

Do professional titles automatically convey authority that is justly deserved? Are we influenced by someone with a prestigious title? It would seem that we are. Con artists will quite often take on a mantle of authority with clothes, cars, and other signs of success, including titles. They may be the vice president of some fabricated company, or a doctor or lawyer. They understand that these trappings of authority are influential in adding credibility to a fake story as they try to get you to part with your money. They have been tremendously successful in gaining the confidence of their marks by this method. By appearing to have authority, we automatically believe what they have to say.

Putting your accomplishments or designations on a business card implies that you are successful and therefore a better choice to deal with than a novice. Many sales organizations include "platinum performer" on their employee cards to indicate they are the best in the business. This gives the potential consumer a sense that the salesperson is successful and therefore has the knowledge required to help them out. Insurance and investment salespeople have specific designations after their name that imply industry knowledge and also infer some authority. Wear these designations proudly, as they are influential with your clients.

Marketing companies will dress up an actor in a white lab coat and call him a doctor and we as viewers believe the advertisement more than we would if the announcer was not called a doctor. Even if we know the actor is not a doctor, it seems we still are influenced by this pitch.

Clothing

Clothing is another influence tool that stimulates an automatic compliance response. Leonard Bickman published an article in the *Journal of Applied Social Psychology* entitled "The Social Power of a Uniform." Bickman conducted a series of studies where he arranged for a researcher dressed in normal street clothes to ask pedestrians to comply with a request to pick up a piece of litter or to stand on the other side of a bus stop sign. They documented the number of times the pedestrians complied with the request. They then changed the attire of the researcher and had him wear a security guard uniform. While in uniform, the researcher made the same requests to the pedestrians and these results were documented. The results clearly indicate that people obeyed the request from a researcher in the uniform far more often than they did when dressed in street clothes.

In a similar study, the pedestrians were told, "See that guy over there by the meter? He is overparked but doesn't have any change. Give him a dime!" The researcher then stepped around the corner so he would be out of sight when the subject reached the man by the parked car. Nearly all of the pedestrians complied with the request to give the man a dime when requested by someone in a security guard uniform but only half did when requested by someone in normal street clothes. This occurred even though the requester was no longer visible. The power of the uniform influenced the subject to comply.

The business suit is another symbol of authority and has an effect on our tendency to comply. In a study by Lefkowitz, Blake, and Mouton, published in the *Journal of Personality and Social Psychology*, the researchers arranged to have a thirty-one-year-old man jaywalk on a busy street. He would cross the street against the light and half the time he was dressed in a smart business suit and the rest of the time he was dressed in casual work shirt and pants. The researchers observed pedestrians' reactions to a blatant breaking of the law and recorded the pedestrians who followed the researcher across the street. The results indicate the power of influence of a power suit. Three and half times more people followed like children behind the man dressed in a suit versus the man dressed in work clothes.

Why would we be willing to break the law simply because a well-dressed man in a suit did it first, and by the same token not break the law when a man in normal work clothes did the same thing? It's the power of the suit. We attribute additional authority to a well-dressed person and therefore believe that what they do must be appropriate. Notwithstanding, the pedestrians knew jaywalking is illegal, yet they still followed the man in the suit far more often than they did the man in normal clothes. This gives a whole new meaning to the term *power suit*.

Clothes do in fact make the man and the woman. We attribute more intelligence to the well dressed; we attribute wealth and success to the well dressed. A good rule of thumb is to always dress up for a meeting rather than dress down. It is more effective to be better dressed than the average attending a meeting rather than to be dressed below average. The next time you attend a meeting or social soiree, check out the attendees and notice what your first reactions are to the well dressed and the not-so-well-dressed.

Gary: As I mentioned earlier, I am a grandfather now, and my daughter Jennifer was over at our home for dinner one evening after she had returned to work. She asked, "Now that we have a baby and I am back to work, my whole life seems to have changed, but my husband's life seems unchanged. I am busy with work, the baby, housework, and cooking. The mornings are very stressful, as I don't know what to wear and I am rushing around like crazy. What can I do?" I couldn't offer any suggestions about her husband (I learned that long ago), but I thought I could help with the clothing selection.

"Why don't you choose your clothes the night before and just have them ready to go? This will smooth out the stress in the morning" I suggested.

Little did I know that this would evoke gales of laughter from both my daughter and my wife, Jan. "There is no way I can choose my clothes the night before because I don't know how I will feel in the morning—and besides, it's all about the hair," Jennifer clarified.

She is a school teacher and must be onstage for her students every single day, and apparently, clothes are an important factor on the presentation and on how you feel to ensure you can be at peak performance.

Have you noticed what professional speakers wear when onstage? Many of them wear black. Why would a professional speaker be dressed all in black? Well, black is slimming, for starters, as any woman will tell you. Second, black and navy blue are trustworthy colours, and people tend to trust those who wear these colours. Authority is enhanced by those dressed in black. If you're nervous about an upcoming, meeting what should you wear? We suggest you wear your favourite outfit—you know you look good in it, and this alone will lift your spirits and your credibility and confidence. When you're tired in the morning after a night out on the town, what should you wear? We suggest bright colours to give you a vibrant lift, helping you look confident rather than bone tired. The brightness takes the eyes away from the weary face.

It is, of course, a huge error to judge others by their clothes. Con men always dress the part to gain your trust just before they gain access to your money. If you're in sales, a primary rule is to never judge a book by its cover. Car salesmen are notorious for assuming a poorly dressed individual will never be able to afford the new Cadillac on the showroom floor. They will try to direct the purchaser to a cheaper model like a Malibu, and some are even rude to the client. Many a successful farmer or Internet millionaire have received less than appropriate treatment simply because salespeople judge buyers by their clothes.

Gestures

Gestures alone can have an impact on the credibility of an influence practitioner. Eye contact has always been used as a method to instill authority. If someone looks us in the eye, we assume they are telling the truth. When people look away, it is believed they aren't being completely honest.

Hand gestures and body language convey tremendous information to an audience and to clients. They also convey information back to the presenter or salesperson. Many of these are common knowledge, but just because we know them doesn't mean we recognize them or use them effectively ourselves.

The gesture of open hands usually means an openness and honesty. Rejection is inferred when the arms are crossed. This usually means a tough sell is ahead. If the hands move to the hips, we are in real trouble, as this is a defiant move. Shaking a leg or wetting lips usually signals stress, and a good salesperson should look to relieve the stress. Lying has many clues for both the salesperson and the client and include touching the face or mouth; downcast eyes, especially to the left; shifting in the seat; or rubbing sweaty hands on the pant leg. Excessive scratching of the nose or pulling at an ear is another telltale sign that a fib is on the way. There are a number of books on this subject that would make good reading if this topic is of interest. We've only scratched the surface of non-verbal communication.

Voice

Voice is also a powerful tool. Remember in the '90s when George Bush was president of the United States? *Saturday Night Live* had a field day with his voice. Dana Carvey created a career out of imitating George Bush's hesitant style, and Bush lost the next election to a man with a more powerful presence, Bill Clinton, a master communicator.

In a mock jury study, researchers had people listen to witnesses as they answered questions about a supposed accident.[13] One of the questions was: "Approximately how long did you stay there before the ambulance arrived?" One group of jurors heard the witness respond in a direct fashion. They said, "Twenty minutes—long enough to help get Mrs. David straightened out." Another group of jurors listened to the witness stumble over the detail as they said, "Oh, it seems like it was about, uh, twenty minutes—just long enough to help my friend Mrs. David, you know, get straightened out." The straightforward witnesses were deemed significantly more credible and confident than the ones who stumbled over the details. It turned out that what the witnesses actually said was of less importance than how they said it.

Decisive and fast talkers are really no more sure of their facts than anyone else, but their style creates the impression of confidence in what they have to say. This confidence is sensed by the audience and it provides more credibility to the presenter. A good communicator is seen as more intelligent, knowledgeable, and authoritative on the ideas they present. This is the reason why many professional salespeople or those in management join Toastmasters clubs or take speaking courses. This enhanced delivery style is a powerful influence tool.

Even voice volume is an influential tool. Louder voices are considered to be more authoritative, and the words being delivered also seem to carry more credibility. When parents raise their voices, the children all of sudden know that they mean business and usually comply quickly. If, however, a raised voice is a normal occurrence, it loses its impact, as many of us know. Judicial use of an elevated voice enhances the authority of the speaker and in turn increases the level of influence.

Have you noticed that those who speak with a loud voice seem to garner the most attention in meetings? Those with quiet soft voices are often asked to repeat themselves because they can be difficult to hear. We generally make the assumption that a quiet voice indicates uncertanty and lacks credibility and authority. Many use the technique of lowering their voice at the end of a sentence, which might indicate that the speaker is unsure of their facts and conclusions. Listeners draw conclusions from voices and as influencers and agents of change, we should be aware of this judgmental quality and take steps to improve. Have you also noticed how some speakers raise their voice to a higher pitch at the end of sentences almost into a questioning tone? Many young people do this and it's often interpreted as immature and much less authoritative.

The next time your watching television, pay attention to the volume level during commercials. Commercials sustain the volume near the maximum, whereas the shows you watch typically have a much greater range, from loud to quiet, or even silence. This technique is believed to add credibility to the information being provided in the commercial. There is a reason for everything, and it's usually to have more influence over us.

To get ahead in sales or management, the ability to speak effectively is an essential asset that should be developed vigorously. Take courses, practice and videotape presentations, and carefully scrutinize all aspects of the presentation. You will enhance your authority and influence and in the process become more successful.

We have presented to thousands of people in the past several years. A lapel microphone is a must, even for small audiences. When showing a video, we suggest playing the tape a little louder than you would normally like. We have tested this approach with groups of various sizes. For the first half of the session, we would have the volume at normal volume for the size of the room. Half way through the program, after a pause, we would increase the volume by 15% and observe the difference in the group reaction. Without fail, the second half of the session was always rated higher than the first half. The attendees were also visibly more attentive and more readily accepted the information presented as the truth during the second half. We have reversed this technique and the exact same results were noted. The louder presentation was more effective. Volume does in fact increase the authority level of the speaker.

Matching the Hatch

One of Gary's hobbies is fly-fishing. He enjoys communing with nature on a quiet river with the rush of water against his waders. The line, rod, and arm all become one with the symmetry of casting and gently landing the fly on the surface of the water in as natural a style as possible. Trout are tricky little fish and quite picky about their diet. You can have the perfect presentation, the perfect float, in exactly the right location and the trout will rise toward the fly for a look and then turn away in disgust. All you see is a flash of silver as the trout has rejected your offering. Why does this happen again and again? Sometimes the fly is too large or the wrong colour, and the trout know this.

The objective is to have the perfect presentation with the fly that closely matches what is occurring in nature at that time. A true fly-fisher will check the water and air long before he wets a line. Turning a rock over and checking the water will reveal what insects are available and where they are in their life cycle. Watching the air reveals the size, colour, and type of insects emerging from the water or landing on the surface. This prep work is essential to increase the chances of actually catching a trout. The fly-fisher then chooses a fly that matches the insects that are hatching both in colour and size.

Now properly equipped by matching the hatch, the perfect presentation will result in a strike and a wonderful battle between fish and fly-fisher. The thrill of the strike is only surpassed by the thrill of outwitting the wily trout.

Matching the hatch is equally important in the world of influence. One must understand the customer before an effective sales strategy can be implemented. If the customer has a type A personality, the successful influencer must accommodate this style into the presentation. There's no point in presenting dozens of graphs and charts in tremendous detail when the client is more interested in the bottom line. If you're talking to the chief financial officer, who is a chartered accountant, the last thing you should be doing is a slick presentation that skips the details. Your authority will be enhanced by matching the style of those you intend to influence. Just like the wily trout who will only strike at the bait that is familiar, so the prospective client will only strike at your bait if it is familiar in style and presentation to theirs.

Additional Detail

An authority figure provides credibility to a proposal. If you don't have built-in authority, what can you do to enhance the credibility of your proposal and therefore your authority on the subject matter? We can learn a little about this aspect of credibility by looking at urban legends. We have all heard of urban legends and most have a localized flavour with specific local details. The escaped convict from the psych ward at the local hospital was seen at the local campground you're staying at. And remember the story of the young couple at lover's lane? The girl gets nervous and wants to go home because she had heard that an escaped criminal with a hook for a hand had been seen in a local town and the police had been alerted. The boyfriend wants to stay, of course, but the young girl insists and so they drive off to the Derby Dip for fries and a Coke. When she gets out of the car, she discovers a hook embedded in the door. These urban legends gain credibility and are remembered and passed on because of the local flavour that is added to each to make the story seem more real.

In 1986, researchers Jonathon Shedler and Melvin Manis created an experiment to simulate a trial.[14] Subjects were told they were selected to be on an experimental jury and were to be the jurors in a prepared trial. They were provided with a transcript of the trial that listed well balanced pros and cons of the case. The transcript contained eight arguments against the defendant and eight arguments for the defendant.

The jurors were to decide the fate of a seven-year-old. Was the mother, Mrs. Johnson, a fit parent and should the child remain in her care? The interesting aspect of this study was in the detail. One group of jurors had arguments for Mrs. Johnson enhanced with some vivid detail, whereas the arguments against did not contain this level of detail. The other group was presented with the opposite combination.

As an example, one argument for Mrs. Johnson contained the statement that she sees to it that her child washes and brushes his teeth before bedtime. In the vivid story, the statement included this additional piece of information: He uses a *Star Wars* toothbrush that looks like Darth Vader.

An argument against Mrs. Johnson included the statement that the child went to school with a badly scraped arm that Mrs. Johnson had not cleaned or otherwise attended to. The school nurse had to clean the scrape. The vivid transcript included the detail that the nurse stained her uniform with mercurochrome as she cleaned the wound.

The researchers carefully tested the arguments. The point of the exercise was to ensure that the vivid details would be irrelevant to the case. They carried no additional pertinent information that would sway the decision. It did matter that Mrs. Johnson monitored her son brushing his teeth before bedtime, but it didn't matter the type of toothbrush he used.

The results were a surprise. Even though the additional vivid details should have had no impact on the jurors' decision, they did. The jurors voted in favour of Mrs. Johnson almost 60% of the time when the vivid details were included with the favorable arguments and only 43% of the time when the vivid details were included with the unfavourable arguments. It would seem that even unimportant details had a big effect on the decision-making process.

In their book *Made to Stick: Why Some Ideas Survive and Others Die,* Chip Heath and Dan Heath explain why certain ideas have a larger impact on us than others. They analyze the jury study in their book. Why did the details make a difference in this case? The details enhanced the credibility of the story. They made the story more believable. If you can visualize the Darth Vader toothbrush, it is easier to see the boy brushing his teeth. It would naturally follow that Mrs. Johnson is a good mother.

The lesson for the influence practitioner is that vivid details enhance credibility and enhance the authority principle in almost any argument or presentation. The details don't have to be valid on their own but should help the listener visualize the point you are trying to make.

Statistics are always a valued tool used to enhance the authority of the speaker or presenter. Advertisers have known this secret for years and inundate us with statistics on their products. Look at the back of a cereal box and you will be blown away by the statistics and detail. We all automatically feel better about a product with all this information. The effective use of statistics adds credibility to every argument. The person using the statistics is also seen as more of an authority on that topic than one who mismanages statistics.

"MBA speak" is also an effective tool for building credibility. Jargon, buzz words, and technical terms are always used to impress. We hate to admit it, but they work on most of us. Combine the jargon with a nice blue pinstriped suit, a clear loud voice delivered with speed and confidence, throw in a couple of statistics, and we all become putty. If the person has a degree from a reputable university and an impressive title, we might as well sign on the dotted line immediately.

Because

A study was conducted to assess the value of having a reason when asking for a favour.[15] It makes sense that people would generally like a reason before they comply with a request. The study involved people lining up to use a photocopier in a public library. A researcher would attempt to get in line in front of another patron and would say, "Excuse me, I have five pages. May I use the photocopy machine? Because I'm in a rush." This request gained almost complete agreement as 94% of the people would allow the researcher in line in front of them to use the photocopier. They had a valid reason that was accepted by the other patrons, so they complied with the request most of the time.

They then tried a different tactic on other occasions: "Excuse me, I have five pages. May I use the photocopy machine?" This change in the question resulted in only a 60% compliance rate. It would appear that the difference was due to the lack of additional information: "I am in a rush."

To verify this finding, the researchers tried a third approach:

"Excuse me, I have five pages. May I use the photocopy machine? Because I have to make some copies." The results of this variation nearly matched the original with a 93% compliance rate. No differentiating reason was provided other than the *because* clause. The people in line simply had an automatic response to *because* and never even listened to the reason. They just assumed that they had a good reason since the word *because* was used. Using the word *because* adds credibility even if the reason itself adds no value to the request.

Another study reported in Robert Cialdini's book *Influence: The Psychology of Persuasion* deals with theatre attendees and is equally surprising. During long lineups at the theatre, a researcher would attempt to get in line near the front by saying, "Excuse me, may I get in line in front of you?" Needless to say, most people told them where to go, and that was the back of the line. But for another group, the researchers asked, "Excuse me, may I get in line in front of you? Because I would like to get in line." Guess what happened? Yes, significantly more people let the researcher in line simply because he invoked *because* and people made an immediate response without thinking or even listening to the reason. They just assumed it was a good reason and they said okay.

We all respond to situations without thinking. Certain words trigger a response in us that is almost automatic. In this instance, the word *because* conveys some type of authority on the person using it and even with no real reason. Now we know why parents are successful in using the phrase "because I said so" with their children. Apparently, all you really have to say is "because."

Three Magic Words

Because is not the only word that has tremendous power over us. There are three words that many salespeople use to support their authority, knowledge, and credibility by simply inserting one of them. During the course of a sales discussion, or any discussion for that matter, a large part is dedicated to discovering the needs of the client. There are many styles and approaches to understanding needs, but it is common practice to discover a client's needs so you can match them up with the features and benefits of your offering and close the sale.

Once needs are identified, many salespeople have difficulty closing the sale. How does one move from understanding to closing? Many people prefer to hint at the close rather than risk an outright request. Many prefer a direct approach: "Can we sign you up right now?" Thousands of books on sales over the years proffer good solid advice on this topic, and it really depends on your individual style. However, some words do have more psychological impact than others.

A prospective client is generally looking for someone to provide honest and knowledgeable information. We discussed several methods earlier in this chapter on how to enhance your authority in the beginning so the prospect will trust you. With trust, the client will be ready to take your advice. This is where the magic words come in to build on this desire for advice.

The three magic words are *recommend, suggest,* and *advise.*

After a needs analysis, a good salesperson will make a recommendation but rarely uses the actual word. These words reinforce authority, trustworthiness, and knowledge and will make a difference in your close ratio. Here's an example: "So, Mr. Jones, based on what we have discussed, I would recommend…because…." You then match the features and benefits of your product to the exact needs the client has just outlined. This is good, as we have used the words *recommend* and *because.*

If you don't like "I recommend," try "I suggest" or "I advise"— they are all powerful. Our personal favourite is "I recommend," but it's up to you. We suggest you practice the phrasing so it feels comfortable for you.

Making recommendations is a powerful influence tool. When Gary's son Michael was a waiter and bartender while in school, he would often make recommendations to clients on what was particularly good that evening. These were based on food that was the freshest or whether the fish just arrived, or maybe it was the chef's absolute specialty and was only served once a month. Whatever the reason, he would try to get the patrons to select his recommendations. The recommendations were not overly expensive, but since he suggested them, the level of trust for his opinion skyrocketed, and when he next suggested the wine to go with the meal, the patrons would usually comply. As you know, the money is always in the alcohol at restaurants and so are the tips.

By being just a little assertive and using the magic word *recommend,* Michael's tips would always exceed that of the others in the restaurant. The patrons always felt they were getting treated in a unique and special way and would reward his caring service with an extra tip.

The three magic words will help you close more sales. They capitalize on credible authority and place you more in control of the outcome. We suggest you at least give some of these ideas a try in your life. You will be surprised to see how simple yet persuasive they are.

Most salespeople are actually selling themselves in any transaction. They sometimes believe they are selling a product or service, but what it really comes down to is the person doing the selling. If this is the case, what are buyers really looking for? They are looking to deal with someone who has both knowledge and credibility. The average person wants to know that the person they are dealing with is both trustworthy and competent.

The world is full of tricksters and shysters who are out to make a quick sale at the expense of a relationship. The long-term salesperson is looking to build relationships through good value and honesty. Referrals for future business occur when clients refer their family and friends to an authority they trust. Become an authority and business will flow directly to your bottom line. A reference from a satisfied customer enhances your reputation as an authority in your industry. Once you are perceived as an authority, the sales and influence process becomes much easier.

People really do want to deal with an authority in the area in which they are looking to spend money. The larger the purchase, the more important the authority component becomes in influencing the final decision. Even in our social lives, this principle of believing an authority is a powerful persuasive tool. Let's look at some best practices we can implement to enhance our own authority in any conversation, be it sales or life.

Best Practices

1. People will say yes more often to someone they see as an authority.
2. The most effective authority is a credible authority with both knowledge and honesty.
3. Present a product or service weakness early in the sales presentation to gain credibility.
4. People buy from people they trust. Gain their trust early in the conversation.
5. Add detail that might not be directly pertinent to your product or service to make it memorable.
6. Learn how to be a public speaker.
7. Speak loudly, forcefully, and with clear enunciation.
8. Don't use PowerPoint unless absolutely necessary, and then reconsider; it takes away from your authority.
9. Showcase your educational credentials and industry recognition.
10. Script an effective introduction that builds your authority. Many call this the elevator speech, as it is about two minutes long.
11. Get written references from satisfied clients. Share these references on your website or with your prospective clients.
12. Get your clients to introduce you to their associates for further business. These situations are like having built-in authority.

Chapter 6
How to Get to "Yes"

We all have a desire for more harmony in our lives. We like things to be predictable. Surprises are a nice change of pace, but if our whole life were full of surprises, the stress load would be enormous. We prefer a degree of consistency. We like to know we have a secure job. We generally perform better if we are comfortable with our job security.

We also have habits. We take the same route to work most of the time because it's familiar. We drink the same beverages, eat the same snacks, and keep the same friends. We want consistency in our lives. With this drive for consistency, we tend to be consistent with the commitments we make. When we make a promise, we all want and need to keep that promise in order to maintain our internal harmony. If someone doesn't keep their promises, there are rather severe social consequences. These people are called liars, welchers, moochers, and other terms that indicate their unreliability. We all like to think that we can be trusted to keep our word, and we are driven to do just that.

We Expect Consistency

We need a degree of consistency in our lives. Consistency brings comfort and predictability. Life must make sense to us. When it doesn't, we must expend energy to try to figure it out. We actually expect consistency. When we flip a light switch, we expect the light bulb to turn on. If it doesn't, we experience some minor stress as we realize something is wrong. We want things to work the same way every time they happen. When we turn the ignition key in our car, we expect the engine to start every single time. What would your life look like if you never knew whether your car would start every time? Your stress level would escalate each time you sat in the car and put the key in the ignition. You wouldn't live with this situation for long. Your solution would be to find consistency in your life and eliminate this unpredictability. You would buy another car that was reliable, or you would take public transit.

We all expect consistency in our lives. We expect it in the physical world as well as the psychological world. We expect our marriages to be intact when we wake every morning and we expect it to be much the same as it was when we go to bed. This might be good or bad depending on the circumstances, but we do expect it to be much the same. We expect attitudes of our friends and co-workers to be much the same as it was yesterday. When mood swings enter the picture, we get confused and have difficulty managing the situation because such behaviour is inconsistent with what we expect. Our expectation for consistency in others is complemented by our own personal need for consistency in ourselves. This is a natural human need that brings stability and harmony to all of our lives.

Inconsistencies

Life sometimes deals us unexpected cards. As we know, things don't always work out as planned, and sometimes things hit us in surprising and unexpected ways. This results in an inconsistency between what we expect and what we are experiencing in our reality.

It's your birthday and you expect a gift from your family, but everyone forgot. It's Christmas and you expect a surprise gift that would demonstrate some personal thought behind it and you instead get a gift card to Home Depot. It's performance review time at work and your raise is half of what you expected. You love your job and respect your boss and you believe you have done an exceptional job, but the outcome of the review is unexpected. How do you feel about these situations? Your natural harmony is disrupted by them.

Cognitive Dissonance

Cognitive dissonance is the reactionary state you're in when things don't go as expected. You love your job and believe you are a good performer and yet your boss, whom you like, has just rated you poorly. The immediate reaction is confusion. This result is outside your comfort zone and so you question what really happened. Soon, a mild form of anger moves into your body as your stress level rises. Your heart rate escalates, your hands get sweaty, your face gets flushed, and your mind races around, looking for some reasons or justification or blame. A defensive response usually appears first, as we need to defend ourselves from this unjustified attack on our performance and character. Is your job at risk? What did you do wrong? Maybe the boss you used to like is not so good after all. Confusion, anger, and stress all combine to totally destroy the previous sense of harmony in your life. It's very uncomfortable and your biggest desire is to get back into harmony.

Rejection is a daily occurrence for salespeople. We will discuss failure and rejection in more detail later in the book. When you get a "no" from a prospective client, the same reaction happens in your body and mind. You are convinced you did an excellent sales job and yet the client refused your offering. The mind goes into analytical mode to see what happened, as the results are inconsistent with the expected results. We all have a tendency to relive that moment again and again as we try to make sense of what went wrong. Many focus on the mistakes that might have been made to determine how to fine tune their performance, and some focus on what went well and try to make those aspects even more powerful.

All of us experience the cognitive dissonance of a result being inconsistent with our expectations, and we naturally feel bad. We feel rejected and often blame ourselves for the lack of results. Confusion, anger, and frustration overwhelm us in the first moments after an experience of rejection. But some type of balance returns as we justify the situation and accept the reality of the rejection. We then attempt to discover new ways to rebuild self-confidence to face another client and get the yes we want next time.

This state of cognitive dissonance is very uncomfortable and stressful. Our natural desire is to avoid this state at all costs and, if we find ourselves in this state, to get out of it as soon as possible.

Regaining Consistency

Being in dissonance is an uncomfortable experience. No one can survive this state for long without risking heart disease or other serious health problems, so the desire to regain consistency in our lives is overpowering. We all must deal with the dissonance and get rid of it as soon as possible. It's not an easy task, since the little voice in your head can be quite judgmental. The little voice is always speaking to you and is quite often supporting the dissonance in your mind by raising all kinds of doubts about your ability to regain harmony. Fear of disruption travels like waves through our mind and body. Stress escalates and compounds the inconsistency between what happened and what we want. What can we do to regain our harmony?

As we mentioned in the self-talk section of the book, you can talk yourself out of this mess. Self-denial is usually the first response. Just pretend it didn't happen at all and try to ignore the situation entirely. Move on to the next issue in your life and convince yourself the situation never occurred at all. Some people are actually quite good at this and tuck bad news away in a drawer of their mind and move on quickly. Those people have control over their doubts. Many others put it in the drawer but never close the drawer, keeping it as a part of their consciousness. Most of us would find this approach almost impossible. Successful deniers simply don't waste their time on things they cannot change and move on with life. If you can accomplish this, it will quickly reassert harmony and your life will move forward.

A second technique is to use the balance approach. Simply pull out the scales of life and overweight the good side to overcome any bad news. No matter how bad things get, look at all the wonderful ratings you have had in the past, such as your personal successes and many contributions. Remember how fantastic your personal life is and all the opportunities that lie ahead of you. One bad situation is simply a bump in the road which is really paved with gold. The "no" in the sale is actually an expected one. A good salesperson cannot close every single deal. Even professional baseball players strike out more times than they hit home runs. Believing you'll win more than you'll lose is much more powerful than thinking you'll lose more than you'll win. It's your choice. A good rule of thumb for assessing the severity of the dissonance is to measure how many good things you must come up with to overcome bad news. If a week of good things non-stop isn't working, you can assume the dissonance is a severe one and might require some serious work to resolve.

A third technique many people use is to simply change the expectation. "I received a bad review this year, but wait until next year; I will be back and recover all lost ground." No need to get too excited this year—performance goes up and performance goes down. It was a particular tough year with unusual circumstances that really aren't your fault at all. In this instance, rationalizing is the tool to resolve the dissonance. It really didn't matter that much of it really wasn't your fault. The boss was wrong and you will be back in no time. The real problem was the economy and everyone in the company had to pay the price. Therefore it wasn't about poor performance at all, it was circumstances outside your control. The "no" in the sales situation was really a "yes" because the client did show some interest and you do have another appointment scheduled. You could convince yourself that you will get the sale next time or you might have a bigger opportunity just ahead with another client. Rationalize the dissonance away and harmony will be restored in your life.

Finally, you could change your evaluation of the event itself. A poor rating could be re-evaluated as a good rating. Focus on the positives in the review and focus on how much the boss really appreciates the value of your contribution to the company. Given the environment, maybe it was actually a great review and well deserved. Rather than creating a negative thought about the results, self-talk yourself into a positive state by changing the results in your mind.

There are many different ways to deal with these inconsistencies in life. We all have a tremendous desire to be consistent with what we have said or done in the past. We need to be consistent with our values. If we make a promise or decision, we all need to act consistently with it. We all want to keep our word and commitments. Making a commitment with someone is almost a guarantee that we will keep our promise. If we don't, we experience cognitive dissonance, which we know is very uncomfortable. A powerful sales and influence tool is to gain a commitment from someone first. A volunteered commitment is most effective and a written commitment is even more effective. We all have a tendency to live up to what we write down.

Changing Minds

Is it possible to get someone to do something that they don't believe in? Is it possible to have someone behave counter to their true attitudes? How can we change attitudes to obtain behaviour we hope for?

A common research study has been used countless times to prove this point. First, a researcher would survey people's opinions on some topic that was against their views, say, capital punishment or universal welfare. One group would be forced to write the essay as a requirement for their educational credit, while another group would be asked to volunteer to write the essay. Both groups were surveyed again on their opinions on the topic after they completed the essay.

The group that was forced to participate showed almost no change in their attitudes toward the topic, notwithstanding their essay was against their normally held views. They were able to rationalize their essay as being forced and therefore didn't change their opinions on the topic.

However, the volunteer group did register a change in their opinions after they wrote their essay which was counter to their previously held beliefs. They volunteered to write an essay that countered their own strongly held beliefs. The action of writing an essay inconsistent with their previously held views produced an inconsistency that was uncomfortable for them. They needed to remove this inconsistency to regain a harmony of thought. The way many of them decided to remove this inconsistency was to change their opinion on the topic and give an alternative view some credence. The key to this exercise is in the participants' ability or inability to find an external source to justify their actions. An external source such as a requirement didn't effect an attitude change, but volunteering did. To regain harmony, if we can't rationalize, we all have a tendency to change our beliefs based on the activity just performed.

Incentives

Will incentives cause people to change their minds on certain issues? Many marketing companies and sales organizations strongly believe in incentives, but what does the research say?

In the previous study, they added another stimulus. Half the students were offered an incentive of $20 to write the essay that was counter to their beliefs, the other half was offered a $0.50 payment to write the essay—a big difference. Which group do you think changed attitudes after the essay was written?

The results were surprising. The group who were paid $20 showed very little changes in their attitudes, while the group who were paid $0.50 displayed significant changes. Why would this occur?

Both groups in this study were volunteers and agreed to write an essay that was counter to their beliefs. During the exercise, they experienced cognitive dissonance, as the words written were inconsistent with their own beliefs. The group that was paid $20 for this essay could justify writing the material based on the fact they were paid. They could therefore remain consistent with their views since they had been paid to write otherwise. They did it for the money and this was enough to regain harmony. Justification was at work to deal with the inconsistent behaviour. The $20 payment actually forced them to write the essay and the dissonance simply disappeared and all was well in their world.

The group who were paid only $0.50 didn't have the luxury of rationalizing their behaviour with payment since it was so low. They needed to resolve this dissonance in their mind, and the only remaining way was to change their attitude and express opinions that support what they write. The essay they write attacks their core beliefs, but they do so voluntarily. How could they do this? How could they write this essay when they don't believe a word of it? The need to be consistent with the action of writing the essay takes over and they suddenly start to question their original beliefs and leave room for a different view. Maybe this other perspective does have merit after all.

We all go through this exercise of attempting to be consistent. This simple study reveals that we can be influenced and persuaded to change our views and behaviour by very simple activities that appeal to our desire and need to be consistent and to avoid inconsistencies. Does this work in the real world or just the research field?

Real Life Dissonance

The process of teaching and learning is a perfect example of consistency in real life. Students come to class with a world full of preconceived notions and attitudes that have been instilled in them since birth. Students walk into class with a desire to maintain these consistencies at all costs. It's the teacher's job to create new learning opportunities that will challenge these strongly held beliefs. How can teachers influence the students to be more receptive to new ideas and concepts? If these inconsistencies are substantial and if the students are having difficulty solving their dissonance, then both the teacher and the learner will have problems with the new material.

The same situation applies when managing people. Managers want to achieve certain behaviour in their employees; however, the employee might be influenced by their preconceived notions and disagree with the approach. How does a manager achieve compliance in the face of disagreement? The usual technique applied in business is to use the autocratic approach and demand compliance using threats. This rarely works long term. Preparing a strong business argument and presenting the case forcefully might only ingrain the previously held beliefs even stronger. If we push too hard and do not get the results we seek, we may end up making the problem far worse than what it was in the first place.

In sales, we are always dealing with preconceived notions. Customers have notions about their needs, about the product, about the salesperson themselves, and even about the future of their business. To close a sale, we need to deal with these preconceived notions and effect an attitude change so the product or service will be of value to the client. We need to change their attitude before we can change their behaviour to buy.

Parents of teenagers have a serious problem. Teenagers will drink alcohol at social events, and in many situations they will also drive. Teenage drinking and driving is a serious situation and causes parents grave concern while they wait for their kids to return home safely. Thousands of alcohol-related accidents take the lives of innocent people each year. Why is it so difficult to stop teenagers from drinking and driving? It seems logical that drinking and driving is a very dangerous activity. It is against the law and the worst consequence is about as dire as it gets: death.

Given this clear consequence and the coaching by parents, why do teenagers continue to get behind the wheel while inebriated and why do other teens get in the car with the drunk driver? It appears that part of the problem is the teens' belief system. They feel they are invincible and nothing bad can happen to them. It might happen to others but not to them. Parental arguments about drinking and driving cause a dissonance between their invincibility and the request of a parent. The desire for independence plays a role in this internal argument for teenagers as well. To be consistent with their beliefs, they discount what the parents are saying by indicating that their parents are just worried about them. The argument of invincibility wins out and the teens jump behind the wheel with their friends and become another statistic in the teen drunk driving annals. Even though it makes no sense that anyone would drink and drive, it happens every day and people die. It is often innocent bystanders or other drivers who suffer the consequences.

A sale is another excellent example. The forceful salesperson might lose a sale for being too forceful and challenging strongly held beliefs that only serve to make those beliefs even stronger. So what is the answer to overcoming someone's strongly held beliefs? The key is to avoid creating dissonance forcefully, as the client will simply justify their position even more so. Such an attack rarely works. We suggest the art of self-discovery. In the above study where the volunteers wrote an article that was against their firm belief resulted in an attitude change, they changed because they volunteered and justified their action. Self-discovery is a similar approach that asks a variety of carefully crafted questions to allow the individual to draw fresh conclusions from the material and slowly generate an attitude shift. This works effectively in management and in any sales dialogue. Salespeople often do most of the talking, thinking they can convince the client to buy. The real challenge is to get the client to convince themselves to buy. We will discuss self-discovery techniques later in the book. Another excellent technique is to get a person to make a small commitment first so they are more likely to make a larger commitment later.

Foot-in-the-Door Technique

Gaining an early small commitment to something has been called the foot-in-the-door technique. Once the foot is in the door, people have accepted that you are there and will allow the rest of your body to enter. This age-old technique is based on very sound psychology.

Charitable organizations and religious groups have used this approach with good results. Charities will often start their first request at a very small amount, and each year they will ask for more. Once an individual has committed to the cause with a small donation, they are obliged to be consistent with this commitment and continually increase their pledge. Once the commitment is well established, the charity might even request to be included in the patron's will, a request that is often fulfilled. The management of this ever-escalating commitment has proven to be quite successful.

Salespeople will often begin the relationship with a small piece of business, just to let the client try them out. Once a client has agreed to do some business with the firm, it is much easier to make further larger requests for business because they have already committed to the product or service. The need to act consistently takes over and a larger sale could very well take place. Once an order is placed, no matter how small, a former prospect is now a customer and will act accordingly if the product or service meets their expectations.

In "Compliance without pressure: the foot-in-the-door technique," published in the *Journal of Personality and Social Psychology,* social scientists Jonathan Friedman and Scott Fraser discuss a study in which they proved the power of making requests that become progressively larger.[16] In this study, a researcher posed as a volunteer worker and went door to door in a residential neighbourhood in California, making a request that was ridiculous in nature and size. Homeowners were asked to install a huge billboard on their front lawn in support of a public awareness initiative on driving safely in residential areas. The homeowner was even shown a photograph of a home with the huge sign already in place. The sign was so large that it virtually blocked the view of the house from the street and took up almost all of their front lawn. The sign simply read "Drive Carefully" in bold letters. In most instances, the request was turned down. Only 17% of homeowners were willing to have the sign on their front lawn.

However, another group of residents in this same study agreed to the request 76% of the time. What was the difference? Why did this certain group of homeowners agree so readily to the installation of such a huge and ugly sign on their lawn that basically disfigured their home? This segment of homes had been contacted two weeks earlier and had made a small commitment to the "Drive Safely" campaign. A different researcher acting as a volunteer had approached these homeowners and asked whether they would put a small three-inch square sign in their window. The sign simply stated "Be a Safe Driver." The request was so small and the cause a good one that most of the households canvassed agreed immediately to this small and inconsequential request. The homeowners dutifully installed the sign in their window and felt good about their contribution to the safety of their streets. Little did they know that this tiny commitment would lead to their agreement to a much larger request later.

These homeowners had made a public commitment as supporters of safer streets. When a researcher returned two weeks later and made the larger request for the huge lawn sign, a full 76% of those homeowners complied with the request. Once they had made a commitment to the small request, homeowners felt the need to be consistent with the "Drive Safely" philosophy and support the initiative with the lawn sign.

Those who made the small commitment first complied with the larger request almost four and half times more often than those asked for the major commitment first. This is a huge difference encouraged by using the escalating commitment approach.

The researchers wanted to extend their research, so they approached a different set of homeowners and asked if they would sign a petition to "Keep California Beautiful." Now who wouldn't sign a petition to keep their state beautiful? Almost everyone who was asked agreed immediately to the request and signed it. After two weeks, the researchers returned with a new volunteer and visited these same homes. This time, they asked these residents to install the same huge sign earlier mentioned with the words "Drive Safely" on their front lawns. The results are an amazing example of how we can influence our target audience with simple techniques. The people in this study agreed to the huge sign almost 50% of the time. The results were astounding at the time of this study. How could a commitment on a totally different subject affect the results of getting a huge "Drive Safely" sign on a lawn?

Even the researchers were baffled by these results. They pondered why people signing a petition to keep California beautiful would lead them to agree to a much larger request that had no relationship to it. They finally concluded that the simple act of signing the petition had changed the view these residents had of themselves. After signing the petition, these homeowners now saw themselves as activists who were interested in their community and had civic pride. They might never have considered themselves public-minded individuals in the past, but the act of signing a petition had changed them. They needed to be consistent with this new commitment and the only way to maintain the harmony was to change their views to support their continued actions. Friedman and Fraser explain:

> What may occur is a change in the person's feelings about getting involved or taking action. Once he has agreed to a request, his attitude may change, he may become, in his own eyes, the kind of person who does this sort of thing, who agreed to requests made by strangers, who takes action on things he believes in, who cooperates with good causes.[17]

We are susceptible to being influenced by our desire to be consistent with our commitments and who we think we are. The professional influencer realizes that a small commitment can and often does lead to a much larger commitment later. These small commitments can change a person's self-image and make them willing to cooperate on issues they might not have without making the small commitment first. This technique is how a salesperson turns a prospect into a client. As soon as the prospect buys into even a small piece of what you offer, their perspective changes from a non-buyer to a customer. This change in perspective for a customer is quite a significant achievement because once a prospect sees themselves as a customer, they become much more willing to agree to a larger request at a later time.

Mortgage brokers in particular use this technique to gain at least one deal from a realtor. Once the realtor agrees to give a broker an opportunity, the realtor's mind shifts. This new attitude means that the new broker is now a source of mortgage financing, and when more business is requested, they will often comply. Using the ever-escalating request approach, the broker might soon request to be allowed to quote on every deal. Once this happens, it is only a matter of time before the realtor agrees to an exclusive arrangement to give the broker the first chance on every deal. When used properly, this foot-in-the-door technique is powerful. The problem is that most salespeople are too eager for the big sale and don't take the time to build the relationship and influence their prospect in such a way to change their perspective on the relationship.

This differs from the concession approach. Both approaches work, and we leave it to you to determine which works best. Generally, if a person has decided to buy, always make the largest request, but with a new potential client, the foot-in-the-door technique might be best to start the relationship.

Consistency Principle

People want to be consistent with what they say and do and will make changes in their lives to ensure this consistency remains. Inconsistency creates inner tension and discord, which causes us to move into action to restore harmony. The greater the inconsistency, the greater the motivation to deal with it. Inconsistency creates feelings of confusion, uncertainty, irritation, and denial, while consistency creates a feeling of harmony, calmness, and satisfaction.

The opportunity for masters of influence is to use this human behavioural quality we all have to effect change in behaviour. This can occur in education, in management, with your children or your spouse, or with a prospective client when you want them to purchase your product over another equally attractive option. As influencers, we know that the drive to be consistent is a powerful motivator that often leads us to act in ways that might not be in our best interests.

The desire to maintain consistency is overwhelming for us all. Smokers know they should quit, but refuse to read any anti-smoking articles in magazines. They avoid dissonance by avoiding new information on why they should quit and the dangers of continuing to smoke. We simply don't want to hear any views that oppose our current view of the world.

Do you know managers who don't like bad news and cut you off if you are about to share some reality with them? Managers who make a bad hire will work twice as hard to help their new hire make the grade rather than face the facts that they made an error. Stock investors are classic cases of justification. They will hang onto stocks that have recently declined and show no prospects of regaining their former price. The correct investment decision might be to take the loss and move on, but they somehow become attached to this loser stock because they hate to admit they made a mistake. They need to act consistently with their initial decision to buy. We have often heard investors rationalize these decisions: "It's not a loss until they sell it—it's only a paper loss until the stock is actually sold." Sorry, folks, your net worth has declined, and we call that a loss.

Thomas Moriarty published a study called "Crime, commitment, and the responsive bystander" in the *Journal of Personality and Social Psychology*.[18] In this study, Moriarty staged thefts on a New York beach to see if onlookers would get involved and stop a crime in progress. The researchers set up an assistant with a beach towel and radio not far from someone lounging on the beach. After a few minutes of relaxing on the blanket, the assistant would get up and walk away from his beach towel and radio and wander toward the water. Once the assistant had left the scene, another accomplice would pretend to be a thief and steal the radio right in front of the subject. The thief would steal the radio in the classic grab-and-run style. This is New York, remember, so you can imagine that few people would react to this staged theft. In fact, hardly anyone was willing to put themselves at risk by attempting to stop the robbery. It would appear that not getting involved is a national pastime, as only four people out of the twenty attempts did anything to thwart the robbery.

The researchers also staged the theft with a slight adjustment to the circumstances. This adjustment in the study produced dramatically different results from the test subjects. The scenario was the same with an assistant lying down on a beach blanket close to a subject and lounging with the radio on. This time, however, when the assistant got up to take a walk, he asked the adjacent subject the following question: "Could you please watch my things?" Each time the question was asked, the assistant would wait for an affirmative answer such as, "Sure." Each subject had made a verbal commitment to a complete stranger and the results will astound you. The subjects attempted to stop the thief nineteen out of twenty times. The subjects immediately responded to the thief by chasing him, grabbing the radio, and even physically restraining the thief, demanding an explanation.

The simple act of making a verbal commitment increased the desired response from 20% to a surprising 95%. Why would people, who normally don't want to get involved, respond dramatically and aggressively to a theft of a radio? In the first instance, the subject made no commitment and was therefore not personally involved and had no requirement to stop the thief. In the second set of studies, the subject made a commitment to watch the radio and therefore had to act consistently with this promise when the radio was stolen—an immediate and automatic response to uphold the earlier commitment. The subject had to be consistent with the commitment they had just made, even at personal risk. This is indeed a powerful influence tool.

Our society highly values consistency. It is reliable and creates a sense of harmony in all of us. Inconsistent behaviour, on the other hand, is seen as dangerous and unreliable, and it isn't valued at all. The management phrase that refers to this is "walk the talk." In this case, the manager's or executive's behaviour needs to be consistent with the words they use to communicate to employees. Many managers don't "walk the talk," they just talk, and employees notice the disparity between words and actions. Actions speak louder than words and an inconsistent manager is seen as untrustworthy, indecisive, or, even worse, an outright liar. People don't like to follow a leader whose words are inconsistent with actions—harmony at the office is disturbed, employees have difficulty performing at their peak, and chit-chat and gossip take over the workplace. The employees try to deal with the inconsistency by dropping their assessment of the leader and the company.

Consistency is a highly valued quality in all of society. It is so valued that we often react automatically because of our desire to be consistent. This approach saves a lot of time in unnecessary research and thinking time as we intuitively know what to do in these situations.

Group Dynamics

As new groups form and tackle a new project, a sequence of events always occurs within the team dynamics. It is called *forming, storming, norming, performing*. These stages of group dynamics seem to occur mostly with a new group.[19]

When groups first *form*, they are all excited about the possibilities of what they will achieve, but personalities soon enter the fray and the *storming* activity takes over. In this stage, people disagree (often vehemently) with each other. This is a stage for commitment and consistency. Early on, people make a decision on the direction of the project, and once they have made their commitment, they must be consistent with this even under duress from others. Some might call this stubborn, and that is exactly what it is—stubborn to preserve their original public commitment rather than change their mind and be inconsistent. Many groups never get out of storming, as some individuals simply refuse to give up their viewpoints. The need to be consistent is overpowering and the entire team and their results suffer. This usually requires a change in the team makeup to eliminate the problem so the team can move forward into *norming,* where they feel comfortable sharing without having ownership of the ideas. Once this is settled, the group quickly moves into *performing.* This is where the rubber meets the road and accomplishments are made.

Team exercises are an interesting aspect of how commitment and consistency can have a detrimental effect on team dynamics. If you're running a meeting, it is never a good idea to take a straw vote on an issue before a complete discussion. If you do, some members might make public commitments and end up in heated debates for all of the wrong reasons. The same goes for making a sale: Never try to close too soon because if the answer is negative, the commitment and consistency factors will come into play to derail your sales presentation.

The Up-Sell Technique

If you can get someone to commit to a product, idea, or decision, that person is more likely to remain committed even after the terms and conditions of the original situation change.

New car dealers use this tactic effectively. Once we have decided on our beautiful new car, we become committed to owning that vehicle. We love the colour, we love the smell, we love the way we feel when we sit inside. Consistency moves in next, and now that we have decided we want that car, we will respond favourably to the undercoating upgrade to keep the car like new longer. We might even go for the permanent wax job to keep that showroom shine for five years. The process of selling a car is all about getting a commitment. The dealer lets you take it for a ride, and some even let you take the car home. Wow, when the neighbours see the new car, you are committed. The paperwork seems endless—all part of enhancing the commitment. Sometimes even the price of the car is low at the beginning and then rises after they see the commitment signals on your face.

Gary: The real challenge for the consumer comes at Christmas. As I mentioned earlier, I have a granddaughter, and this past Christmas, an updated version of "Tickle Me Elmo" was the must-have gift for young children. In December, I thought I had best get to the store and buy Tickle Me Elmo before the real rush began. Well, much to my surprise, the store was sold out. They expected more in stock before Christmas but couldn't take an order. I searched another five stores over the next two weeks and the answer was always the same: sold out. What was I to do? I had promised my daughter I would take care of Elmo, and here it was only a week before Christmas and no Elmo in sight.

How was I to handle this challenge? I couldn't break my commitment to my daughter and granddaughter, and yet I couldn't find Elmo anywhere in the city. Here is what I had to do in order to be consistent with my promise: I created a Tickle Me Elmo voucher that could be redeemed for a new Tickle Me Elmo in January. Now a voucher isn't much of a gift for a granddaughter at Christmas, so I had to buy something else for her to open under the tree. It had to be nice, too, no cheap gift, as all grandparents crave that look of excitement on the child's face when they open your gift. Avery couldn't even read yet, so the credit voucher was no winner.

I did redeem the credit voucher for Elmo in January and young Avery ended up with more gifts than she would have normally, and I spent more money than usual. As I thought about this, I wondered who was the big winner here. Why, it must be the toy stores and young Avery, of course. They managed to get me to buy more product than I would have normally by having Elmo unavailable just before Christmas. Their store sales were high in January with sales of Elmo, even though January is often a bad month for toy sales. The store had capitalized on my desire to be consistent with my commitment. They had helped with my commitment by making Tickle Me Elmo such an attractive gift that kids around the world craved this little guy. Much to my chagrin, however, when we opened the box, young Avery was scared to death of Elmo and started to cry when Elmo started to laugh and roll around on the floor. Even eight months later, she still cries just looking at his face. Even the words *Tickle Me Elmo* bring a look of fear on her face. Now it appears only the store was the winner.

Why is the desire to be consistent with a commitment such a powerful driver in all of us? Why do we feel such an urge to follow through on our promises? It is cultural. People who don't meet their commitments have a definite reputation in most societies. They are called untrustworthy, liars, and even worse when they don't deliver on their promises. Gaining a commitment is a powerful way to get someone to say yes and to actually do what it is you wish them to do.

Will You?

In the banking business, February is RRSP (Registered Retirement Savings Plan) month in Canada and 401K time in the U.S. During this period, financial planners and advisors make appointments with customers to discuss their retirement plans and help them to make deposits to their plans in order to earn tax deductions for the previous year. There is a sense of urgency around these appointments, given the deadline and the competitive nature of this type of business.

One of the problems that advisors have is no-shows: People make appointments and don't show up to meet with the advisor. We have discussed this with many of our workshop participants over the years. One advisor, Julia, had an interesting story for us.

For years, she had been documenting cancelled appointments and recording her success rate with clients. Her statistics indicated that during February, her no-shows increased to over 30% and this was costing her valuable business and commissions. She decided to try a different approach to reduce the no-shows.

When making appointments with clients, she would always end the conversation with "Please call me if you have to cancel your appointment." Her new approach was to get a commitment from the client to call if they had to cancel. She simply added two words to her normal closing. When she implemented this small change, the results were amazing. No-shows dropped from over 30% to less than 10%. Those who wanted to cancel actually phoned to reschedule and then showed up. Her customer volumes skyrocketed and so did her commissions.

She changed "Please call if you have to cancel your appointment" to "Will you please call if you have to cancel your appointment?" What is the difference between these two approaches? In the first instance, Julia made a statement and the client felt no obligation to respond. The client did not have to make any commitment and therefore didn't feel obliged to notify Julia if they wanted to cancel. Under the revised scenario, Julia changed the statement to a question. When you turn the statement into a question, the person feels compelled to answer. As soon as the client answered in the affirmative, a little switch flipped up and a promise was made. We all want to keep our promises. The clients wanted to keep theirs and they did.

By changing a statement to a question, Julia engaged the principle of commitment and consistency. By doing so, her no-shows dropped significantly and her income rose accordingly. A simple change of having to make a verbal commitment has increased the probability that the client will act consistently with that commitment and follow through on their promise. The key is to pause after the question and give the client a chance to respond. The challenge, of course, is to get a commitment first. In this instance, it was quite easy and the results proved to be dramatic. We all want to be true to our word. Our word is our bond, after all. We are not born liars; we want to keep our promises and will act diligently to keep them.

Most salespeople seem to prefer making a statement when requesting a sale rather than actually asking a question and getting a commitment. It is a simple shift in approach but the results can be astounding. Most of us are humble and don't want to appear too pushy, so we give our clients an easy out by making a statement rather than a question. If you want improved results, turn the statement into a question and you will see an immediate change in your results.

Making Powerful Requests

Connie: You sometimes have to ask for what you want in return. Heck, it's your life. Who else should be asking for this? You should always be making powerful requests for what you want. Make powerful requests to get what you want. No hinting—ask specifically for what it is you want.

"I do make powerful requests," you say. Let's be sure. Here is an illustration of how garbage day used to go down in my home.

On Tuesday nights, I would say to my husband, "Honey, tomorrow is Wednesday—garbage day!" I would get no response from the TV room. Hmm. Why not? The drama in my mind would begin. Why is he not jumping into action to get the trash? He is not even moving during the commercials. Well, it's not my job. I am not taking the garbage out. It's his job! After all, he agreed to be the garbage man around here. It's his responsibility, and he is going to do it, not me. Heck, he even gets angry with me if I put the garbage out.

Let me ask you this: Did I make a powerful request? Did I make a statement, or did I ask a question? Did I get his commitment to the action I wanted to see? No, I didn't. I made a statement. No wonder I didn't get an answer. I didn't ask a question, so he didn't have to respond. This statement technique left me disappointed and wondering why he wouldn't take out the trash. Was it his fault? Nope. I need to turn that blaming finger back at myself and ask whether I made a powerful request.

It's incredible just how many people think they are making requests when they are simply making statements. A question involves a question mark (?). What could I have said to my husband? How about this? "Honey, tomorrow is garbage day. Will you please put out the trash tonight?" He would have said, "Sure, I will."

Begin listening to yourself. I bet you will find you make statements and only hint at the actions you want more often than you realize.

Most salespeople seem to prefer making a statement when requesting a sale rather than actually asking a question and getting a commitment. It is a simple shift in approach but the results can be astounding.

Real Life

Do you have teenagers? Any parent with teenagers always faces the challenge of having them come home on time. Let's say you want your teenager home at eleven in the evening. What do you normally say to your son or daughter? We ask this question in our seminars and the answers range from "Be home at eleven" (sometimes adding the formidable "or else") to "You had better be home by eleven or you're grounded for two years." It seems we like to make threats to encourage proper behaviour. The common quality among all the responses we hear is that the request to be home by eleven is always a statement, never a question. When the statement is "Be home by eleven," the response from the teenager is usually a mumble. Even teenagers know enough not to give a commitment because they know the consequences of commitments already.

We suggest to our seminar participants that they try following in the footsteps of Julie the financial advisor: "Will you be home by eleven?" followed by a pause while looking at them and waiting for an answer. And what will the son or daughter usually say in response? "No", "I won't be able to be home by eleven," or, worse, "I will try to." As we know from the previous chapter, the word *no* is a moment of opportunity available to you. You must know what to put into that moment in order to capitalize on it. We like to hear "no" because this means we can make a concession and we will be more likely to get compliance.

What could you as a parent say to your son or daughter who has just said, "No, I can't be home by eleven"? Here are some responses we have heard over the years from participants who are parents and actually use these techniques:

"Will you call if you're going to be late?" What does this imply? We want you home by eleven, but if you don't want to, you can come home anytime you want as long as you phone. Two or three in the morning? It's all okay as long as you phone. Don't forget our objective is to get the teen home at eleven; this is like a sale where we want the buyer to do what we want them to do. This technique fails miserably and we tell them so.

"Well, if you won't be home by eleven, then you can't go out." This causes severe confrontation and the teen will often just leave anyway, halting all communication. This is not influence, this is autocratic parenting at its best. There is no way the teen will be home by eleven. The rebellious stage has arrived and the results are unpleasant for everyone when we replace influence with a dictatorial approach.

Some use concession, but in reverse: "Will you be home by midnight then?" This concession is going the wrong way. If the teen says no again, your next response in concession is one in the morning—not a good solution. Remember, our influence goal is to get your teenager to agree to come home by eleven, not later. And you don't want to force them to stay home.

Try this: "Well, if you can't be home by eleven, will you be home by ten thirty?" This is using the concession approach of influence, and your teen will usually say, "Oh, alright, alright, I will be home by eleven." If you don't smirk in self-satisfaction, they will be more likely to be home at eleven than they would if you used your normal statement. It's all about getting a positive response to the question. When a teen says yes, that little switch flips in their head. They do want to keep their promises.

In our sessions, participants ask how they can get their children to clean their rooms. The same approach applies. It's Saturday morning and you want to influence your child to clean their room. You haven't had a great deal of success with this in the past with your usual approach. Here is what most of the participants say to their children: "Okay, it's Saturday morning; I want you to clean your room because it's an absolute mess and I am fed with up with it looking like a pig sty." The usual response is, "I will do it later." The question becomes: How much later? Two years later works for them. Some parents use the demand technique: "Clean your room today or else"—no response, and the room remains messy.

Here is a suggestion to try: "It's Saturday morning; will you tidy your room, clean the bathroom, vacuum the main floor rug, feed the dog, and change the cat litter?" The usual response from the child is, "No, I can't do all that today; I have way too much to do with my friends." As you will recall, the word *no* is a moment of opportunity and we should be ready to make a concession. Try this next time: "Well, if you can't do all that today, will you clean your room?" The child will often say okay and actually clean their room.

Connie: In Peterborough, one of our clients shared her frustration in making a request of her young child. She hated the cold snowy winter months because of the extra work in getting her son dressed in his snowsuit and boots. I asked her what she said to her son as they got ready to leave the house. She replied, "Get your snowsuit on—do it now! Stop fooling around!" She stopped. She heard the words as they came out of her mouth. She was even a tad embarrassed as she shared this in front of her peers. She gave an order, and never made a request of her child. It would take over ten minutes of nagging and complaining to get her son dressed, so she was willing to practice making a powerful request.

She wrote back a few days later. "I'm shocked it works." She said she tried making the request the day after the workshop. She called out sweetly to her son, "Honey, will you do Mommy a favour?"

"Sure, Mommy," her son replied.

"Will you please put on your snow suit?"

"Sure, Mommy." The morning battles were a

thing of the past. Here we have a powerful request in action.

We receive many emails from attendees at the various seminars we conduct and the response to this one is the most popular. Mothers especially will express their amazement that the influence technique actually works. They ask, "How long does this last?" We tell them we don't know how long it lasts but to enjoy it while it does. Sooner or later, they might figure out what you're doing and then you will have to apply another influence technique to get what you ask for.

Call Me Back

This influence approach is equally effective in business. Most customers will shop around for the best product and the best price. In the mortgage business, customers always want to shop for a better rate. You have interviewed the client, understand their needs, and made your closing presentation, but what if the client indicates that they would like to look around first before they finally decide on a mortgage provider? This happens frequently in any sales role and yet few sales professionals are truly prepared with what to say. Scripting is critical; a good salesperson should know exactly what to say and how to say it at these powerful moments of opportunity.

When you know in advance what's going to happen, you should be fully prepared to enhance your chances of gaining that customer's business. The challenge is that the customer will be leaving you to shop for rates, giving someone else an opportunity to close the sale without your getting a second chance.

What do you say when the client is leaving? Many of our students of sales have said things like, "Thank you for giving us the opportunity to present our product and I hope you will decide to bring your business to us." This is a statement, but not all that bad, except it doesn't get a commitment from the client to do anything.

It's just a short prayer hoping that you will get more business. Praying to be successful doesn't work all that often.

Some salespeople are worried about the rate, so they say, "Please call me if you find a better rate." This is even worse. Now what you're saying to your prospect is that your rate is not the best and there is a better rate out there: If you don't find it early, just keep on looking because a better rate is waiting to be discovered. Once they find a better rate (and they will), what do you do now, reduce your rate to compete? The client will wonder why you didn't simply do that in the first place. It's an ugly place to be when you have to reduce your rate to compete after a client comes back with a better rate. Credibility suffers, as does future business.

What do you say in this instance? We always ask the participants what they want the client to do. They often say to call if they get a better rate or call after they decide on another company, and some want to follow up on the customer with their phone call a week later. None of these are as effective as: "Will you please give me a call before you decide?" This is a simple request to which the client will usually say yes, therefore making a commitment to you. If you build even a little relationship during the dialogue, the client will actually call you before they decide. They need to keep their promise and they will. If you don't make the request and simply make a statement, there will be no need for the client to make a commitment. No commitment? No need to act and therefore no phone call and no business. It's that simple.

Which is better when developing business, you phoning the customer or the customer phoning you before they decide? No question here. It's much more effective if the customer phones you to give you a second chance. They are already 70% sold and only need to meet with you to close the deal. The objective should be to get the client to agree to call you back before they decide. Give it a try. We know you will be impressed with the results. It doesn't work all the time, but it will work more than your current approach.

This strategy is based on the simple fact that if we make a promise, we feel bad if we don't keep it. We work quite diligently to keep our promises to avoid this feeling. This principle is at our fingertips, but few apply it effectively to build your business and your relationships. We challenge you to try it on for size in the safety of your own home and check the results.

Effort Extra

Another interesting aspect of human nature is what we call the big-effort syndrome. It would appear that the more energy, time, or money we put into a commitment, the more we want to stick with it. We see this in business all the time. Executives get tied into a bad idea because they have made a public commitment to it and included significant resources to support it. They would sooner send good money after bad rather than admit the idea was wrong. Cutting your losses is extremely difficult if the commitment has involved significant resources both personal and financial.

When a manager hires someone, they want to ensure that this new employee is successful. The higher the level of management that chooses the new employee, the greater the degree of commitment to ensuring this person works out. There is a real hesitancy to fire an employee that you have hired personally. These new hires will experience more chances to fail and will receive more encouragement to succeed than those who have been hired by someone else. The public commitment displayed by the hiring will force the manager to try to justify the decision and find ways to keep that employee on staff long after they should.

About fifteen years ago, one of our executives hired a new assistant, George. The new hire to the company had wonderful credentials, a good resume, and experience. It didn't take long for the people reporting to George to realize that the cultural fit was terribly wrong. The company had been an entrepreneurial one and encouraged employees to be independent and empowered to do the right things for the customer. The staff had previously been encouraged to share customer issues up the ladder to resolve them quickly. George, on the other hand, had an autocratic approach and wanted to ensure that his people made him look good. Staff were told to follow the chain of command or face termination.

The team reporting directly to George started to go underground rather than be open and honest. They talked among themselves and complained constantly. Many started to look for work elsewhere. The executive was told by human resources of the management problems the team faced, but he stated it was just a transition and that all would be fine shortly. He said he would work with George and bring him around.

Well, as you can expect, things went from bad to worse. In order to feel that his hire had been the correct one, he had to find performance problems within the staff.

This went on for two years with ever-escalating issues surrounding George's lack of management skills. The autocratic approach became more pronounced when he started to see he was getting into trouble. George blamed others in the company for his problems and the executive actually believed the problem lied elsewhere in the organization. Interviews with some disgruntled staff members merely led to more coaching but no tangible results. George simply was not a cultural fit for the organization. After a year, the executive finally had to admit he made an error and terminated George.

Why did this take so long for an intelligent and effective executive to make a decision to terminate? The branch staff always wondered why the executive couldn't see the damage George was causing to the culture and to the morale of the branches. They started to lose confidence in the executive after six months of inaction and soon started to lose confidence in the company. This is a severe consequence of not dealing with an ugly situation early. The reason George lasted as long as he did was the simple fact that the executive had made a public commitment and needed to act consistently.

The extra effort involved in hiring a new executive influenced the executive's ability to make the right decision. He felt compelled to justify his decision. If he fired George too soon, he would feel his judgment would be in question, but by waiting too long, both his judgment and integrity were in question. It's a catch-22, really. A good rule of thumb might be to do the right thing based on facts, not on the effort put into the decision. If we are aware of the power that this type of influence can have on us, we will be empowered to deal with it more effectively and make the right decisions quickly.

Gary: My family and I like to go to concerts. Many of the concert ads in the paper or on TV rarely have a price attached to it. Even when you go online to look at the upcoming concerts, they will often not include the price. Why do they not include the price? I suggest that that they are using the big-effort syndrome on us. I have found that when researching concerts, I rarely know the price. Tickets go on sale on Friday at 8 a.m. I am on the phone, waiting in the queue for twenty minutes, until I finally get an operator and enquire about the price. The price seems steep, but because I have been on the phone for twenty minutes, I want the tickets. I have just invested twenty minutes into this concert already and therefore want to attend, so I buy the tickets. It seems that even the exercise of going online on Ticketmaster is enough of an effort to increase the chances of me buying those tickets. The more trouble I go through to get tickets, the more I value getting them. In fact, the more trouble, effort, and even pain we endure to obtain something, the more we value it.

What is the message here for salespeople? If someone has to do something extra in order to buy from you, they will value that purchase far more than they would if it were easy to obtain. Also, the word of mouth on the quality of the item will be significantly higher. This is one reason why salespeople who make house calls are encouraged to stay in the home as long as possible. The longer you stay, the more likely you are to make a sale and the more likely the client will be delighted with the purchase. The same theory applies to the phone. Call centres are urged to keep people on the phone at all costs. The longer they are on the phone, the more committed one becomes to purchase something.

Low-Balling, or Bait and Switch

Most sales professionals are aware of the technique known as low-balling, or bait and switch. It happens when a product is listed below the regular price, but when you make a commitment to get this product, the salesperson throws a curve and indicates either an error or stock shortage but suggests another item that costs more. It's surprising how often we fall for this tactic. We decide on the product, make an effort to drive to the store, and now we face a different product with a higher price. Most will comply with the higher price. This is unethical in many instances and usually leads to a one-off sale but not a relationship. We should, however, be aware of how this influences us as consumers and how we as salespeople could use this to gain an early commitment to a larger commitment later. This might be seen as just good salesmanship. If things are above board and honest, then the low-ball technique of gaining compliance with a smaller request could be effective in gaining further business and building the relationship.

In his book *Influence: Science and Practice,* Robert Cialdini conducted an interesting study on compliance. Cialdini wanted to see if offering a good deal, which would produce a commitment, could be maintained if he added an unpleasant feature to the deal. The low-ball technique is designed to get a person to stick with a deal even after circumstances have changed to make it a poor deal.

The experiment asked students to perform an unpleasant activity. They were asked to wake up at 7 a.m. to attend a study on "thinking processes." As you can imagine, this is an unpleasant task for university students—getting up early is rarely enjoyed. One group of students were called and informed of the 7 a.m. start time. Only 24% of the students agreed to participate, given the unpleasant time feature of the request. A second group of students were called using the low-ball technique. They were first asked to participate in a study on thinking processes and 56% agreed under the conditions. After they responded, they were told the session begins at 7 a.m. and were given a chance to change their mind. In this study, none of the students changed their mind, and since they had made a commitment to attend, 95% of the students showed up at 7 a.m. as promised.

As Cialdini notes, the impressive thing about the low-ball tactic is its ability to make people feel pleased with a poor choice. Salespeople who only have poor choices to offer are very adept at the low-ball technique. You will find the low ball in all situations, not just sales. It is prevalent in business, management, and even in your personal life.

We all generally need to be consistent with our words, actions, beliefs, and attitudes. We don't like to be perceived as erratic or unreliable. Consistency allows us to take shortcuts on decisions. There's no need for significant research for each decision if we look back at previous decisions and act consistently.

With this personal requirement to be consistent, the influencer's job becomes to gain an initial commitment on an issue or product; this way, the individual will be more willing to agree to further requests that are in line with their initial position. These smaller commitments are most effective when they are public, require some effort, and come from within rather than forced by another. These commitments are powerful. Even when they are wrong, they have a tendency to be supported long after their usefulness has expired.

Personal improvement strategies by the gurus of self-help always suggest the same key strategy: Make a personal commitment. They suggest making a goal, making it public, making it freely, and making it in writing. Making a public commitment to lose weight, quit smoking, or improve self-esteem—and keeping it in your face all the time—makes us more likely to comply with it and change our behaviour to match it. Sales professionals use this same approach to gain a commitment from a client and increase the chances of closing a sale. Parents can gain a public commitment from children and change their behaviour to match it. When applied effectively, this simple technique, combined with other principles of influence, will have a significant impact on getting people to say yes to your requests and you will be more successful in getting more of what you want.

Best Practices

1. The best commitment is a written commitment.
2. Share your commitment publicly. We all want to keep our promises, especially when we make them publicly, as there is more pressure to act consistently with what we say.
3. Ask for a commitment. Most salespeople don't ask for the business—they make a statement instead. Be bold and make powerful requests. "Will you call me before you decide?" This gains a commitment from a price shopper to call you. It is always better to have clients call you than you call clients.
4. When the answer to your request is no, be prepared and make a concession.
5. Gain a small commitment first and then ask for larger commitment later.
6. A small purchase turns a prospect into a client.
7. People become more committed to an action if they have dealt with a concession. Clients are more likely to buy (or provide referrals) after a concession has been made.
8. Write your personal and professional goals down. Make them visible and read them four times a day.
9. Keep your commitments and others will keep theirs.

Chapter 7
Monkey See, Monkey Do

The Lemming Factor

Lemmings are rodents found in Arctic tundra regions. Like other rodents, they experience population explosions at times and disperse en masse to find new feeding grounds. When these population explosions occur, lemmings migrate in large numbers, and when they reach a cliff, they have been known to simply jump off into the ocean and start swimming, usually to their deaths through exhaustion. This unusual sight of thousands of lemmings running off a cliff to their demise has created the myth of lemming mass suicide. This is a frequently used metaphor in reference to people who go along with popular opinion without question. People often get caught up in a herd mentality, with potentially dangerous or even fatal consequences.

Many wonder why lemmings would leap to certain death just because the first one did and then the next five hundred did as well. This metaphor of being influenced by what others are doing explains much of what happens in our society. Peer pressure is a very real persuasive factor. The power of crowd psychology has been investigated by countless psychologists with surprising results. It would appear the lemming factor does influence our behaviour and can therefore be used to increase your effectiveness as well as a tool to influence others. It would seem that we are more likely to behave in a certain way if we believe others like us are behaving similarly. We often look to the actions of others to confirm whether our own actions are appropriate.

Consensus Theory

Drive past any schoolyard filled with teenagers and you will notice various groups of students gathered in small clusters. The individuals within each cluster seem to have the same taste in clothing and hairstyle, but these choices often differ in style compared to other groups. It seems that teens in particular have a desire to be similar to their friends but different from their parents. They want to conform to the group's standards and are strongly influenced by their peers. They are responding to the common need within all of us to be followers. If others are doing it, it must be the right thing to do, and so we follow suit. We all have a basic need and desire to be connected to others. We are social animals, after all.

Let's say you and your spouse go out for a romantic dinner to a restaurant that you have never been to before. You thought you would be adventurous and try a new taste in food. You make a Saturday reservation for 7 p.m. You both get dressed up and ready for a nice romantic evening. When you get to the restaurant, you notice how easy it is to park, as there are few cars in the parking lot, but the restaurant looks quite nice from the outside. You and your spouse head to the main entrance and open the door and step inside.

The place looks lovely with candlelight and a warm decor. As you look around the room, you notice there is no one else in the restaurant. It's empty except for two waiters standing by the bar. What do you do now? You and your spouse look at each other with the same quizzical look. What should you do? Most people will make a feeble excuse about having to cancel and leave. Why would you do that? The fact that no one else is in the restaurant has conveyed a message to you. The message is: If no one else is eating at this restaurant, the food must be terrible. You have just been influenced by the actions of others and "the others" aren't even there. Yes, what others do or don't do has an influence on our own behaviour. You have just judged this restaurant by the opinion of others and not by your own judgment. This is an example of the power of consensus in our lives. We are greatly influenced by what others say or do.

How to Behave

When we are in a situation where we don't know how to behave, we look to others to determine the correct behaviour. If you have ever been to a fancy dinner party or restaurant where they have a number of eating utensils displayed on each side of your dinner plate and several others located at the top, you will know what we mean. What fork goes with what food? Many of us have been in this embarrassing situation and the easy solution is to watch what others at the table are doing. We assume that others at the table who actually reach for a fork are more socially astute than we are; therefore, we choose the same fork as they did for the same item on the plate. We look around nervously to see if anyone notices our apprehension about eating. In this situation, we are able to hide our lack of social graces and escape the embarrassment of choosing the wrong fork. We are influenced by the actions of others because we are unsure of what to do next.

Apathy

Much research has been conducted to study the effects of bystander apathy. When someone is in trouble or needs help, as the number of bystanders increases, the number of people who actually help decreases. The more people present in a crisis, the less responsible each person becomes in aiding the needy. We have a feeling that others are more capable to help and we don't do anything. We don't know what to do, so we wait to see the reaction of others to determine if this is in fact a crisis. It's only when someone moves to assist that anyone else will.[20]

One actual case that took place in New York City stands as the

classic example of bystander apathy and has been studied and reported on for years. Catherine Genovese was murdered one evening
on her way home from work. On March 27, 1964, the *New York
Times* ran a front page story on the incident and the alleged reactions of the neighbours near the killing:

> For more than half an hour, thirty-eight respectable, law
> abiding citizens in Queens watched a killer stalk and stab a
> woman in three separate attacks in Kew Gardens. Twice the
> sound of their voices and the sudden glow of their bedroom
> lights interrupted him and frightened him off. Each time he
> returned, sought her out, and stabbed her again. Not one
> person telephoned the police during the assault; one witness
> called after the woman was dead.[21]

The nation was in an uproar over the apparent apathy of New
Yorkers. How could they sit by and watch this murder and not
phone the police? Actual responses from the neighbours indicated
that they couldn't explain their inaction. Comments at the time
ranged from, "I don't know," "I was afraid," "I didn't want to get
involved." Other media jumped on the case and tried to find an explanation for the behaviour of the witnesses to this crime. After significant research and study, the general feeling was that the
neighbours "simply didn't care." New York City was a big cold city
and the citizens didn't want to get involved. "Apathetic New Yorkers" was the statement often heard across the country.

A. M. Rosenthal was the metropolitan editor of the *New York
Times* and it was he who broke the story. He later authored a book
on the subject.

As outlined in *Thirty-Eight Witnesses: The Kitty Genovese
Case*, he also believed in the apathy of big city people as the reason for their inaction. He writes:

> Nobody can say why the 38 did not lift the phone while
> Miss Genovese was being attacked, since they cannot say

themselves. It can be assumed, however, that their apathy was indeed one of the big-city variety. It is almost a matter of psychological survival. If one is surrounded and pressed by millions of people, the only way to prevent them from constantly impinging on you is to ignore them as often as possible. Indifference to one's neighbour and his troubles is a conditioned reflex in life in New York as it is in other big cities.[22]

The story continued to attract a great deal of attention in the media as big city apathy came under careful scrutiny. Bibb Latane and John Darley published an article entitled *The Unresponsive Bystander: Why Doesn't He Help?* which tried to explain the Genovese case in different terms.[23] A bystander to an emergency situation may be unlikely to assist when there are a number of other bystanders witnessing the same event. They reasoned that each individual's responsibility was reduced with other people present who could assist with the crisis. "Perhaps someone else will give or call for aid, perhaps someone already has." In large groups, the witnesses to an emergency start to feel that someone else will do something or has already done something and so no one does anything.

Latane and Darley have another theory on bystander apathy, which involves the theory of social proof. Sometimes an emergency or crisis situation is not really an emergency at all. A car pulled over on the highway could just be a tired driver rather than out of gas. A man sleeping on a park bench could be a homeless person rather than a victim of a heart attack. As mentioned earlier, when we are uncertain, we look to the actions of others to determine the right course of action for us. The behaviour of others will determine whether something is a crisis situation. The insidious aspect of this concept is that everyone involved will look to each other for understanding as to the severity of the incident.

During an emergency, a bystander might look around at others to determine what they are doing, even though the others might be looking around too. No one jumps in to help. This "social proof" dictates that this is not an emergency situation, so the people simply walk on by and do nothing. Since no one else appears to be concerned about the situation, there must be nothing wrong. Later research on the Genovese case has presented other alternatives and differing facts. The message for us is that groups of bystanders are less likely to act than if the bystander is alone. We seem to judge the severity of situations by what others are doing. In influencing others, it is critical, then, to demonstrate group support for your products or ideas.

Latane and Darley conducted a study of their own in 1968. They had a college student fake an epileptic seizure and monitored the results of people who would move to help the student. When a single bystander was present, they would assist the student 85% of the time, but when five bystanders were present, the student was assisted only 31% of the time.

Why was there such a large difference in bystander response to the exact same situation? When alone, the witness has no one to look to for social proof that something was wrong. They must take action and full responsibility, and they did most of the time. With a small group of bystanders, the opposite occurred. They all look to each other to determine whether this is a crisis, and no one takes responsibility, so no one does anything. We are motivated by the actions and non-actions of others.

If we happen to be a victim of a crisis, we should hope there is only one witness. That way we will get help more readily. If we want help from a group of observers, however, we should point to one individual and ask for their help specifically. This will break through the social proof context and they must now take action because they have been selected to do so. How can we apply this to our world of selling? When clients are undecided, testimonials from other clients might bring social proof into play and make the client feel more comfortable with their decision. Statistical data about how many clients have chosen an option could also bring social proof to bear on the decision. People are influenced by what others like them have done, especially when they are undecided.

Social Proof

Social proof is a psychological phenomenon that occurs in social situations where people are unable to determine the appropriate form of behaviour on their own. In these situations, people will look around at what others are doing and assume that others have more knowledge or experience; they will believe that this behaviour is appropriate for the situation and will act accordingly.

This phenomenon can be expanded to include most situations we find ourselves in. We look to what others are doing in order to determine the appropriate behaviour for ourselves. It is the power of crowd mentality. Most of the time, we don't even realize how we are being influenced. Sales and marketing are prime areas that use social proof to to increase sales and to actually get consumers to change their behaviour.

Laugh Tracks

If you watch any television sitcoms, you will notice that they often include an audience reaction to the show. You will hear laughter on a regular basis during most sitcoms. Most of us are now aware that this laughter is pre-recorded and inserted into the sitcom when the writers think something is funny. Even when they are wrong, they do it anyway. Why would TV producers have fake laughter inserted into their television shows? What could be its purpose?

The producers know the rule of social proof. They know that we will quite often trust the opinions of others—especially a group of others—more than our own logic. When we watch a sitcom and the canned laughter is inserted, we can't help ourselves, we find the humour in the situation as well. We might not laugh as loud or as long, but it appears that a laugh track causes us to enjoy the show more than we would otherwise. The producers are using the power of consensus to help us to enjoy their show and in turn increase ratings and advertising revenue.

Applause tracks do the same thing for television shows. Audiences at shows that are either live or taped are flashed a sign that reads "Applause," and they comply with the request. Have you ever been to a concert, play, or perhaps a political speech? If the event was okay but certainly not spectacular, at the end of the presentation, we all applaud generously. But if a few people stand to provide a standing ovation, what happens next? Exactly, everyone stands and gives a standing ovation. This is the lemming factor in action. Once a few start, a few more join in, and soon everyone is obliged to participate in the standing ovation. We have a need to belong to the group. This is the persuasive power of consensus and social proof.

Auctions

Auctions are an interesting social setting, as we can observe human behaviour at its finest. A number of influence techniques are operating during an auction, including the principles of scarcity and consensus. If somebody else wants it, it seems we want it even more. Second, if more than one person wants it, then we assume it must be a great item. Auctioneers know this about us and have implemented a technique called a shill into the bidding process. A shill is a person who actually works for the auction house and their job is to get the bidding started and to ensure that it's infectious. It's exciting to be in competition with someone else for an antique vase. Once others join in with the bidding, the shill can relax. If the price is too low, the shill might come back into the picture and provide another bid to keep the bidding going. The auctioneer is using a time-tested method to encourage you to buy at elevated prices and yet to believe you got a great deal.

The Art of Dating

When we perceive a man or woman as being popular with the opposite sex, they immediately become more popular. We like people who are popular because it means that others have already approved their social worthiness and we assume they are correct. Have you noticed that the more friends people have the easier it is for them to get friends? A man who walks alone into a bar, looking for action, has no friends with him and so has no social proof working for him and will find it extremely difficult to build. A man who walks into the same bar with four or five other good-looking guys, on the other hand, will have immediate social proof of popularity. Now if the same guy walks into the same bar with two good-looking women, one on each arm, he has immediate celebrity status. People automatically wonder what is it about him that gets two lovely women to join him for the evening. They attach attractive character traits to him and would like to be a part of the action.

Let's say you go to a bar and get turned down by several women and this is noticed by other women in the bar. What do you think your chances are of getting to talk to anyone else in the bar? The other women have just observed your rejections and assume you were rejected for good reason and will therefore reject you as well. They will have no other reason than the simple fact that others rejected you. Time to go home and wait for another evening.

The iPhone Phenomenon

Apple has used the method of social proof and the power of the crowd to create a major buzz around their iPhone. Go see the iPhone "Day One" gallery pages on Apple.com for an amazing marketing strategy that has paid off handsomely. This gallery, along with news reports, shows incredibly long lines of fans waiting for stores to open so they can purchase an iPhone. Some people even stayed in line all night to be the first to get this phone. They show reporters and TV cameras recording the event. All the people are excited and happy, especially after they walk out with their purchases. News articles appeared on a regular basis and bloggers were providing commentary every day on the marvels of the iPhone.

This is social proof at its finest. We are inundated with footage and commentary about the thousands of people who are so excited about this new iPhone that they wait in line to purchase it. If these people are so excited, this must be one marvellous phone and we had best get one too. Apple created a crowd mentality around the iPhone and now millions have been sold, which simply reinforces the social proof of this item for those of us who don't own one. Everyone has one, so we need one too.

The Dot Com Craze

The stock market provides ample evidence of how social proof has an impact on the investment habits of normally prudent investors. The late '90s was a crazy time for Internet stocks, and the NASDAQ skyrocketed. Stories appeared everywhere about investors making millions in the market. More people soon began investing in these "dot com" companies and the stocks went even higher. As the stocks grew, even more people decided to jump on the bandwagon to make some big money. Investment decisions shifted from the quality of the company and its earning to what other people were buying. Cab drivers were even providing investment advice to their passengers and telling stories of how much they had made. Before long, reality hit and it all came crashing down, dropping some 90% in a matter of a year.

Why were so many rational people induced to set aside their logic and risk assessments to invest large amounts of their money in this highly volatile sector of the market? Others were doing it and making money, so it must have been the right thing to do, and so they did. The power of social proof in action. The more people engage in a particular behaviour, the more acceptable this behaviour becomes.

Marketing

How do marketing companies use social proof to influence our decision making? When browsing a bookstore, are you more likely to pick up a book that has a banner on the cover that reads, "*New York Times* Best Seller" or "Over one million copies in print"? These statements are designed to capture our interest. If a million people liked this book, then it must be good, right?

Many products have claims in bold print on their packaging: "Biggest selling," "fastest growing," or "number one." These claims might be true, but their real value comes in the form of social proof. The average purchaser is swayed by this information, and most of the time, we don't even realize the impact this phenomena has on our decision making.

Would you buy the toothpaste that was approved by six out of every ten dentists or toothpaste that wasn't approved by any of them? Other products might have nine out of ten doctors recommending it. We are swayed by the consensus of medical professionals.

Conformity

We are all influenced by what others think to some degree. Sometimes it's quite subtle and we don't even realize we are being influenced; other times, it is as direct as peer pressure. Conformity has its good side effects. We all drive on the right side of the road, and when walking, we always seem to walk on the right side of the sidewalk to avoid mass confusion. Some negative side effects to conformity, however, include such things as abusing drugs and alcohol and other dangerous behaviours.

We are influenced by what others do, and the closer we are to those influences, the more power they exert over our own behaviour. Cigarette smoking is a perfect example. Most of us know that smoking is bad for our health, yet many continue to smoke. Recent evidence regarding teen smoking has indicated that if the parents smoke, a teen is about 15% more likely to smoke than a teen from a non-smoking family. When smoking in teens is compared to friends who smoke, this number skyrockets to almost a 1,000% increase in the likelihood that they will smoke. Generally, teens smoke if their friends smoke. Teens have a need to belong to a group, so if a group smokes, so will those joining the group. The influence of peer pressure on smoking is astounding.

Robert Cialdini sponsored a seminar in Phoenix, Arizona, a

number of years ago. The session was called a "pop," which stands for "power of persuasion." During this seminar, Cialdini shared a recent study he had completed for a hotel chain. One of the issues and opportunities all hotel chains face is the cost of laundry for towels and the environmental impact of washing thousands of towels. Hotels would generally like guests to use their same towels on the second day of their stay rather than have them laundered. The cost savings would be huge and the environmental impact would be greatly reduced.

The hotels in the chain had tried a variety of methods to induce guests to keep their towels for one more day. Many had installed signs in the bathroom that extolled the environmental virtues of reusing towels. Take a look the next time you're in a hotel and see if these signs are there and have an impact on you. Apparently, this environmental call to action had minimal effect on the guests.

Cialdini was called in to provide some insight on how to influence guests to be more environmentally friendly. He suggested using the principle of consensus, or social proof, as a way to encourage guests to use their towels for their second day. He said that extolling the virtues of the environment would have little effect, and he was right. He then suggested putting up a small sign that reads: "The majority of guests who have stayed in this hotel have used their towels for a second day." An even better approach suggested by Cialdini was: "The majority of guests who have stayed in this room have reused their towels."

The results were immediate. Guests would read the sign and be moved to follow the suggestions because other people just like them in this very room had done the same thing. It must therefore be the right thing to do. The number of towels being laundered on a daily basis plummeted. By using the theory of consensus, we are all influenced by this social pressure to do the right thing. It is interesting to note that we are more likely to change our behaviour because others just like us are doing it rather than our individual concern for the environment. Perhaps we are all skeptics at heart and believe that hotels are more interested in reducing costs than helping the environment. In any case, this simple change in wording had a dramatic effect on the behaviour of the guests and the desired outcome was achieved by using the theory of consensus. We all like to conform to what others just like us are doing. This is clearly a powerful influence tool that we as salespeople should consider using.

Everyone Agrees

In her article entitled "Everyone Agrees," published in *Psychology Today*, Melinda Wenner reveals that an often heard opinion seems popular even if it comes from only one person.[24] The 2008 presidential election is a case in point. With so many candidates and so many differing opinions, how can the general public sift through all this media information and decide who they would like to vote for?

The research suggests that we judge a particular viewpoint by how familiar it is to us. Apparently, it doesn't matter if we've heard it ten times from one person or ten times from ten different people. Researchers gave volunteers records of opinions from a staged focus group that had met to discuss the preservation of open spaces in New Jersey.[25] In some cases, multiple people expressed the same viewpoint and, in other cases, the same person repeated their viewpoint several times. Based on this information, the group was asked to determine how the focus group and the population in general felt about this issue.

The study participants rated an opinion as popular if it had been expressed several times, even if only one person in the focus group had expressed it. Follow-up research confirmed that an opinion's familiarity was an important factor for determining whether subjects considered it to be common. The risk is that a vocal minority can sway public opinion merely by stating their message repeatedly. Repetition does have an impact on our decision making. Television commercials are repeated several times during the same show. This is all done with the intent of influencing your purchasing decisions.

What does this mean for the average salesperson or employee wanting to influence others? Repeat the same message and you will get converts to your side. The undecided will be swayed by a familiar message. The familiar is comforting and leads people to believe that it deserves consideration.

The Bandwagon Effect

P. T. Barnum, the famed huckster, once said, "Nothing draws a crowd like a crowd."

Many of us have heard of the bandwagon effect and have probably used the term to explain behaviour in others. People often believe things simply because many other people believe the same thing. We have a tendency to follow the crowd and assume that the crowd is demonstrating the proper behaviour or making the right decisions.

"Jumping on the bandwagon" refers to those of us who join with the perceived winner and associate with those in power. In elections, many voters will cast their ballots for the candidates who are perceived to be winning the popular vote, thus increasing that candidate's chance of winning. This is why pre-election polling has such a powerful impact on results. We all like to back a winner. This effect can be seen with music and sports teams as well. Many people become major fans of a musical group only after they become popular. Sports teams who are winning gain more fans than those who are losing.

What Does This Mean?

As salespeople and influence professionals, we need to realize that people are motivated by what others are doing. In his book *The Cavett Robert Personal Development Course,* Cavett Robert said it best: "Since ninety-five percent of the people are imitators and only five percent initiators, people are more persuaded by the actions of others than by any proof we can offer." The message is clear. Obtain social validation for your product or service and people are more likely to buy it. We all look to what others are buying to provide additional support for our purchases. If we become confused over features and benefits, we are more likely to conform to the group standard. This is why products with highly recognizable brand names outperform less popular brands even though the quality might be comparable. Businesses spend enormous marketing dollars protecting their brands because they know that branding is all-important for future sales.

Referrals

Every successful salesperson would love to increase their referrals from satisfied clients. We have discussed the various methods of increasing referrals from these clients. Social proof is the main reason referrals are such a powerful tool in growing your business.

Putting letters of accommodation on your website sends a clear to message to prospects that others just like them have received exceptional service and find the product or service to exceed their needs. The more letters on the website that confirm your expertise, the more likely an undecided prospect will decide to go with you. They will be influenced by the actions of others.

A letter of introduction by another satisfied client is an excellent way to open doors. The best letter of reference would be from someone at a senior level in a company that is in a similar business as your potential client. If the letter of reference comes from a well-known individual in the business, this is even more powerful to convince the prospect to meet with you.

A personal introduction from a satisfied client who actually knows your prospect is equally persuasive. The theory of consensus kicks in and the prospect is influenced by the fact that a highly respected friend has used your services, meaning that you must indeed bring value. They judge your ability not on what you say and do but by what others see you bringing as value that will increase their results.

A business card that showcases your success is another way to use social proof on the job. If you're looking for a real estate agent, what criteria would impress you? The agent with a platinum award in sales or an agent with no sales results reflected on their card? Social proof suggests that we would be more persuaded to use an agent whom others have used successfully rather than an unknown entity. Previous success and the power of consensus will breed further success. People simply want to deal with those who others have found to be of value.

The Power of Words

Scripting is a vital ingredient in every sales discussion. Certain words will evoke the power of the crowd to support your proposition. McDonald's used to show how many burgers they had sold worldwide until the number got to be too large and they simply started saying, "Billions Sold." Declaring that billions of burgers have been sold is quite a message to the consuming public. These burgers must be darn good and have great value if so many people are buying them. We then stop off at the local McDonald's more often than we would if they didn't indicate "Billions Sold."

Introducing a product or service as the "fastest selling" or the "most popular" will automatically increase sales. The social validation of these offerings have been enhanced because many people are purchasing them. When something is widely popular, we will spend more money to acquire it. Sometimes it's just the salesperson's word we trust. It seems that we all want to be on the inside track with the most popular items so we can be with the in-crowd and more readily accepted by those around us.

Consumer crazes have included hula hoops, Cabbage Patch Kids, the Nintendo Wii, the iPhone, and much more. When we realize that others wanted these products, they became much more desirable. The general population went wild over these products. People would line up for hours and search stores for days trying to find these extremely popular items.

Financial planners will often include words in their sales presentations to prospective investors that suggest others just like them are "doing the same thing." If you want a client to invest with you, what could you say that would invoke their power of consensus? We have heard comments such as, "Many of my clients in the same kind of financial position as you have invested in…" or "Many of my clients just like you have decided to consolidate all their investments with me." See what we have done here? By using the simple phrase "many of my clients," we have provided social validation. The fact that other similar investors have chosen the planner increases the chances that the prospective client will also choose them. No client wants to feel they are alone in choosing an advisor; they want to know that others have chosen and profited from the relationship. The power of words allows you to capitalize on the need we all have to be part of a group.

Open Houses

In real estate sales, an agent will often hold an open house to allow other agents and prospective purchasers to come and view the home. The increased number of people viewing a home increases the chances of someone being willing to make an offer on it. If people of the same financial standing all like the home, then it must be of good value.

If this is the case, what could a real estate agent do to enhance the perceived value of the home? Many agents invite the neighbours to an open house. The neighbours are curious people and want to see the inside of the house and the list price. They will show up at the door, take the full tour, and usually make positive comments about the home. Potential purchasers will notice that many people seem interested in property and, based on the theory of consensus, they too will like the home.

This simple approach of capitalizing on the predictability of human behaviour will result in more sales at higher prices. If you're the consumer, however, you also need to be aware of the predictability of this behaviour and try to downplay the need for social validation and purchase the home based on your needs. Most of the time, we are completely unaware of the effect social proof has on our decision making.

Trade Shows

Trade shows are a great way to meet many potential clients and to demonstrate your wares to those who have attended the show specifically to gather information. We have attended many trade shows over the years and we are always surprised at how little pre-planning goes into them. Most booths are quite attractive and many of the sponsors working each are dressed in similar outfits to draw attention to themselves. This in itself is a good idea to identify and differentiate one company from another, especially a competitor. The problem arises when the people running a booth stand around and talk amongst themselves.

This social chatting is most evident when the employees are all dressed alike. What message does this convey to the potential clients browsing the booths? Will they interrupt a social conversation between co-workers? Will they feel you have a product worth investigating if all they see at the booth are employees? Social proof would indicate that if no clients are talking to the staff, then the staff has nothing new to share with consumers and the product itself is not worth investigating. It's much like going into an empty restaurant at 7 p.m. on a Saturday night. No one is there, so we assume people are avoiding the restaurant because the food is terrible.

What should we be doing at a trade show to garner attention from passersby? The lemming factor indicates that people will go with the crowd. If people are crowding around a booth, then something exciting must be happening and we will all be drawn to this booth to find out what is going on. You therefore need some type of attraction that will get people to your booth but not so entertaining so that all the prospects want to do is play your game and leave. You want to draw them to your booth and you want them to stay and talk.

A simple solution is to have some of your employees dressed like clients. As they stand around your booth, they look like prospects rather than employees. Someone walking by will think a business conversation is taking place and will be much more likely to stop by your booth. Planning ahead and knowing the challenges of a trade show will greatly assist in getting more people to your booth. Once at the booth, the real sales challenges begin and the rest of this book will provide some real insights in how to turn a trade show booth visit into an appointment.

Voicemail

Voicemail is another key persuasive tool we have. Stop right now and dial your voicemail and listen to the entire recording. Check your office voicemail and check your cell phone voicemail. What did you hear? Where you impressed with what you heard or did it sound just like everyone else?

During our seminars, we quite often get participants to phone their voicemail so we can play it over the sound system. Most are dismayed by what they hear. They usually are way too long and go into way too much detail about what they are doing and why they can't answer the phone right now. If you're going to say what you're doing, you should never say, "I am in a series of meetings." No one cares about your meetings. We have heard some say, "I am with clients most of the day but will return your call within two hours." This is much better than meetings. At least it looks like you actually have clients, which is a good thing when we think about consensus.

The voicemail message should be short and to the point. Smile as you record it. Don't be a pain to your clients, because they will avoid the pain. Find a way to reinforce your expertise in your message in a concise manner. Take notes of other voicemails that seem to have an impact on you. We often see voicemail as a pain ourselves rather than an opportunity to communicate with a potential client. This call could be a huge piece of business and the voicemail can help or hinder the sales process. It's up to you to make sure everything you do augments your business favourably.

Answering the Phone

When someone actually gets through to you directly and you pick up your own phone, what do you say? This is a moment of opportunity and most of us don't take this moment seriously. Try a few different approaches and assess any change in the impact on clients. Thank them for calling and use your own name in the introduction. People want to know they have connected with the right person and the right company.

If someone on the phone wants to make an appointment, what do you say immediately after they ask for one? This is your opportunity to provide social validation for the client's decision to choose you. Well, what you don't say is, "Thank God you called—I haven't had an appointment in four months and, yes, I could be available anytime day or night." You have just informed your potential client that you have absolutely no customers and no pipeline of sales. You have just become that empty restaurant and the client will be tempted to leave and cancel the appointment.

Many salespeople do use the consensus technique here, as they inherently realize that they want the client to think they are in demand and therefore an expert in the field. Many people respond to a request for an appointment with, "Let me check my calendar; I have been extremely busy this year.... How about Tuesday or Wednesday between three and four?" If the client wants a better time, the salesperson will often suggest an evening appointment because their days are filling up quickly but not too quickly. Balance is required. Clients want a busy expert working with them but they don't want someone too busy to meet their needs. Social proof can be a double-edged sword and must be used carefully, but if used effectively, it will increase your closed appointments and your sales volumes.

Managers

It isn't only customers who are affected by the principle of consensus—it's actually all of us. A simple test anyone can try is to walk out on the street at lunch in any major city with pedestrian traffic and stand in the middle of the sidewalk and stare up at the top of a building for three minutes straight. What do you think will happen? You're right; you will soon have a small crowd around you looking at the top of the building. As the crowd grows, more and more people start looking up. It spreads across the street and even down side streets as everyone is moved to look up. Why are they doing this en masse? The lemming factor. If everyone is doing it, it must be the right thing to do. Even if it seems stupid.

Managers rarely believe the huge impact they have on employees. Higher level managers and executives have the most impact. Employees are always looking to the leaders of a company to determine proper behaviour within an organization. The rules and regulations only go so far to describe the culture, so employees look to the leaders for clues. They watch every single movement a manager makes to help them determine what to do.

A manager who routinely goes home right on the clock will usually have a group of employees who are clock watchers too. If an executive takes Fridays off to go the cottage or play golf, Fridays become a normal sick day for many employees. Extended lunches by management results in extended lunches for employees.

The behaviour exhibited by managers is mirrored by the employees. This is why "walk the talk" is so critical to the success of a manager and their company. Many managers believe managing is telling people what to do and then following up on them to ensure it is done correctly. This works, but all of the other messages the manager conveys to employees are equally powerful influences on employee behaviour. Social proof in the office is just as effective as it is in sales. The reactions of people are predictable and, as such, a good manager needs to be aware of how their behaviour affects the behaviour of employees and the performance of the company.

Simple things such as a manager picking up a piece of scrap paper off the floor sends a powerful message to the company that cleanliness is important to the organization. Greeting employees in the morning and actually making a point of saying hello will have a huge impact on customer service. Politeness and personal touches are important qualities.

A manager who is early for meetings will consistently have meetings start on time. A manager who is always late will have all meetings in their department start late. Our behaviour sets the tone for what is acceptable. We look to each other to determine what the correct behaviour should be.

Actions do speak louder than words. Your actions have an impact on the behaviour of others. Actions of others affect your behaviour. Our responses are predictable. As masters of influence, we can use this natural tendency to increase our results and improve our persuasive powers.

Best Practices

1. When looking for referrals, ask for personal introductions rather than simply hand out your card.
2. When a key client compliments you, get it in writing and post it on your website. Display thank-you cards you've received. Share the fact that others have enjoyed working with you.
3. Where appropriate, get a letter of introduction to a new prospect from an existing client who is well regarded in the industry.
4. Use statistical data to support your case.
5. Use the power of crowd mentality to enhance your credibility.
6. Use phrases such as, "Many of my clients just like you…."
7. Refer to the most popular brand, mortgage term, or investment products.
8. Find a reputable source, such as service rating agencies, to support your case.
9. Listen to your own voicemail weekly to ensure it meets client expectations.
10. Update your voicemail daily and include the date.

Chapter 8
We Want What We Cannot Have

Connie: It was a terrific finish to the old year and a terrific start to the new. On New Year's Eve, we hosted a blessing ceremony. In the ceremony, we invited each family member to reflect on his or her past and share what they were thankful for. The energy level in the room grew as each person spoke. Next, each family member shared their dreams for 2008 and the coming years. After each person shared their dreams, they stood in front of each sitting family member, with a small open satchel. The sitting family member placed a token into the dream speaker's satchel. This token was a representation of the giver. As the giver placed the token into the satchel, it symbolized their support for the dreams to come true. The dream speaker wrote down their dream declaration, sat down, and then the next person went.

The Blessing Ceremony was deeply moving and inspiring. The gratitude and dreams shared by my family made it a magical night. During the ceremony, both my father and stepmother expressed similar dreams for their future. This couple has it all. They are in their seventies, have been married thirty years, and are in good health. They have a lovely home, good friends, great families, and spend the winters away in warm climates. They are content most of the time and in love with each other. What more could anyone ask for? It was Dad's turn to speak. His voice cracked a little as he said, "I just hope we can keep everything we have today. This is my dream for 2008." There was not a dry eye in the house. Dad really gave me something to think about with his words.

Many people aspire to have what my father and stepmother have. Why are they concerned about losing it, so much so, that they declared that their dream for the future was to retain what they had? In the face of scarcity, their concerns are quite natural.

In this chapter, we will look at this predictable response and how the principle of scarcity influences our decisions and actions. We will explore ways to put this well-known principle to use to increase your effectiveness at work and home. Subtle changes in your choice of words and your presentation will affect your results significantly.

The principle of scarcity says that we value something more when it is limited, and we want what we cannot have. Psychologist Anthony Pratkanis of the University of California said, "As consumers, we have a rule of thumb: If it is rare or scarce, it must be valuable and good."

Imagine you are in a meeting with a client and your telephone rings. The client continues talking, but you cannot hear what they're saying. The little voice in your head is louder than the client's voice. Indecision has taken over. Should you peek at the call display? Should you answer it? Your thoughts drift: "I wonder who is calling. I would hate to miss an important call. Maybe it's the radio station and I will win something if I answer. I wonder who it could be." You interrupt your meeting and answer the phone; after all, you can return to your client shortly, but you might never have this chance again. This is the principle of scarcity at play. Answering the phone suddenly occurred to you as a scarce opportunity, one you just could not bare to lose. You were afraid that if you didn't answer the phone, you might have lost an opportunity for more business or a new client who will help you to meet your sales targets.

Do you ever have these thoughts? "If I only had more time, better health, or a better job. If I only had a million dollars, or if I only had a body like hers. Why is the grass always greener on the other side?" It's the principle of scarcity at play. We want what we cannot have. This is a predictable human response.

"This is the only one left; time is money; and if I could only get my hands on that last antique, my collection would be complete." The principle of scarcity says we want it more if it is limited or in short supply. So why are "diamonds a girl's best friend"? Diamonds are rare. We assign a higher value to the things we deem rare and we want them more! Higher value also implies higher quality.

This sense of urgency to buy scarce commodities is where the power of persuasion comes into play—antiques, family heirlooms, "we're in your neighbourhood today, if you get your driveway sprayed now, you'll save forty dollars." Knowing an item is scarce is what actually calls us into action. In the face of scarcity, we tend to make decisions more quickly. We are all familiar with the sales mantra: Get the client to buy now.

In his book *Maximum Influence,* Kurt W. Mortensen writes, "The law of scarcity works because it makes people feel like they will lose their opportunity to act and choose if they don't do so immediately. The threat of such loss creates urgency in our decision making."[26] Have you ever suffered from buyer's remorse? You are caught up in the buying frenzy at the flea market. You make all kinds of great buys only to get them home and wonder why you wasted your money on this junk. Scarcity is at work. Think back to a first date. As the date ended, you walked her to her car and pondered, should I kiss her? The voice of scarcity in your head says you might never ever have this chance again—don't lose it, and do it quickly!

"If you don't clean your room, you won't go out on Friday night with your friends"; "If you don't lose thirty pounds and get your blood pressure down, you will have a heart attack"; "If you put all your money in one basket, you'll be sorry." These statements are really threats of possible future loss. We are afraid to lose what we already have. As Connie's father and stepmother expressed at the blessing ceremony, their hearts are heavy with sadness as they face the scarcity of time they have with friends and family.

"The tax-filing deadline is approaching soon," "The offer expires today," and Boxing Day Only sales illustrate a scarcity of time. We are afraid of missing out on an opportunity. Opportunities become quite valuable when they are limited in some way. As our time on this planet grows more precious, we activate the principle of scarcity to appreciate certain moments in our lives.

Have you ever been caught up in the excitement of an auction, bidding higher than you promised yourself you would? Does the countdown window on the Home Shopping Channel make your heart race when you see the dwindling quantity of something you think you might want? Marketing companies are fully aware of this predictable consumer response. We are well aware of their use of the principle of scarcity as they sell and market their products to us.

In cards, sports, and work, we see all kinds of people who want to win, and in some cases, at any cost. Competition heightens our desire for the limited, sometimes so much that we might even forget we really didn't want the item in the first place. The principle of consensus combined with the principle of scarcity increases our competitiveness.

People Want What They Cannot Have

If you are a parent of a preteen or teenage girl, you will know Miley Cyrus, the daughter of musician Billy Ray Cyrus, and the star of *Hannah Montana*. This Disney television show is about the life of

Miley Stewart, a regular teenager by day, and Hannah Montana, a famous pop star by night. Miley's pop star identity is a secret in her public life, with the exception of a few close friends. Miley is no longer just on the pretend TV concert stage but on real live concert stages around North America now.

Last fall, tickets went on sale for Hannah Montana's Toronto concert. Many people had their credit cards in hand and sat ready at their computers waiting for 10 a.m. when the tickets went on sale. Thousands of people attempted to buy the tickets online. They tried repeatedly, to no avail. The tickets sold out in three minutes. Many young girls were disappointed with their parents' failure to come through with what they wanted.

In the school halls, girls boasted about having concert tickets, thanks to people their parents knew. Others lamented about how badly they wanted to go. The "have not" girls wanted what they couldn't have. Girls who never had an interest in Hannah Montana began watching the show. They were caught up in the excitement of this once-in-a-lifetime opportunity. They hatched plans to coax parents to buy outrageously priced scalper and eBay tickets. It is the rule of the rare, in the face of scarcity: We want what we cannot have.

If we know something is scarce, we have a propensity to want it more, just as with the girls in the school hall. They were unable to get tickets through the regular channels and looked for other options. Scalpers and secondary market ticket sellers have created an industry based on the principle of scarcity. Seeing that the quantity of concert and event tickets is limited, they buy up all the tickets they can and sell them in the secondary market at inflated prices.

American Express has an exclusive privilege package for their credit card holders called Front of the Line. All card members receive preferred access to concert, theatre, and sporting events. Cardholders can purchase tickets before they go on sale to the public. If you are an avid concert attendee with no connections to the secondary markets, do you have an American Express card in your wallet? If you do, you will not lose an opportunity to buy tickets to the high-demand events. American Express will even send an email notification of the coming events and give you the option to decide in advance what you want and they will take care of it.

Last year, it was *Guitar Hero III* and the Nintendo Wii. In previous years, it was Cabbage Patch Kids, Tickle Me Elmo, and Beanie Babies. As Christmas approaches, your children put this year's "most wanted" toy or game on their Santa wish list. You scour the neighbourhood, the city, and the province in search of that evasive toy. The search becomes all-consuming. This is the last thing you need to accomplish to ensure your child has their best Christmas ever. If you come back empty-handed, what will you do?

Toy companies know the principle of scarcity and they use it well. In the end, the desperate parents end up spending more money on other gifts and write up a Christmas promise to put under the tree to buy that evasive toy when it becomes available again. In January or February, we fork out more dough and finally satisfy last Christmas' wish list.

Our lesson here is to pay attention to the commercials that advertisers aim at our children. Shop in October to buy those well advertised toys before they are gone and save your time and money. You will avoid disappointment, fierce competition of eBay auctions, and credit card bills continuing into February.

The term psychologists use to describe when people act to protect their sense of freedom is "psychological reactance." Professor Jack Brehm of the University of Kansas first introduced a widely acclaimed theory in 1966. He says if we believe our freedom is threatened, we are aroused. That arousal sparks a fear of further loss of freedom and motivates us to act to restore it immediately. When we lose something, we want it more.

The Coke/Coke Classic debacle of the mid-'80s is a good example. You might recall when the Coca-Cola Company changed their formula and introduced the taste of the "New Coke." When Pepsi began to outsell Coke in the supermarkets, Coca-Cola's marketing division conducted numerous blind taste tests, focus groups, and surveys and concluded that the vast majority of people surveyed preferred New Coke to the original. New Coke was bound to be a winner.[27]

On April 23, 1985, the company announced the launch of New Coke and that same week they halted production of the old Coke. This was big news! The company stock prices went up on the initial news. Marketing research revealed within a mere 48 hours of the announcement that 80% of Americans were aware of the change. Three quarters of those surveyed said they would buy New Coke again.[28]

However, contrary to Coke's research, consumers began to oppose the change in the formula. These consumers switched to Pepsi when they could no longer buy the original Coke. The media caught wind of it. Roger Enrico, PepsiCo's Director of North American Operations, declared a companywide holiday and took out a full-page ad in the *New York Times,* proclaiming Pepsi had won the long-running cola wars.

At their Atlanta headquarters, Coca-Cola received over 400,000 calls and letters in protest of the change. The company hired a psychiatrist to listen to the concerns expressed by the disgruntled callers. He reported that it sounded as though these people were describing the death of a family member.[29] In response to the public outcry, the Coke chemists ever so slightly changed the formula again. However, even that didn't seem to help.

Gay Mullins, a Seattle retiree, formed an organization called the Old Cola Drinkers of America. He lobbied Coca-Cola to reinstate its old formula or to sell it to someone else. His organization took over 60,000 calls from unhappy Coke drinkers. He even went so far as to file a class action lawsuit against Coca-Cola to make the old Coke formula public. The courts dismissed the suit without a trial. In two informal blind taste tests, Mullins either failed to distinguish the New Coke from the old or expressed his preference for the New Coke.

True to the scarcity principle, consumers bought up remaining inventories of the old Coke from North American stores and set their sights overseas, where the new formula had not yet been introduced. What was going on here? If it was neither the taste nor quality of the product that perturbed people, what was it? Coca-Cola's worst fear came to pass. It appeared that their top competitor had pulled into the market top spot.

Why did this happen? Consumers had their freedom to buy something they had been buying their entire lives taken away from them. It was even Coca-Cola's 100th anniversary that year. The problem was not the product quality but the perceived loss of their favourite drink, the original Coke. This loss caused Coke drinkers to rise up and protest the change. It happened because the scarcity principle was at play.

Coca-Cola Director Carlton Curtis finally realized that it was the withdrawal of the old formula that upset consumers, not the taste of the new one. On July 10, 1985, just seventy-seven days later, Coca-Cola announced the return of the old Coke.

Many thought the original decision was a major disaster for Coca-Cola; however, by the end of that year, Coke Classic sales outstripped both New Coke and Pepsi. Six months later, Coca-Cola's sales increased at more than twice the rate of PepsiCo's. When consumers got their favourite original Coke formula back, they responded with their wallets and Coca-Cola's sales skyrocketed to overpower PepsiCo.

There is an important message for us to take away from the New Coke saga. When people perceive a loss, they act. When taking something away from our customers, we must consider it very carefully. Consider the possible impact. The voice of the customer is important, even if they are in the minority. Taking something of value away could cause customers to rebel by taking a pass on your product and moving to your competition. If possible, involve your valued customers in these key decisions. Lead them through the thought process and ask for their help in solving the problem.

Do you have a confidant? Gathering insights from a special client you can trust with confidential information is critical when considering a business change or new product introduction. Many companies use focus groups to collect customer feedback on proposed changes. However, the danger of focus groups is that one or two people tend to be outspoken and dominate the discussion. You miss the feedback from the quiet or shy types. An opposing view from a soft spoken or silent client could hold crucial insights for your company. Innovation comes from the few, not from the masses. When considering a significant change, also consider collecting your feedback from a series of confidants one on one.

Question: Is it better to tell a prospective client what they stand to gain by dealing with you or your company, or what they stand to lose if they don't? Take a minute and think about this. How do you make your recommendations to your clients right now? Do you present what they stand to gain? Do you present what they stand to lose?

We have presented this question to thousands of salespeople in the past several years at our seminars and we always have excellent discussions. We have never had an entire group of participants actually agree on one answer, which is good when you are trying to introduce new sales concepts to the audience.

It seems like a simple question on the surface. Many participants opt for what they will gain. They usually go on to explain that people are much more interested in what they will get from their buying decision. It's the old WIFM argument: What's in it for me? Most salespeople will talk about all the features and benefits and build a strong case for the client to buy from them.

Others in the groups will choose what the client will lose by not dealing with them. They explain that the client will lose the salesperson's personal expertise and that no one else in the marketplace can match it. They indicate that many people are risk adverse by nature and are more motivated by the thought of losing something. We have an interesting conversation for a few minutes as the groups try to convince each other that their decision is the right one.

When hired for a new position, most of us learn the basics of how to do the job. We learn the products' features and benefits and/or we learn the features and benefits for our services. Finally, we finish our training and land at our desk or cubicle, or hit the road or sales floor. When we first get in front of a client or prospect, and recognize a need for one of our products or services, we immediately explain the features and benefits. How does the customer respond to this dumping of information? You either get a sale or you get the elusive "I have to think about that." So how can we get clients to act now rather than just walk away and think about our recommendation?

PG&E conducted a study several years ago in California. They went door to door in various cities, offering an energy audit on homes. For half of the homes in the study, the homeowners were told that if they implemented the recommendations for energy efficiency, such as weather stripping and more insulation, they could save $0.50 a day on their energy bill. The other half of the homeowners were told that if they *didn't* implement the recommendations, they would *lose* $0.50 a day. Significantly more homeowners agreed to the recommendation under the loss conditions. It was the same fifty cents. When the recommendation was made highlighting what the homeowner stood to lose, many more people were motivated to take action. Why did this happen? People are more motivated by the thought of losing something than of gaining the very same thing.

Let us put the scarcity principle to work for us. Think about your favourite product or service offering. What is a feature or benefit you promote most about this offering? Simply take that feature or benefit and just turn it upside down. Now add another sentence or two to your usual client discussions. This extra mention will state what your client will lose if they don't follow your recommendation. It is the same feature or benefit they stand to gain, but positioning it as a loss will motivate the client to take action rather than walk away to think about it. The story that follows will help you understand.

Debt Consolidations

Connie: The Queen of Credit Lines, as I like to call her, works for a major bank and refused to change

her method in presenting debt consolidation recommendations to her clients. She was already
very successful, doing more than twice the volume of the average lender. "Why should I
change?" she thought. She had great success explaining how much her clients could save by consolidating their debts into a secured line of credit.
She understood the principle of scarcity and the
concept of presenting the loss rather than just the
gain, but was still reluctant. Her boss was in the
presentation and twisted her arm. She reluctantly
agreed.

Three days later, The Queen called me to
share her experiences. In the past, she would
present her recommendation, showing the client
how much she could save them by consolidating
their debts. She would then wait for the client's
response. The client would often say, "That's nice;
I'll think about it." She would ask permission to
follow up with a call in a week or two. The client
normally agreed.

During her follow-up call to the client, she
would recreate the appointment that they had
had. She would say, "This was the problem you
came in with. This was my recommendation based
on your needs that we discussed. What are your
thoughts on our discussion?" She had a high rate
of success in booking the deals. She was pleased
with her current results and could not imagine it
getting any better for her.

The Queen continued, "You will never believe
what I've got to say! You were right! This technique really does work!" I asked her what she
was doing differently. She said, "I pretty much do
the same as before. However, I have made one

very small change. Now when I present my recommendation, I tell the client how much they stand to lose by maintaining their current financial situation. Even before I can make a powerful request asking for their business, the client asks me, 'Where do I sign?'" She was tickled pink with her results. She no longer had to play telephone tag with the client, nor recreate their last appointment over the phone. She presents what the client stands to lose and signs them up right away!

Most lenders say something like, "If you consolidate your loans with us, I can save you two hundred and twenty dollars a month." This was the line previously used by the Queen of Credit Lines. A simple shift in her wording produced dramatic results. She now says, "If you don't consolidate your debt into a line of credit today, you will continue to lose two hundred and twenty dollars a month." It's the actual amount of money mentioned that grabs our immediate attention. Clients will actually lean a little closer to you because you have really gained their attention. They are much more interested in the thought of losing money than they are of gaining the same amount. When a client is attentive, the sale is almost closed.

We learn the features and benefits of our product and service offerings, and, unfortunately, our natural tendency is to tell people only what they will gain by working with us or in choosing our offerings. Telling a client what they stand to lose will motivate them into action much more often than telling them what they stand to gain or save.

During workshops, we survey the participants. Most are salespeople earning straight commission or a salary plus bonus, and most have sales targets or quotas to achieve. We ask if they would be interested in receiving a $20,000 bonus from their company this year, provided they meet their sales targets. Naturally, most participants get pretty excited about this opportunity. Next, we inform them that if they don't achieve their sales target this year, they will have to send the company a cheque for $4,000. Well, their faces turn downward immediately as they think about it. They weigh their options. "Do I want to make an additional $20,000 if I meet my sales targets and take the chance of losing $4,000 if I don't?"

The results to date are that 90% of the participants don't want to participate in this kind of an incentive deal. They are more worried about losing $4,000 than they are motivated about gaining $20,000. If you want to increase your influence and persuasion abilities with your clients, present what they stand to lose as well as what they stand to gain and watch your results increase.

Take a Test

Try the scarcity factor on for yourself, and then try it on others around you and discover the results first hand. Where do you feel this in your body? When we say to you that we can save you $220 a month, where do you feel it? What does the little voice inside your head say? Now, when we say to you that by keeping your financial situation as it is, you are losing $220 a month. Where do you feel it in your body? What is the little voice in your head saying after each statement?

Most people have a greater reaction to the loss statement. The majority of seminar participants say that they feel the savings statement in their head. They raise their eyebrows and that little voice in their head says, "That's nice." When responding to the loss statement, participants say they feel the impact in their gut, as though somebody punched them. Their eyebrows raise and the little voice says, "Oh my gosh, what can I do?"

Knowing this, feeling it for yourself, and testing it out on others, the question to consider is: What can you do with it? How will you present your recommendation to your clients now? Do you want them to think, "That's nice?" or "Oh my gosh, what can I do?" The response is predictable. Choose your words carefully to stimulate the response you want.

Sample Phrases

"I can offer you the benefit of monthly payment flexibility on this loan. If you don't choose our company, you lose the option to skip your January, post-Christmas payment."
—A finance company lender

"I will ensure you get the right mortgage for your particular needs; however, you might lose access to multiple lenders if you don't stay with me."
—An independent mortgage broker

"I have the perfect mortgage for you. It has a biweekly payment option to pay off your mortgage faster. However, if you do not take this mortgage, you might lose the lump sum repayment privilege. I would hate for you to lose this valuable option with our company. In fact, without it you will lose thirty-four thousand dollars over the life of the mortgage."
—A bank mortgage specialist

Independent financial planners state that by not dealing with their company, you will lose the expertise of certified professionals reviewing every aspect of your financial affairs.

Investment experts tap into the scarcity principle by reminding us that the tax deadline is looming. "It's time to contribute to your retirement plan. The deadline is just days away. If you don't have the money, that's no problem; I can lend it to you. May I help you right now while I have you on the phone?"

A billboard outside of Toronto advertises a well-known realtor in the community. The message is that Dan will buy your house if he doesn't sell it within ninety days. If you don't choose Dan, you will lose the guaranteed sale of your house.

A mortgage professional quotes the client a mortgage payment including life and disability insurance. Many lenders have a bulletin on their desk, indicating that one in three people will inevitably suffer a disability at some point in their careers. "I would hate for you to lose your house if you got hurt or, heaven forbid, cause hardship for your family should you die."

A title insurance account manager will let their lawyer clients know they are losing out on trips anywhere in the world by not paying their monthly bills with their Air Miles credit card.

A bank advertises the opportunity to earn Air Miles for using your debit and credit cards. By banking elsewhere, you are losing free trips anywhere in the world. The branch staff brings to your attention that your regular banking habits could be causing you to lose free merchandise by failing to collect their Air Miles.

Practice for yourself now. What does a client stand to lose by not dealing with you? If you are a financial planner, how can you flip the benefit of dollar cost averaging into a motivating loss statement? If you are a realtor, how can you flip the benefits of "this particular home" into a motivating loss statement? If you are a lawyer, what will a customer stand to lose if they die without a will?

Human Resources

A young woman in the human resource department of a company shared her frustration in getting the managers to take action on filling their job vacancies. The short-handed departments bombarded her with employee complaints. Workloads were too heavy now that a cohort had quit the company or left on maternity leave. The manager knew of these complaints but was also working hard to pick up the slack for the missing employees and just could not get around to making hiring a top priority as he tried to cope.

The HR officer shared her new technique. She told a short-handed manager that he had many good people in his department who are hardworking people and are clearly committed to the company but are also showing signs of wear. She went on to let him know what he stood to lose by dragging his heels in the hiring process. He stood to lose the goodwill and dedication of the remaining good people. Where would he be if another of his great employees left because of being overworked?

The insurance industry has many masters of influence. Per capita, Canada has one of the most-insured populations in the world. An insurance company will indemnify you from loss as outlined in their particular policy, be it life or disability insurance. We can insure our homes against fire and flood damage. We have high-ratio mortgage insurance to protect the banks from consumer loan defaults. We have title insurance to protect us from fraudsters stealing our homes. There is business liability insurance, errors and omissions insurance, health and dental insurance, and even pet insurance. The fear of loss motivates us to take action to protect ourselves.

What is your competitive advantage? What tangible differences exist today between you and your competitors? Some companies offer people hours, not bankers' hours; free second opinions on your investments; or Air Miles for daily banking accounts plus bonus points when you have other company products. Share what you have that is exclusive to your company and position it as what the client will lose by not working with you.

Hearing Loss

A recent study looked at the impact of different messages on a sampling of miners.[30] In the mining industry, one of the well-known consequences to working while exposed to loud noise is hearing loss. Up to 90% of miners suffer significantly.

The Mine Safety and Health Administration of the U.S. Department of Labor initiated a federal law in 2000 establishing noise standards for employers of mines. The law encourages miners to wear hearing protection and to get regular hearing tests. With the most recent advancements in technology, miners can protect their hearing. Though this study took part in the mining industry, its conclusions are valid for every line of work.

To increase awareness about voluntary hearing protection in the miners, the study used a variety of messages. The messages were positive, negative, or neutral. The study also considered several other pieces of research, one of which looked at positive and negative television health ads from a variety of health contexts—AIDS, smoking, alcohol use, blood pressure, etc. In this study, they concluded individuals were more likely to pay attention to positive ads, but the memory was better for the negative ones. It also found "low-involved" participants remembered emotional messages more and "high-involved" participants, which showed no difference between the rational or emotional messages.

In the miners study, they selected twenty-three mines. They assigned six mines a positive message condition, six a negative message condition, six a neutral message condition, and five were in the control group. The researchers exposed the miners to their assigned message conditions in two ways: by postcard and by posters placed in areas they frequented such as locker rooms, drink stations, and time card sites.

During week one, they mailed a postcard to each miner. A week later, they mailed a second postcard. Each postcard contained a colour picture with an accompanying experimental message. All types of message cards had the same text message on the flip side addressing voluntary behaviours miners could use to protect their hearing. The negative emotion message read: "Peace and quiet is not an option when your ears ring all the time." The positive emotion message read: "The sound of falling leaves is relaxing. Always wear hearing protection on the job." The neutral emotion message read: "Hear today, and tomorrow. Always wear hearing protection on the job."

A survey was mailed a week after the second postcard. They promised the miners a custom-printed mining decal in exchange for their completed survey. About six weeks later, the miners received a second survey for those who responded to the first survey.

The study concluded that all three message condition types generated a similar attitudinal outcome. The attitude of the miners who received the postcards and were exposed to the posters was significantly more positive than in the no-message control group. Positive attitudes are nice, but what we really want to know is how to get people to act, not only think about our requests. The study concluded that the negative message condition was no more effective than no message at all. The smokers we polled say that the grotesque photograph on their cigarette package does not deter them from smoking the contents. In a similar way, the miners just disregard it as a negative message only.

The positive and neutral messages had some impact. However, the most significant behavioural results came from the miners who received both positive and negative condition messages. Both the first and second surveys confirmed this.

As our workshop research suggests and as this study confirms, it is not the benefits alone that get people to act, it is also what they stand to lose if they don't. As salespeople, we need to let people know what they stand to gain and what they stand to lose if we genuinely want to spur them into action rather than just think about it.

Now you know how to better use the principle of scarcity and increase the likelihood that you will close the sale immediately. How you present your recommendations will get a predictable response. People cannot stand to lose something they perceive is valuable to them.

When you want to be influential and get someone to go with your recommendation, clearly point out what that person is losing by their inaction, and offer up your proposed solution.

Competition Heightens Our Desire

Have you ever tried to book a limousine for a Friday night in June? Between weddings and proms, limousines are scarce commodities. The desire to contract one heightens when your teenager says, "But everyone else is going in one; I need one too!"

When something is scarce and there is competition, we occasionally lose sight of the value we are really willing to pay. An inflated ticket price for popular concerts is an example. How do we take advantage of the simple economics of supply and demand?

Even if we initially had no interest in the rare commodity or event, like the Hannah Montana tickets, when coupled with the consensus principle—others are doing it, so it must be right—we tend to want it more and are willing to pay a higher price.

Many people get caught up in hype and excitement of buying a new issue of small capital stock, only later to ask themselves, "Why did I make that purchase? I don't buy small capital stocks. I buy mutual funds as a rule. Who is this stockbroker guy anyway?" That is the voice of experience speaking. The stockbroker on the phone was engaging. His firm had only a limited quantity of stock to sell. They could hear the phones ringing like crazy in the background. This must be a popular judging by the buzz of activity. They had better buy now before he runs out.

Poseidon Adventure

In 1973, Barry Diller, who was VP primetime programming for the ABC network, paid $3.3 million for a single showing of the movie *The Poseidon Adventure*. This amount exceeded the previous most expensive movie, *Patton,* by $1.3 million. This represented a 60% increase over the previous amount. The cost was so excessive that ABC actually anticipated losing $1 million on the transaction.[31]

You might wonder why TV executives would buy a one-time showing of a movie and expect to lose money on the transaction. The movie studio had decided to offer *The Poseidon Adventure* to the networks in an open-bid auction. This was the first time this process had been used and the networks were forced to compete with each other for this one-time showing. This added to the scarcity of the product and so each network wanted it more. They captured the attention of the networks and the competition to win overcame their own common sense to make a profit.

After ABC won the auction, they realized that this process was not to their benefit, as they had severely overpaid for this product. After the auction, Barry Diller said, "ABC has decided regarding its policy for the future that it would never again enter into an auction situation."

Robert Wood, then president of CBS television, nearly outbid ABC in the heat of the auction and explained the process:

We were very rational at the start. We priced the movie out in terms of what it could bringing for us, then allowed a certain value on top of that for exploitation.

But then the bidding started. ABC opened with $2 million. I came back with $2.4. ABC went $2.8. And the fever of the thing caught us. Like a guy who had lost his mind, I kept bidding. Finally, I went to $3.3 million and there came a moment I said to myself, "Good grief, if I get it, what the heck am I going to do with it?" When ABC finally topped me, my main feeling was relief. It's been very educational.

It is interesting to note in this exercise that the loser was relieved to have lost and the winner of the auction vows never to do it again. They both realized that even executives can be swayed by the power of scarcity and by the excitement created in wanting that scarce item. This is a lesson for all of us.

When someone tells us something is rare, it triggers the principle of scarcity. If it's limited by quantity or time, the effect is accentuated. If something is exclusive to us or exclusive of others, we want it more. When we are in competition for something, it becomes even more desirable.

As a homeowner trying to sell a house, book your showings back to back, if possible. As one potential buyer sees another potential buyer leaving the house, the buyers feel they want it more.

In the Leaside area of Toronto, scarcity flourishes. Realtors often have multiple offers for those prestigious homes. When someone shops in Leaside, they know they face steep competition and that they will likely have to offer more than the asking price to cement the deal. This is scarcity in action.

As homeowners negotiate for their mortgage rates, they use the competition aspect of the scarcity principle too. Borrowers come in with competitors' offers and ask for the best rate possible. A lender is under the scarcity influence when they feel they must compete with another financial institution.

What we must be clear about is whether we want the business at any price. What price are we willing to pay? At what point do we no longer deem this a valuable transaction?

We all want what we cannot have. This natural response will build your success or it could turn on you as others apply this principle on you. This is the power of these influential tools. They are really a double-edged sword. We are all susceptible to the persuasive powers of scarcity. Find a way to use these approaches in your life and you will be more successful. The choice is yours to make.

Best Practices

1. Ask yourself what it will cost the customer if they don't buy from you.
2. Take a pertinent feature or benefit and simply turn it over to highlight what the client will lose by not dealing with you or your company.
3. When presenting features and benefits to be gained, always include a statement about what the client will lose.
4. People are more motivated to act by the thought of losing something than of gaining the very same thing.
5. Be bold in your statements.
6. Practice scripting and speaking with co-workers.
7. Make the words come from your heart, not a book—not even this book.
8. Create a sense of loss and an urgency to buy.
9. Competition creates urgency and desire.
10. Try it and you will be surprised at how effective this approach can be. Just do it.

Chapter 9
Rejection:
How to Handle "No"

In sales, as in life, most of us are afraid of rejection. We fear rejection—we fear the word *no*—and generally will try to avoid any situation where someone could say to no to us. We are all relatively humble people and our self-confidence is a sensitive thing. We seem to want to protect ourselves from rejection because it could damage our self-image and our projected image of what others see. This fear limits our potential in so many ways that in order to be more successful in life, we must learn to deal with this aspect of our character.

You are certainly not alone in your fear of rejection. It raises its ugly head in so many situations it almost becomes a part of our daily lives. One of the biggest fears most people have is the fear of speaking in public. Why are so many afraid to do it? Is it because we fear being embarrassed? Do we fear we will make an error? Do we fear looking stupid, that people will laugh, that we will trip on the way to the stage? Maybe we fear we will forget our speech. These and several other fears overwhelm most of us when we do get an opportunity to speak in public.

Rejection is just a part of everyday life, especially in the world of selling. Salespeople will be out on the road, offering their products and services, and people will simply say "no thanks." How we handle this rejection and move forward separates the successful from the unsuccessful.

Gary: Remember the dance events back in grade school? It's our first time attending a dance. I remember the event very well. I lived in a small town in a rural setting. Since it was a small town, I knew literally everyone in the school and had many best friends. As close friends often do, we went everywhere together as a small gang. We played ball together, we played cards together, we rode our bikes to the park together, and swam and fished together. We would talk about girls most of the time.

The afternoon of my first big dance was fast approaching and I didn't know how to dance. Luckily, my older sister Sheila was a dancing queen. She knew all the latest music and dance steps, and after some cajoling agreed to teach me some rudimentary dance steps so I could at least look like I knew something. I was a good student. After a few days, Sheila announced that I was ready to rock 'n' roll.

The day of the dance arrived and I went with a bunch of my friends. I certainly couldn't go to the dance by myself, what would everyone think? That I didn't have friends! We walked into the room huddled together and looked around at everyone else. Young boys seem to derive some energy and confidence when they have good friends close by, and I was no exception.

As I entered the room, the music was playing, the lights were dimmed just a little but not too much, so I could still clearly see that there were boys lined up on one side of the room and girls lined up on the other side. The middle of the room where the dancing was to take place was empty, a vast void that put an absolute fear through my heart. The boys and girls looked across the room at each other and they would whisper to their friends, but no one ventured across the room to ask for a dance. My friends and I glanced casually across the room to check out the girls, but in a non-interested way. We couldn't give away our desire to the girls too quickly. The open space across the dance floor loomed like a mountain range that was virtually impassable. The floor held red hot coals that would incinerate anyone foolish enough to venture onto its surface. Everyone huddled tight against the wall for support; no one was ready to make that dangerous trek across the open floor to face destiny.

Why not? This is what young boys and girls have been waiting for. Nature has prepared us to move across the room and begin the ritual of wooing the opposite sex. My friends looked at me and whispered, "You go first," and I, of course, replied with the creative response, "No, you go first." We all looked longingly at the girls and the girls looked longingly at the boys, but the girls maintained a certain look of disinterest. They seem more interested in chatting with each other than with providing the signal to the boys that will give us the courage to walk across the room.

All of the boys were eager but afraid—I was eager but deathly afraid. What was I afraid of? I knew most of these girls by name and had spent social time with them in class, during recess, and even after school. I had no problem approaching them outside of the dance floor. Why was it so difficult here?

The answer lies in the fear of rejection and the consequences this rejection will have on me personally and in front of all of my friends. All of the young boys, myself included, had this male swagger that was full of self-confidence, but underneath the swagger lay a fearful young boy not wanting to be centred out in front of others as a loser if the girl says no.

Back then, our self-confidence level was still quite delicate and could easily be crushed. I honestly felt that if rejected, I would be crushed for life. All of my friends would laugh, the girls against the wall would laugh and point their fingers, and I would be ostracized as a loser. I would never be able to approach another girl for as long as I lived, and life as I knew it would be over forever. It's interesting how young people attach lifelong consequences to minor activities. Perhaps it's the fact they have such little experience in life that they assign such grave consequences to relatively inconsequential events.

So, what to do next? The next phase for my friends was to move from asking to ridicule. They started to say, "What are you, chicken?" They started to make these little clucking noises in my direction. Well, as a boy growing up in a rural community, being called a chicken was about as bad a slur on your character as it gets. We were men, after all, and being called a chicken was a challenge to our own self-worth, and few boys could resist this influence tool. Even children know the tools of influence well and certainly know how to apply them. I rose to the bait like a trout for a fly on a calm evening. They knew I would, and I suppose I knew I would as well. Perhaps this was the incentive I needed to walk across that bed of hot coals.

Not to be outdone by the name calling, I used the same tactic on several of my friends: "I'm not the chicken; you are." We did have a way with words in our youth. Finally, after several minutes of inane name calling, three of us agreed we would lead the way to get the party going—we were leaders after all. A little self-confidence pumping ensued amongst the three adventurers. We all gathered our courage from each other and stepped forward into the limelight. With our first steps onto the floor, all eyes turned toward us. I was convinced all eyes were on me and I could feel the palms of my hands starting to sweat. A flush ran from my neck up onto my face and I was sure I was as red as a beet and everyone could see the fear on my face. I switched to that little boy swagger and filled my chest with false bravado and continued into the void.

I targeted Sarah, a cute little blonde that I had been teasing lately. It seems that young boys think teasing girls is a good way to woo them. The three of us ventured into unknown territory as we crossed the halfway point. No turning back now; we were committed to our task. This commitment helped a bit, but it did feel like water was pouring off my hands and leaving a trail of drips behind me on the floor.

As we approached the girls, they looked demurely away and whispered to each other. I was the first to reach my target. I gathered my courage and finally squeaked out, "Would you like to dance?" There, I had finally made the request and now I was fully exposed to the whims of this cute little blonde. Fear bubbled up into my throat as I awaited a response. I had already convinced myself she would say no and I would have to crawl back to the other side of the room embarrassed beyond belief and committed to never asking another girl to dance for the rest of my life. I was prepared for the worst, but much to my surprise, she looked up at me and smiled—the most beautiful smile I have ever seen or will ever see—and she responded with the finest words any salesperson will ever hear, "Yes, I would, thank you."

Wow. It was over, and I had been successful. I had made the sale and it wasn't all that hard after all. I took her by the hand and walked out onto the floor and we started to dance. My friends were equally fortunate, and as soon as the rest of the boys and girls saw that the ice had been broken, mayhem ensued. The boys rushed to their favourites and the girls started to dance with each other as well. The dance was a great success, and my first big public test had been a success as well. This was one of my finest moments that stuck with me for a long time. I had faced my fear; I had overcome the obstacles and made the powerful request. And the best of all, she had said yes. I will never forget that Roy Orbison song—"Running Scared" for our first dance. How appropriate.

Overcoming the fear to begin is one of the keys to success. Getting started is always the challenge. Procrastination is so much easier. "I will do it next time" is the number one reason why success never arrives. If you don't start, you can never finish and never accomplish. Fear is only a state of mind and you can control your mind if you want to. It's your choice. Just starting is the best way to overcome fear.

This first success with the girls was followed up by a series of rejections. I attended many dances as a young man and was surprised that many of the young ladies would simply say no to my request for a dance. Now, I wasn't a bad-looking young boy, and I was on the basketball team, but it seems some girls prefer to decline. I had always wondered why they would attend a dance and not accept invitations to dance. I still don't know, by the way, and it has haunted me to this day. Here, the situation was reversed: I had no problem asking girls to dance, but now I wasn't successful every time. I did have my share of successes, mind you, but I faced a great deal of rejection. The key for all of us is how we deal with rejection.

Salespeople face rejection on a daily basis. How do they wake the next day with a song in their heart and a smile on their face to tackle rejection once again? Parents dealing with teens face the word *no* almost daily. Some people can cope well with rejection and others are stuck in recrimination and self-blame. Parents use "no" with little children a great deal. Children are trained what not to do by phrases such as, "Don't touch that or you'll break it," "No, stay out of the cupboard," "No, you can't do that," "No, no, no, and more no." Children begin by living with rejection, so it's no wonder we face problems with rejection as adults. To be truly successful as an influencer, we need to understand how to deal with rejection and failure.

Explanatory Style Theory

Professional athletes are paid huge amounts of money. They are paid these sums by the sports club owners, who intend on winning. And how often do they win? Many teams win less than half the time they play, meaning they lose more than they win. A handful of teams win more than average. All but one team loses out on the playoffs, with only one team becoming champions. How do professional athletes deal with these losses when they are paid to win? Does a loss have an impact on their performances in future games? Are they more likely to win after a loss, and, if so, what is the difference between those teams who overcome a loss and those who don't?

Martin Seligman attempts to answer this question in his book *Learned Optimism*. He investigates what he calls the "explanatory style theory." He and his students have spent thousands of hours reading the sports pages and testing his theory against sports statistics. He believes there are three basic predictions for sports. First, everything being equal, an individual with the more optimistic explanatory style will go on to win. They will win because they will try harder, particularly after a defeat or under stiff competition. Second, the same thing should hold true for teams. If a team can be characterized by its level of optimism, the more optimistic team should win if talent is equal. This phenomenon should be most apparent under pressure. Third, and most exciting, when an athlete's explanatory style is changed from pessimistic to optimistic, they should win more, particularly while under pressure.

When things go wrong for an individual, they use a specific style of explanation to deal with it. We all have a style of seeing causes and over time, these styles become habits of explaining to ourselves and others why the events occurred as they did. We become adept at explaining the failures we face on a regular basis. Seligman divided these styles into three forms: permanence, personalization, and pervasiveness.

Generally, people who give up easily after a failure believe the causes of the failure were permanent. The bad situation will persist and will always hinder their success. However, the people who persist look at the same situation as temporary rather than permanent. We can look at these two styles as pessimistic and optimistic, respectively. Seligman contends that optimistic people are more successful at overcoming failure than pessimistic people. He suggests that we can change our behaviour to enhance our optimistic qualities and become more successful.

The permanent pessimist uses words such as, "This always happens to me," "Diets never work," "I will never make a sale," while the temporary optimist uses words such as, "This sometimes happens to me when I don't prepare," "Diets never work when I eat out so often," "I missed this sale today, but I won't tomorrow." Notice the difference in the explanatory styles of dealing with failure? The permanent style is debilitating while the temporary style is opportunistic.

This is important to consider because failure hurts everyone, even the most optimistic. We don't like to fail because the pain is deep, but the hurt will go away. For some, the hurt dissipates almost immediately, while for others, it lingers, affecting future activities. Some feel helpless in certain situations and the initiative they need to move forward grinds to a halt. They have a little voice in their heads telling them there is no point in trying again. We have all heard that little voice trying to protect us from failure, but it also limits our ability to succeed and to try again.

The other side of the equation is how we interpret good events. The permanent explanatory style is optimistic with words such as, "I'm always lucky," "I always put out a big effort," or "I'm talented." The temporary explanatory style deals with good fortune as though it were a one-time thing with phrases such as, "It's my lucky day," "I try hard," or "I won because my rival got tired." The difference is confidence in one's ability. The temporary style believes it was just this time only and it will not likely reoccur, while the permanent style has confidence they can repeat this good fortune because they are good at what they do.

Another aspect of the style is called personalization, which deals with how we use either internal or external reasons for explanations. When bad things happen, we can internalize and blame ourselves or we can externalize and blame others or circumstances. People who blame themselves when they fail usually have low self-esteem as a consequence. If this approach becomes a habit, low self-esteem hinders their ability to move forward. They slowly become helpless because they feel worthless, talentless, and unappreciated. People who blame external sources don't lose self-esteem when failure strikes. Their personal self-worth remains intact. These people generally like themselves better than do those who internalize.

Internalizing bad events includes phrases such as, "I'm not that bright," "I have no talent in selling," "I can't close and never could," or "I don't have self-confidence." People who externalize use phrases such as, "The client wasn't too bright" or "I'm not having much luck at selling this week."

When things go right, the same principles applies. The pessimist externalizes good fortune as just luck or the efforts of other people. The optimist, on the other hand, takes some credit for good fortune by saying they took advantage of opportunities or it was their skill that closed the sale. Two approaches to the same thing, but one approach leads to power and one leads to defeat.

Finally, the aspect of the explanatory style known as pervasiveness makes the failures universal or specific to one time. Some people who face a significant failure such as being fired or divorced make a universal explanation for the failure and give up on everything. Their life implodes and they use phrases such as, "I'm useless," "All men are animals," or "Life is unfair." These people are extremely pessimistic about themselves and the world around them. Their little voice is now on a tirade and they relive bad moments for months on end, sometimes years, and the voice inside their head tries to protect them by limiting any future activities.

On the other hand, some people make specific explanations for the failure and give up on that one activity, but the rest of their life continues normally. They use phrases such as, "I am simply no good at golf," "This man I married was no good," or "My boss who fired me was unfair." These people are optimistic about themselves and experience failure in only one aspect of their life. Their little voice is justifying the action but not personalizing the action as a personal fault. The voice in their head is busy preparing for the future rather than protecting from the past.

The permanence dimension determines how long a person will

give up and remain a little depressed about the failure. Permanent explanations such as "this always happens to me" will result in long-lasting problems in that area. The pervasiveness dimension predicts whether the failure will affect other aspects of your life. Universal explanations leak into all aspects of life, while specific explanations are limited to the specific area of failure.

This is only a general overview, but Seligman has done significant research to assess the optimistic style vs. the pessimistic style in sports and its effects on winning the game after a loss.

Baseball

Seligman and his researchers wondered whether optimism leads to victory or vice versa. They studied the New York Mets' 1985 season by reviewing comments made in the media after a losing game. He applied a score from his optimism and pessimism scale to determine how they explained failure and then analyzed the results of those games and the entire season. Here are some examples from his book[32]:

Manager Davey Johnson: "We lost because they made the plays tonight."

Darryl Strawberry after he missed a fly ball: "The ball really carried, I almost got my glove on it." Strawberry also commented on why they were shut out: "Sometimes you go through those kinds of days."

Keith Hernandez on why they won only two games on the road: "All the time on the road began to tax us." Hernandez on why their lead in the league had shrunk to only half a game: "[The other team] made a bad play and came up smelling like a rose."

Star pitcher Dwight Gooden on why he threw a wild pitch: "Some moisture must have gotten on the ball." Gooden on why a batter hit a home run: "He hit well tonight."

As you can see from these few examples, when the Mets lost, it was just for that day. It wasn't their fault, it was the just these opponents. The 1985 Mets had an optimistic explanatory style as a team to deal with failure and losing games.

Seligman and his researchers also looked at the St. Louis Cardinals in the same way. Reviewing thousands of interviews by the players in the media throughout the year. Here are some examples of what the Cardinals had to say about losing:

> Manager Whitey Herzog on why the team lost: "We can't hit. What the hell, let's face it." This explanation is permanent, pervasive and personalized. A high pessimistic rating.
>
> Herzog on why they had trouble winning after days off: "It's a mental thing. We were too relaxed."
>
> Willie McGee, the 1985 National League batting champion, said he didn't steal as many bases as he should have: "I don't have the expertise."
>
> Jack Clark on dropping a fly ball: "It was a real catchable ball. I just didn't catch it."
>
> Tom Herr on why his batting average dropped twenty-one points: "I am having a lot of trouble concentrating and keeping my mind on the job."

The Cardinals had an extremely talented team on paper—far superior to the Mets. However, the Cardinals' explanation style for failure was much more pessimistic than the Mets. Under Seligman's theory, the optimistic Mets should have excelled the following season and the more talented but pessimistic Cardinals should have floundered. In 1986, the Mets win percentage went from .605 to .667 and they won the World Series. Less talent, but more optimistic. The Cardinals, on the other hand, crumbled and won only 49% of their games, finishing out of contention.

To prove a point, the researchers completed the explanatory analyses for the entire National League in 1985 and predicted how they would do in 1986. The results were astounding. The optimistic teams exceeded their 1985 win/loss record, while the pessimistic teams didn't. When under pressure, the results are even more impressive. The optimistic teams hit well, while the pessimistic teams fell apart under pressure.

Seligman repeated his study the following year for baseball and again the results were the same. He next studied explanatory style within the NBA Atlantic Division with the same results. The basic conclusion: Success on the playing field is predicted by optimism and failure is predicted by pessimism.

This works well in sports, but what about the real world of selling face to face to clients and dealing with the daily challenge of being rejected and losing sales? Will explanatory style help predict who will be good salespeople and who will not?

Met Life

A life insurance sale is one of the toughest games in town. Thousands of people are hired into the field each year and over half of them quit during the first year. The turnover is painful for insurance companies, as they invest significant money in hiring, training, and paying these new recruits. Seligman wondered if he could provide some insight into this high turnover business by using his research. He went to Met Life to investigate.[33]

He was told by the executives that selling is not an easy life. The key ingredient is persistence in the face of continual rejection. Few people can really do it well over time. The turnover was a serious problem. At the end of four years, 80% of the original hires had left, so it was critical to find a way to reduce turnover. The agents face a "no" every single day and often many rejections. The rejections begin to weigh heavily on the agents and they second guess their ability. They usually start to procrastinate in making calls and seeing new prospects. They find meaningless things to do to keep busy and avoid making calls and facing further rejections. Sales start to dwindle, incomes drop, and the new hires decide to move on to another career. It appeared to be a classic case of how the new hires explained their defeats to themselves. The previous studies of the explanatory style would indicate that the more successful agents were more optimistic in their approach.

The executives were well aware that optimism is a key to sales success but had no real way to measure it before they hired someone. Seligman had the tool available and they questioned two hundred of their experienced salespeople. Half were top performers and half were underperformers. The results of the test confirmed the power of optimism. The agents who scored in the optimistic side sold 37% more than those who scored in the bottom half. However, agents who scored in the top 10% sold 88% more than the most pessimistic tenth.

In 1985, Met Life sponsored a full study on 15,000 applicants. The goal was to hire 1,000 agents, using their existing methods and the ASQ (American Society for Quality) score was kept secret. The objective was to see if optimists would outsell pessimists. The second goal was to hire 1,000 applicants who had barely failed the existing testing criteria but had scored in the top half of Seligman's ASQ test to assess optimism and pessimism.

So Met Life hired 1,000 new agents—half were optimists and the other half were pessimists. They also hired another group of 1,000 who had failed the companies tests but scored high on optimism. Over the next two years, these groups were monitored carefully.

In the first year, the optimists outsold the pessimists by a mere 8%, but in the second year, the optimists outsold the pessimists by 31%. The team that was hired based solely on the model outsold the pessimists in the regular field by 21% in the first year and 57% in the second year. They even outsold the average of the regular force over two years even though they had failed Met Life's existing testing criteria. Met Life has implemented the optimist testing approach across the board. Applicants must be in the top 25% of the ASQ results to be considered even if they ace the existing testing. They also hire applicants who just missed passing their existing tests but scored in the top half on the ASQ. The result: Met Life is one of the leading life insurance companies in the world, and they have reduced turnover and increased average sales across the board.

Optimist or Pessimist

The optimist is more successful in sales because they are more persistent. They can deal internally with rejection and put the right spin on it to get back in the saddle again. Once thrown from the saddle, the pessimist will walk away from the horse and look for work elsewhere. So what are you? Are you an optimist or a pessimist, and to what degree? We suggest you read Seligman's book and do the various tests he has included inside. They're enlightening.

Connie: Once you know what kind of tendency you have what can you do about it? My then eleven-year-old son Ryan is an athletic boy involved in all kinds of sports. He loves hockey and plays in the local league, but that summer he failed to make the more competitive hockey league that he had played in the previous year. As a result, he had time to try out for the school volleyball team. When he had tried out for the team as a grade five student, he was cut on the first day of tryouts. This year, at five foot two and eleven years old, he tried out again and was fully expecting to make the team.

That Tuesday, Ryan had to be at school earlier than the country school bus would deliver him, so I drove him and a neighbour's boy into town. As Ryan sat in the back seat of the car, he practiced some of the finger exercises the neighbour had taught him to strengthen his fingers. Ryan played piano for years, which had given him strong hands and fingers. The neighbour, one of last year's team members, went on to explain that they even have to do pushups on their fingertips! The boys were excited and I wished them good luck and dropped them off at the door of the school.

At the dinner table that night, I asked Ryan how his first round of tryouts went. Ryan said, "There were a lot of kids from grade four and up, there this morning." He sounded pretty confident despite the numbers.

I nodded and asked, "So how do you think you did?"

He went on to share, "Being a tall grade sixer, I think some of the shorter grade fours won't make it, but they are still pretty good!" It's usually pretty hard to get Ryan to give answers in full sentence form rather than grunts and short answers, and tonight he had a lot to say.

Ryan ate some more of his dinner and shared even more, much to my surprise. He went on to say, "A lot of kids have to be cut. Twice as many kids tried out as there are spaces on the team. But I can tell my two or three buddies are back on the team this year because they were on the team last year." And that was the end of the conversation on volleyball for the night.

The second tryout day arrived and Ryan was ready with his volleyball clothes and running shoes packed away in his knapsack. Off to school he went. Tryouts were over lunch hour that day. I kept my fingers crossed, hoping Ryan would still be in the running at the end of the second tryout.

Just before dinner, Ryan didn't seem like himself. My husband, Greg, and I could sense what was coming. We almost didn't want to ask, to save Ryan the pain of sharing his failure. I asked anyway, "So, little buddy, how did the tryouts go today?"

Ryan had his head down almost in his plate. He heard the question and waited patiently to respond, making woeful eye contact with his dad across the table. He finally spouted, "I didn't make it."

I was ready to see how Ryan responded to this failure. What was his explanatory style, given he really wanted to make the team? After a short pause, I asked, "Ryan, can you tell me how you feel about that?"

Ryan's response surprised me with the clarity as he said, "There were so many kids on the team and the coach picked some of the shorter grade fours, and, besides, it wasn't fair." He wasn't finished with his explanation and went on to say, "I'm a good athlete and, besides, I want to be on the basketball team coming up next. And, Mommy, will you watch *Malcolm in the Middle* with me at seven?"

I was delighted by his explanatory style and replied, "Of course I will. We love that show, don't we?" He smiled and ate his dinner and it seemed like the matter at hand had been dealt with and Ryan had moved on.

This is an excellent example of a young boy who faced failure and rejection and yet his explanatory style is optimistic, so he can easily manage the failure and move on to the next school sport. I was quite pleased with how well Ryan handled this rejection and very pleased with his statement that he was a good athlete and he would make the basketball team. It is interesting to observe how people deal with failure and, more important, how they explain the failure. Ryan is an optimist and will therefore do well in school and sports, and will be healthier and generally more successful. Failure hounds all of us, even those in professional sports.

Cold Calls

We will all face failure, rejection, and disappointment in our lives. How we explain these failures to ourselves determines how quickly we can bounce back. Salespeople, as we know, face this dilemma every day. Making cold calls might be the toughest of all sales roles. In interviewing the thousands of participants in our programs, the cold call is always an area people require the most help. One of the attendees in particular was a classic case. His job was to cold call potential clients from a list provided by his company. The objective was to obtain an appointment. He would call night after night, and after a few months, he was getting depressed about his job. He was finding it more difficult every night to make the calls and he would procrastinate excessively. He would get a coffee to pick him up, and then he needed a cigarette. Maybe just watch a little TV to relax. His income was terrible and he was wondering why he was even in this business anymore.

We asked him how he felt after his calls were completed. He responded that he was turned down most of the time. The people just didn't want the services and he wasn't any good on the phone. He had no excitement about phoning and thought it was a waste of his time. There was little chance he could make a sale on the phone or even get an appointment. People were rude to him all the time. He went on and on about all the things going wrong in his life and his job. His pessimistic explanatory style caused him to spiral down under the weight of his own negative thoughts. He was talking himself out of the business and finding everything that was wrong with the job. The odds of his lasting in the job were very slim. In fact, two months later, we met him in another program we were offering and he was with a new company and doing quite well. "So far," he said. The pessimism was still there and we expect he will change jobs again.

One of the young women in this same class with a similar job faced the same daily failures and rejections on the phone. The difference was in her explanatory style. She was pleased that she managed to get a conversation with ten people on the phone. Although she had not achieved any appointments, it felt good to get a conversation going. Her objective was to get ten conversations and, she hoped, one appointment. Making twenty-five calls was an accomplishment for her and getting ten to stay on the phone was a real win, and she felt confident that the next ten calls would lead to at least one appointment. The next day, she got right at it and managed to make two appointments that both later turned into sales. Her explanatory style was one of finding the positives and the small wins. This gave her the energy to face the challenges of the job again the next day. She liked her job and enjoyed making the cold calls and finding those opportunities to make an appointment. She loved the company and she loved the product.

These were two people with the same difficult job and yet two totally different ways of looking at rejection. Our young man buckled under the weight of his own explanatory style, while our young woman was persistent based on how she looked at failure. The power of positive self-talk can't be overemphasized. It has a huge impact on everyone's ability to overcome the failures and rejections we all face every day. Build failures into a mountain and they will rule your life, build them into a molehill and you will rule your life. It's your choice! The little voice in your head can be controlled.

Optimistic people tend to distort reality in a self-serving direction, while pessimistic people tend to see reality a bit more pragmatically. The pessimist is really at the mercy of reality, whereas the optimist has an effective defense system that maintains a positive outlook even in the face of a reality that's negative or indifferent.

Self-fulfilling prophecies play well into this scenario. If we believe we are failing, we will ultimately fail. If we believe we are winning the sales battle, we will ultimately win. Self-talk is the determining factor in changing a self-fulfilling prophecy into an asset or a detrimental force. Again, you choose how to interpret results that will help you be more persistent and get back into the saddle. Persistence pays off in the long run. Giving up early is the true sign of continual failure.

Dealing with Failure

If optimists are more successful salespeople, how can we as influencers capitalize on this aspect of bouncing back from adversity? Seligman again offers us some clues that might help develop the skills necessary to be more persistent and, in turn, be more optimistic and more successful in getting what we ask for.

Life does not play favourites. It deals as many setbacks, failures, and tragedies on the optimist as on the pessimist. The optimist is simply better equipped to handle these setbacks that life delivers. They have a better way of bouncing back from defeat and picking up the pieces and starting again because they believe they can. Remember the baseball locker room and media chatter by the players after a game? The team with a positive mental attitude who didn't blame themselves totally for the loss went on to win many more games after a loss than those teams who looked at the loss as an indication of how poor a team they really were. Bouncing back is difficult if you blame yourself and your team for poor skills and poor play. Finding a reason that points to a one-time situation is far more beneficial than saying you're a lousy player. Bouncing back quickly is a sign of a winner, wallowing in defeat is a sure sign of a loser.

The pessimist thinks that preparing for the worst is the safest way to handle rejection. That way, they are ready for it and won't feel too bad if it happens. They can say, "See, I told you it wouldn't work," or, "I couldn't sell that client." Even when the pessimist wins, and they do, they are still thinking about the next time and how it probably won't work out.

"'Tis better to have loved and lost than never to have loved at all" is a famous quotation from Alfred Lord Tennyson's poem "In Memoriam." What does this mean to an optimist and to a pessimist? The pessimist will attempt to protect themselves from loss by never gambling on falling in love in the first place. They never really give themselves, nor do they give love a chance to blossom. The optimist, on the other hand, is willing to gamble because the love gained is worth it all. They don't think about failure in love and they give the relationship all they've got. You do the math. Who will fall in love and find the true happiness that only love can provide?

The pessimist looks for reasons why it will fail and the optimist looks for reasons why it will succeed. In a relationship, what perspective do you want to take and what perspective do you want your partner to take? These are powerful influences that affect literally every aspect of our lives. The secret is to choose the path that leads to success and happiness rather than failure and loneliness. We know many people who have resigned themselves to never finding a partner. A good question to ask them is why they haven't found one. This will give you a clue as to their level of optimism.

If they say, "I just haven't found the right person yet and it's hard to meet new people in the kind of job I have," this is a more optimistic response and they do have hope that they will find a partner. If they say, "I am too old now, who would want me now? And, besides, I never meet anyone anymore," this is a universal statement that indicates a pessimistic attitude and there is really no chance of finding someone. Both of these statements will probably come true. The optimist hasn't found one *yet,* while the pessimist will never find one.

Self-Talk

Self-talk has a tremendous influence on how we look at life and, in turn, influences how we behave. Let's look at some ways we can all enhance optimism and reduce pessimism. If we can accomplish this small task, we will all become happier, healthier, and more successful.

An interesting aspect of this exercise is that if you're pessimistic by nature, you like it that way. In fact, you don't generally like optimistic people. You often see them as unrealistic, always blaming others for their mistakes, and always bragging about their accomplishments. The optimists are boring, unreliable, overconfident, and irritating. So why in the world would you consider becoming one of those bothersome people? Some of us are accused of being aggravating in an overconfident fashion on occasion. When something goes exceptionally well, we sometimes brag a wee bit, and why not? It feels good to have a success and we like to share it. The pessimist looks askance at this behaviour and never wants to take credit for success but is more than willing to take credit for failure.

Can we alter the pessimist's view of failure so they'll be able to try and try again? The Little Engine That Could was an optimist or he never would have been able to climb that mountain. When we encounter problems in our lives, we normally react by thinking about them over and over again. These thoughts change over a short time into beliefs and they become a habit in how we deal with adversity in our everyday lives. Most of the time, these habits are automatic responses without any conscious thought. These beliefs have consequences. They determine the difference between giving up and feeling dejected, and feeling good and taking action.

Think about being on a diet. One night, you decide to go out with the people from work and have a few drinks and some chicken wings. What is the first thing a dieter says to themselves? They usually say, "Uh oh, I blew the diet! I just can't go out without eating everything in sight. I give up on this diet stuff; I just can't do it, so I might as well have dessert too." The diet is over until next time. The consequence of the self-talk about failing to keep the diet has resulted in the diet's failure and going back to eating junk food. Pessimism wins the day: "I'm weak. I have no will power. I'll never lose weight." This is the automatic response and it soon becomes a habit, which partially explains why most dieters fail in their quest to lose weight and fad diets flourish in bookstores and on infomercials.

A new habit could be applied in an instance where we might

experience the situation of a few drinks and chicken wings, but instead of hammering ourselves, we could stop for a moment and explain the situation with phrases such as, "I only had two drinks and three little chicken wings; the calorie count wasn't all that bad and I'll walk home tonight to burn them off. I guess I slipped a little today, but I'll be back full-bore tomorrow with the diet. It's not the end of my diet just because I slipped a little; it's the first time in six weeks that I slipped, and I am still under control of my diet." The consequences of this approach are that the diet stays intact and no late-night food binge follows the chicken wings. We remain committed to the diet.

What a difference in consequences, using a simple little change in how we explain our activities to ourselves. The impact is quite significant and happens on a daily basis for most of us. To get a better handle on this exercise, we suggest writing down a negative experience and then document how you feel about the situation. Next, write about the consequences of how you feel. If the consequences seem rather harsh after a second look, you can change the way you feel about the situation. This will change the consequences and shift your actions to a more positive outcome.

Distraction

There are several ways to deal with pessimistic responses to adversity. Many people have a great deal of success by using the distraction method. Parents are quite effective in using distraction when children are involved in things they shouldn't be. The interest shifts to a new task. In real life, you simply have to say, *stop!* This will cause a pause in thinking and give you a chance to take control again. Any signal will assist in this exercise. Some ring a bell, some pinch their arm, and some carry cards that encourage reconsideration of the impulse to be pessimistic. The bottom line is that you have control of how you respond to situations. If you let the response be automatic, you have given away your freedom over your life and success.

Write your thoughts down in a notebook and refer to these notes later to consider your actions at a later date. Schedule time to go over the feelings and consequences that arise out of failures rather than spend hours going over it again and again in your mind to no benefit. Take control.

Disputation

Another common technique is to dispute the results in the first place. Be argumentative with yourself on the results. You failed to make a sale today that you thought you should have. The immediate response might be that you failed because you aren't much of a salesperson, you were ill-prepared, and you won't make any more sales that week. You are devastated by missing out on this sale. You needed this sale to cover next month's mortgage payment. Sales is not for you. The consequences of this belief are quite dire. You slow down your efforts to make other sales because you might feel there is no point, and you consider leaving the industry.

The disputation technique shifts the blame away from your inability to close a sale to one of reality. You might say, "I have really blown this one loss of a sale out of proportion. I've made many sales this month; I've been successful in the past. I've been busy with the family lately and this has taken some of my time, but next week it's back to normal—I already have several appointments lined up that look very promising."

The outcome of this approach is totally different than the consequences of the pessimistic approach. You feel better about your performance even though the results are the same. The future looks much better with a commitment to move forward and find more time to develop more business. Sales skills are confirmed rather than derided. The method of distraction allows the salesperson to tackle the next day with enthusiasm and a positive attitude. Success comes with persistence.

This method of arguing with yourself might seem unusual at first glance. We have all become quite competent at arguing with others and debating issues of interest, so it should be easy to translate this skill onto ourselves. You must use your influencing skills on yourself to develop a new set of optimistic habits.

Tools of Argumentation

• Evidence.   Have a good hard look at the facts. The easiest way to win an argument is to disprove the negative. Ask yourself: "What is the evidence for this belief that I am a total failure?" The fact is you lost one sale, not every sale. Eliminating negative thinking is sometimes enough to win the day. You don't have to turn everything rosy to make changes happen. The influence of stopping negative thoughts can be just as effective as the power of positive thinking. Your behaviour will respond to this shift in thinking through action rather than passivity, and success will follow. Try it on for size next time you face a setback. As soon as your thoughts shift to the negative and everything that's gone wrong, tell yourself to *stop* and begin an argument with yourself to look at the situation from a factual perspective rather than an emotional one. You can control the little voice in your head much more than you think.

• Alternatives. Most negative experiences have more than one justifiable cause. If the sale didn't go through, there will be various reasons why it happened. Perhaps the buyer didn't need the product, had to delay consideration because of budget constraints, or was shopping before deciding. Perhaps you were ill-prepared this time out, the material you provided wasn't updated by marketing, or the client wanted to buy from his brother-in-law. There are a number of viable ways a sale can fail that have little or nothing at all to do with the salesperson. Pessimists focus on the worst case scenario and usually include a personal attack on their own skills and abilities. Alternatives provide evidence of more than one answer to why the sale was rejected. This allows the pessimist to practice disputing their own personal failure and give them the initiative to keep on going the next day with enthusiasm.

• **Implications.** Sometimes the facts of a situation aren't on your side. Maybe there are indications that you did blow the sale and no amount of effort can diffuse the fact that you blew it. The challenge then becomes to tone down the reaction. The loss of one sale is not the end of the world. It might feel like it at the time, but if you ask yourself what the implications are, a little respite might seep into your mind. You lost a sale—what does that really imply? You lost a sale, but that doesn't imply that you will lose every sale in the future. The pessimist says it repeatedly: "I'll never sell anything ever again." Using these simple techniques empowers you to assess bad situations and find a balance between negativity and reality. The negative implications are a one-time occurance and you will try again tomorrow. If you can do this successfully, this approach will become a habit over time, after which the debilitating effects of rejection and failure will become mere bumps in the road to success.

• **Energization.** After dealing with your own pain, reviewing negative situations, and winning the argument with yourself, it is time to become energized again, which requires a commitment. Rather than saying you will never sell another item for the rest of the week, make a commitment to get appointments before the week is through. Set a goal of eight appointments perhaps. Doing this will cause the negative vibes of failure to be replaced with the positive vibes of action-oriented commitments. How you deal with adversity is your choice. These approaches work, but your decision to take charge are what make them happen.

These approaches are equally effective in the world of sales as they are in the worlds of management and life. Children face adversity on a regular basis and you can influence their future behaviour by how you help them deal with it using an optimistic approach. Optimism can be learned, and the younger we learn, the easier it is to apply. The explanatory style will tell you where your child is on the spectrum of pessimism and optimism. Optimistic children do better in school, have healthier lives, have more social interaction, and are generally better behaved. Being a teenager is still a challenge, but optimistic children are easier to communicate with and seem to maintain a better life balance during this tumultuous period. *The Female Brain* by neuropsychiatrist Louann Brizendine is an excellent book on the various stages we all go through during our lives. *Learned Optimism* by Martin Seligman is a must-read if you enjoyed the ideas expressed in this chapter.

It has been suggested that one of our basic needs as human beings is to be accepted in groups. All humans and many other animal species require a certain amount of social acceptance and interaction to be psychologically healthy. Even amongst varieties of primates, being a member of a group is important for safety and social identity. Rejection by individuals or an entire group can be especially brutal to our self-perception. The fear of rejection is what causes us to conform to peer pressure. Teens in particular are swayed by a fear of rejection to conform to peer pressure. No one wants to be ostracized by the crowd they belong to. Those who are ostracized experience significant personal anguish and become a target for those who do "belong."

The difficulty of peer rejection in teens is that once it occurs, it is virtually impossible to overcome and the teen might spend years in personal isolation. This can lead to low self-esteem, internalized problems such as depression, and externalized problems resulting in overly aggressive and abusive behaviour.

A fear of rejection can be a serious hindrance to your overall effectiveness. Rejection in the political arena means more than just losing a sale, it means losing your job or not getting the job in the first place. A provincial election was held in Ontario in the fall of 2007. The Ontario New Democratic Party (NDP) held ten seats in the last three provincial elections and expected to see significant gains in 2007. The results left the NDP and leader Howard Hampton with just ten seats. They had made no progress under Hampton's leadership.

Some would call this a failure to improve the representation of NDP elected officials in Ontario, while others might call for a leadership change to improve their standing with the public. Howard Hampton, on the other hand, saw this election as a victory for the NDP and his leadership, and stated he would continue as leader. "We have improved our percentage in the popular vote, and if we had a thousand votes distributed differently, we would have won four more seats, but that's the way it goes," he said. A little shift in the voting pattern and he could have increased his results by 40%. How is that for an optimistic view?

Hampton's explanatory style is one of optimism and he found a way to explain his performance in a positive manner and convinced himself the party was really a winner. This approach allows Hampton and the party itself to keep on fighting election after election for what they believe in. A defeatist approach by Hampton would have meant expulsion from the leadership, and the party itself would have suffered tremendous internal fighting as they would attempt to put the blame on someone. Instead, he found the silver lining and the party is pleased with itself and its future prospects. Howard Hampton retained the leadership of the NDP.

The power of explanatory style is amazing when we delve into the reactions of those who face defeat and rejection. We have a need for acceptance. When this acceptance is in jeopardy, our emotional response can be quite severe. Practice an optimistic approach and you will find a better way to deal with rejection and build your self-esteem, which will improve your success in future endeavours. This will give you the persistence and courage to go on after a defeat. Self-talk can either pull you out of depressive moods or pull you down into more depressive ones. Use self-talk to your advantage.

On the Job

So how does all this apply to the real world of day-to-day sales, and what can we do as salespeople to enhance our performance? We all fear being rejected and facing the prospect of a client saying no to a proposal. As mentioned earlier in the book, "no" can be a moment of opportunity, as it gives us a chance to make a concession. This aspect of reciprocity works in many instances, but certainly not all the time. This approach increases the likelihood that a client will say yes to the second request, as they want to give back to you the form of behaviour that you have just given them. Most of us are so fearful of "no" that we retreat from the situation and allow the negative vibes to overtake us and reduce our enthusiasm and the other positive feelings that keep us going.

The other technique discussed earlier was the commitment and consistency principle. By gaining a small commitment first, we can increase the chances of getting a larger commitment later on. If you are suffering from doubt about your career and having some difficulty dealing with the rejections you face, we suggest revisiting the chapters on concessions and commitment/consistency. The more often clients say yes, the less they will say no. The best way to deal with rejection is to simply win more often.

This chapter has dealt with the personal internal challenges we all face when we experience rejection or failure. Sales success comes from within. It's not a product or feature that sells, it is the salesperson. Your mindset going into a sales opportunity will determine the success or failure of the outcome. If you can buy into the concept that you can control how you feel, then your success is assured in whatever field you try.

Self-talk helps you reframe the rejection through a more positive explanatory style. Here are some best practices to help you deal with rejection, especially if it is a reoccurring event in your life.

Best Practices

1. Find a job you love! Happiness is the best guide to success.
2. Set short-term goals. When dealing with rejection, the short-term goals will provide useful feedback to help you remain persistent.
3. Set achievable goals. Find a win every day. Build on strengths and you will gain control over the fear of rejections.
4. Understand the power of the little voice in your head, and then learn to control it rather than let it control you. Remember, this internal voice is trying to protect you from failure, but it also limits your ability to act.
5. Self-talk is the best answer to dealing with your inner voice. Self-affirmation will bring to bear the power of self-fulfilling prophecies in a positive way.
6. When adversity strikes, write down your beliefs about the situation. Next, write down several other possible explanations for what happened that aren't so pessimistic about your abilities.
7. Practice arguing with yourself and disputing what your own little voice is telling you and explain the situation in different more optimistic terms.
8. Make it a habit to find a positive explanation for every single

bad thing that happens in your life.

9. Remember that everything that goes wrong is not your fault. The future is indeed bright and full of promise if you simply open your arms and welcome it.

10. Persistence is the number one criteria for success. How you deal with adversity will determine the degree of persistence in your life.

11. Be positive as often as possible. If you want something bad enough, you will get it.

12. It's your choice. "If it's to be, it's up to me."

Chapter 10
Sales Conversations

Influence and persuasion are accomplished with words and deeds. The words we choose have a significant impact on the effectiveness of our conversations. We are firm believers in scripting to enhance the conversations we have with people. The right words at the right time can and do change behaviour. The right influence principles used at the right time also change behaviour. Scripting our responses requires practice and coaching.

There are many instances where we know what the customer will say or how they will respond. As sales professionals, we should know how to capitalize on this and know the moments during a conversation where we have an opportunity to be more influential. We need to recognize those moments and know what to put into them. The words we choose can determine the success ratio of our conversations.

Sales conversations—and most other conversations—follow a predictable pattern. We will review that pattern in some detail and offer ideas and suggestions that will enhance that conversation to increase the probability that you will get "yes" to your requests.

Greeting

The first stage of any conversation is the greeting, especially if this is the first time you have met a client. If it is a client you have known for some time, the same principles apply but not as crucially, as you have already established rapport and some credibility with past experiences. The greeting is broken down into three stages: preparing, the greeting, and permission to proceed.

1. Preparing

Preparation is a critical stage of any discussion. You need to be ready to present your case—you need to be ready mentally and you need to be ready to meet your goals. Something to ask yourself before you meet with a client is: "What do I need to be fully prepared to meet with this client, and what is my objective for this meeting?" If this is your first time meeting the client a little research would be in order.

Pre-Call Planning

You first need to determine your overall goal. It might be to make a sale or to understand your client's needs so that you can get another appointment. A simple goal is easy to achieve, and you will feel successful after the meeting. Success builds success. Once the goal has been established, do some research. Look up the company on the Internet to find out about their products, volumes, profitability, and goals. The Internet is a tremendous source of information. Find out about the person your going to see. Google their name and see what happens. Ask others in the business if they know this person and check your own company files to see if they are or have been a client. Personal and professional information is invaluable in building rapport immediately.

Materials

What do you need to bring to the meeting to enhance your discussion? Is the material up to date? Do you have enough brochures if several people attend the meeting? Backups are a great way to be prepared for the unexpected. Are you bringing a gift along to try the reciprocity theory by giving first? Do you have business cards in your pocket? Is your name tag on and is it on the right side? The name tag must always be on your right lapel. When you shake hands with the right hand, the body moves to the left and the name tag moves toward the client so it is easier to see and read. Politicians have perfected the art of the name badge on the right lapel and it is a lesson well learned.

In the Car

Okay, this is a field call and you're in the parking lot of your client's company. What are the things you should do to better prepare yourself for this interview? Look into your briefcase or purse and assure yourself you have all the material you need. Pull down the visor and have a look in the mirror. Appearance is a critical influence factor and you need to look good. We always suggest you give a big warm smile into the mirror. This has two practical elements. We all feel and look better when we smile, so it's a good warm-up before the real smile in front of the client. Second, a big smile shows your teeth and you get an opportunity to look for any foreign matter that might be lodged there. Perhaps a piece of lettuce from lunch is stuck between your teeth. Research has indicated that people lose credibility in direct proportion to the amount of food that is visible inside your mouth when meeting new people. If you find something, get rid of it quickly and then have a breath mint just to be sure you're fresh.

A comb or brush does well to make us look better before a meeting. Unless we're blessed with natural beauty, we need all the help we can get. Neat hair and a bright smile does wonders. As mentioned earlier in the book, good-looking people are often considered to be more intelligent, more successful, and are more persuasive. Appearance is the first effect you have on a client. The moment of truth is when the client first lays eyes on you. They can't help themselves; they begin to judge you immediately and often spend the rest of the meeting looking for reasons to justify their initial reaction to you. Therefore, look as good as you can: conservative, well-cut, and well-fitting clothes and a bright smile with teeth—always show those teeth. Clients love people with teeth.

Goals

While in your car, review the purpose of the meeting. If you don't have a goal, don't get out of the car. The objective should be attainable yet challenging. You could even have several goals. The fear of hearing "no" has a stranglehold on many salespeople, and they believe they will fail before they get out of the car. They set an objective that is virtually impossible to attain and therefore face negativity all day. By 3 p.m., they're emotionally drained and unable to function effectively. Their self-esteem has been beaten down to nothing and all they want to do is go home, have a drink, and lie on the couch to sulk over the horrible job they have. Don't do that to yourself. Set your goals and objectives so that you'll win. A goal of a second appointment is a good one, as are understanding the client's needs or meeting more than one decision maker in the office. If it's your first visit, don't set yourself up for failure by demanding that you close a sale during that meeting. This is a relationship business and it takes time to build a relationship. You want a long-term business relationship with this client, not a one-time sale. But if it is a one-time sale, you want referrals from this client. Relationships count in business, which means getting the client to like you and your product or service is also a good goal.

Self-Talk

Selling is a tough business and we all need to be at the top of our game when we meet with clients. Take a moment before you get out of your car to review your successes, sales skills, and personal qualities. This a good way for you to build self-esteem before you meet the client. Salespeople generally work alone and don't get enough positive feedback from supervisors. People who work in an office see their bosses every day and have ample opportunity to showcase their worth and receive acknowledgements on their abilities and contributions. Salespeople rarely meet face to face with the boss—maybe once a month if they're lucky—and so they face reality every day on their own. The only one to provide positive feedback is the person looking back at you in the mirror. Take this opportunity for some self-affirmation. Review the chapter on self-talk for more detail on this subject. It is absolutely critical that you walk away from your car with a sense that you're indeed the best you can be and that you're excited about this opportunity with this client.

Gary: Being positive about yourself and your product will reflect well on your client. There will be an aura of confidence around you that will enhance your credibility. The words you use will have much more impact if the client senses your confidence in your product or service. This requires practice. I have one of those small, yellow, smiley face air fresheners hanging from my mirror. I look at it every time I go in for a meeting and speak directly to the smiley face about how great the meeting will go and how the services will fit right into the business plan for my client. "I am knowledgeable and darn good at what I do. When I get out of the car, I am ready to rock 'n' roll."

2. The Greeting

Now you are face to face with your client or referral source for the first time. What do you do and what do you say? This requires some prep time so you know exactly what to put into this moment of influence. People judge you in the first ten to fifteen seconds, so you need to make a positive and powerful first impression. Your appearance has been finely honed in the car, so you know you look good. Your self-talk gave you a confidence boost, so you look and act like a knowledgeable authority. This all helps, and now you must open your mouth.

Let's see those teeth right away. Your winning smile will help create the positive first impression. Have a firm handshake and use the client's name immediately: "Mr. Jones, so nice to meet you; I'm Gary Ford, your account manager for ABC Company." This is a simple beginning, and you can certainly augment this with additional words, but let's look more closely at what took place. Using the client's name twice in the first minute is critical to build some comfort level. People love to hear their name and have a tendency to like you better if you use it. Introduce yourself and your company. Most people will say something like, "Gary Ford, an account manager from ABC company." There is a big difference in the reception between *an* account manager and *your* account manager. A connection occurs when you indicate that you are their account manager or sales representative. Try this simple shift in wording and we guarantee you will notice a different look on clients' faces.

When do you hand out the business card? Many salespeople prefer to hand out their business card at the end of the sales call as a closing. We suggest handing out your business card during the initial greeting. Again, there is a big difference in the response from the customer. When you say your name, the client might not remember it. When you hand your business card at this time, they look at it and it reinforces your name and your company's name. There is nothing worse than having a client forget your name and then spend the next ten minutes of your sales discussion trying to remember it. Instead of paying attention to what you're saying, they're busy trying to remember your name. Give your client a break and let them hear and see your name.

Small Talk

Small talk is okay when you're walking back to the office or getting settled. This can build some rapport between you and your client—you're using the liking principle to find some similarity. If your client golfs, you could comment that this weekend's weather is going to be great and that you're planning a round of golf. Don't overdo this part of the conversation, as both you and the client are busy. There are many ways to observe an opportunity for similarity if you're observant or if your pre-call planning has included some personal research. Items around the office will also give you a clue. Look for something to like.

3. Permission to Proceed

After building some rapport, you are ready to get to work. Checking with the client whether to proceed allows a smooth transition to the task at hand. A check to proceed can be as simple as, "We had booked forty minutes today, is that still okay?" What does this little technique really do for the conversation? It shows respect for your client and respect for their time. That's a good start in building a relationship. It almost always gets a yes response. A yes response is always a good sign. You have also confirmed the amount time dedicated to this meeting and your client now is fully prepared to pay attention for the duration.

This transition leads into our next phase of the sales conversation, which is understanding your client's needs. An excellent transition to this next phase could be, "In order for me to provide the best advice I can, may I ask you a few questions about your financial affairs?" This works well for banking staff. Another might be, "In order for me to see how we can help, may I ask you a few questions about your business?" This check to proceed gets another "yes," and your client is actually giving you permission to ask questions that they might otherwise be hesitant about providing. You have opened a door to more conversation and your client is now expecting some questions rather than a sales pitch. This process is not a sales pitch. The intent is to have the client speak more than the salesperson. This technique prepares the client to do just that. It's amazing how well it opens up a client to a wide variety of questions, and they will be more than willing to comply and participate in the conversation. In fact, they will enjoy it. People love to talk about themselves.

Understanding Needs

This second phase of the sales conversation process is the most critical and most difficult component. It allows the client to discover their needs. It's surprising how many clients don't really know their needs. They have symptoms of real needs that are rarely fully expressed in the early stages of a conversation. The average salesperson wants to close quickly, and many sales books recommend that you should always be closing. This is a huge error in judgment.

The average salesperson discovers a tiny need and immediately goes to the close and to helping the customer. When this doesn't work, they return to the needs analysis, and when another one is discovered, they go to the close again. This happens so many times in a row that the client is totally confused and frustrated and starts to get irritated. This is one of the most difficult challenges for the sales professional. Don't close too early.

This same process plays itself out in personal life too. Married couples are known for not understanding each other's needs. They rarely spend the time to discover what their partner really wants. The whole relationship becomes based on symptoms, while the true issues never get resolved. Spouses are often heard saying, "You just don't understand me." And it's true, they don't because they are so busy responding to symptoms and not taking the time to listen. Listening is a key skill in understanding your client's needs and the needs of your spouse, your kids, your employees, and literally everyone in your life.

The key to understanding and having the client discover their needs is a simple process that includes asking questions, listening carefully to the response, and then restating part of what they said. This will guide them in the direction you wish the conversation to go, and then you do the most difficult task in sales: *pause*. A five-second pause seems like two seconds to your client but seems like thirty seconds to you.

Asking the Questions

This is the first thing you do after your check to proceed with the client. The key to helping others in self-discovery is to ask open-ended questions. These are wide open questions that require much more than a yes-or-no response. Remember, the objective here is to assist the client in discovering their real needs. Open-ended questions usually begin with the words *what, where, why, when,* or *how.* Open questions encourage the client to provide their true feelings about their business, which will give you a better understanding of available opportunities.

What is a good opening question? It all depends on what you need to know and who you are dealing with. A good start might be, "Will you tell me a little bit about your operation?" We really like the phrase "tell me a little about…." This opens the door to a wide range of responses and the client will usually say much more about their business than they would under specific questions. If you're selling clothes, you might say, "Will you tell me a little about your wardrobe?" You can also try, "Will you tell me about how you see your financial needs for retirement?" and "Will you tell me a little about your home purchase?" Mortgage people always focus on the mortgage because they believe that's what the customer wants, but what they're really buying is a home. This process entails so much more than just a product or service and yet we limit ourselves with our questions. Give the client the opportunity to talk and they will show you how they would like to be sold.

Never begin a sales conversation by asking specific questions around volumes, problems, or who they use. You will get short answers and really never learn anything about how the company functions, their priorities, and the opportunities available to you.

Listening for Clues and Restating for Clarity

The client's answer to your first question will usually take up to two or three minutes. Let them talk and don't interrupt, no matter how tempting it seems. You will learn a great deal about this client, their needs, their business, and their opportunities. A good sales-person is in charge of the conversation and will effectively use the restate technique to direct the conversation smoothly. Select something from your client's statements that you want to investigate further and simply restate what they said and then *pause*. There is no need to present another question at this stage; just let the restate technique do its magic.

Restating does several things in the sales conversation. The most important being that it shows respect and understanding for what your client says. Psychologists call this mirroring and suggest this technique for couples who are having difficulty communicating. As communication seems to be the number one problem for married couples, this is a popular approach to getting back in harmony with one another. If one spouse simply waited while the other finished speaking and then restated the key message of the communication, life would be much richer. Instead, we usually listen for an opportunity to refute what was said rather than listen to understand. Both spouses wait for the opportunity to jump into the conversation and take control. It's no longer a communication but a competition. Many people have an amazing knack for being able to finish their partner's sentences. They must have lived together so long that they are both mind readers.

Do you find yourself listening for opportunities to attack the speaker or to refute their ideas? Do you lie in wait for opportunities to close so you can jump into the conversation and start doing all the talking as you lay out your features and benefits? Or are you polite and let the other person finish their thoughts? We all could be more polite and let others complete their thoughts. When you practice this approach, it's quite surprising what you will learn. Communication is designed to travel two ways and enhance understanding. Try this simple technique the next time you're heading into communication hell with your spouse or partner. You will be amazed at the results and we believe you will win the sale at the end of the day.

Let's look at an example that demonstrates this approach. You are a financial advisor and looking to convince a prospective client to invest with you. The client has significant assets with various institutions. You're meeting them for the first time, and after building some rapport and checking to proceed, you might say, "What can you tell me about your financial affairs and long-term financial goals?" The customer might respond with, "Well, I have twelve more years to retirement and no pension plan at work. My investment portfolio is about a million dollars right now in a mix of mutual funds spread around five different companies. I like to diversify my investments. The rate of return has been okay lately, but a few years ago, I took a bit of a bath and it has taken me a couple of years to recover. I don't want to go through that again. My plan is to have two million dollars set aside in investments both in RRSPs and outside RRSPs. I'm a conservative investor, and the closer I get to retirement, the more conservative I seem to get. I think I'm on the right track but came to you to see if I'm going to be comfortable in retirement and to review some of my current investment strategies."

The client pauses here, so now what do you do? Most advisors or salespeople will either ask a specific question or immediately go for the sales pitch, since the client has laid out some concerns. What do you normally do at this stage?

The key to understanding a client's needs is to get them to talk more and to talk with little direction. We call this the funnelling technique. An open-ended question gets a general response at the top of the funnel. The funnel then gets narrower as you move down it with more questions. The questions and restatements are designed to get the client to discover their real needs and share them with you.

As an advisor, you could ask another question. Some will ask, "Where are your investments located now?" Do you really need to know this at this point? We didn't think so. If you move in to close too quickly, the client will get nervous and could either bolt or refuse to answer at this stage. This will evaporate your rapport, which is tough to get back. Be patient; this is a big sale.

Others ask, "How much are you saving for retirement? I can map out a chart to see what rate of return we will need to achieve the two million dollar target in twelve years." Too specific again—be patient. Others might ask, "How is your money invested today? We can do a risk assessment and compare that to your risk profile."

We suggest you simply restate something that the client said that will direct the conversation in the general direction you want it to go. The restatement process keeps you in charge of the conversation. You are able to direct the conversation, not by asking questions, but by restating the areas that are of interest for you (and ultimately the client) to explore further. This approach keeps the dialogue conversational rather than having it seem like an interrogation. A staccato series of questions makes most of us feel uneasy and pressured. There is no need to use police tactics of shining a bright light in your client's face and firing questions at them to get a confession. We are discovering needs, not discovering criminal intent. Many salespeople smell blood and want to move in for the kill long before the gun is even loaded, and then wonder why the client doesn't buy. Be patient!

Using the restating technique, what do you want to know more about at this stage? Once you decide what areas to investigate further, you simply restate what the client has said and then pause. Give the client a moment to think and digest and they will always carry on the conversation with you. It's amazing to see. We've both had entire sales go from one question to five or six restatements and had the client convince themselves to buy without another question or even a closing statement. This is a powerful sales tool, but it requires a great deal of patience and excellent listening skills. You have to hear the phrase that will move the conversation in the direction you wish it to go next. We suggest you practice this technique with your spouse. You can practice with impunity because you aren't selling and the side benefits will amaze you as your spouse opens up to you like a flower in springtime. Your communication will be enhanced, and your spouse will think, "Wow, we are really starting to communicate and understand one another."

Getting back to the client, what can you say? You could say something like, "So, you took a bit of a bath in the market downturn a number of years ago." The challenge here is to pause and not continue with a question. Many will ask a question here by adding something like, "How has that affected your investment strategy?" The problem with most salespeople is they want to interpret what events mean for the client rather than let the client tell you. By adding this question, you have just eliminated any other comments the client might have made about his reaction to the downturn. Leave the funnel wide open at this stage and let the client answer for themselves. Sure, restatements aren't questions, but clients will listen to a restatement and will want to expand on it for you. It's how effective conversations develop. The client might go into a story about how an investment advisor talked them into a bad investment and now they don't trust advisors and manage all their money themselves. This takes you down a different road than if the client says that they got caught up in the dot com bubble and didn't diversify properly, and now they're committed to diversification within Canada. This is a totally different perspective that reveals your clients needs and aspirations.

The client also might get specific and say they lost $200,000 and had to get a part-time job to get his portfolio back but still has the job and is enjoying it. You never know what the client will say, so don't assume you do. Give them enough room to tell you their story. As the conversation continues, you will restate and pause enough times until the client has revealed their true needs. You will also discover how you can help them. This is the magic of self-discovery.

Listening

The understanding stage isn't easy. Most salespeople want to close their client rather than understand them. To be an effective closer, you need to understand your client. If you do, the close is often done for you. A true salesperson is a good listener. Salespeople usually have a pitch and think they know what clients need and what clients will say. This easily leads to poor listening habits. Salespeople often jump to conclusions before all the facts are in because they don't listen to their clients. They become so focused on what they want to accomplish that they ignore the subtle messages a client is giving about what they really need and how they would like to buy.

To enhance your listening skills, we suggest you take notes while the client is speaking. Avoid taking copious notes and instead record key points that will require further investigation. You can restate these points as you work down the communication funnel. Watch the client's body language in between notes. This is why you shouldn't hunch over your notepad and write every word.

The next key to listening is to listen to yourself. Your inner voice will tell you when you are drawing conclusions and formulating responses to the client's comments. A red flag should pop up in your mind, but you need to remind yourself that you're listening to understand and eventually to restate. You aren't listening for an opening to respond. Practice with your spouse or close friend and you'll notice a tendency to want to jump in and take over the conversation. Don't do it! Fight the urge to interrupt. Your time to close will come soon enough. Be patient.

To encourage more conversation from your client, maintain eye contact and use the age-old technique of nodding your head in agreement or making acknowledgement noises such as "uh huh" or "yes" or even "oh." It will keep a client talking and divulging more information about their needs.

In his book *The Sales Bible,* Jeffrey Gittomer teaches how to listen: "Learn to listen in two words...shut up!"[28] It's amazing how much you can learn by just keeping quiet. People think you're smarter if you're quiet. You can learn more by listening than by speaking. This is why we have two ears and only one mouth.

Let's say you're a mortgage broker trying to get referral deals from a real estate agent. The agent already has several mortgage brokers they use on a regular basis. Another agent who uses your services introduced the prospect to you. You meet the prospect for lunch. After your initial greeting and building some rapport, you're ready to talk business. Your objective is to get this agent to refer business. In fact, your number one objective is to develop a relationship with this agent so that you will be their exclusive source for mortgages on all the real estate transactions they process. What is your first question?

We have heard many responses to this first question over the years with the thousands of participants in our seminars and workshops. Here are just a few:

"So, how many real estate deals do you do in a year?" This is too far down the funnel. The client could say twelve or so, but now what do you do? This is almost like a qualifying question to see if the agent is good enough for you to deal with. You should have done your pre-call planning and determined the value of this prospect before sitting down for lunch.

"Who do you refer your mortgage business to now?" This is too far down the funnel as well and might seem a little too abrupt early in the conversation. No need to go for the throat right off the bat. Besides, does it really matter who they use? They don't use you at the moment, which is the key point, so why do you care who they use? This could cause some early resentment in your prospect because it looks like a sales pitch. It's important to remember that life is sales, and many people you talk to are, in fact, in sales and so are watching how you sell. This agent is in sales and doesn't want to be sold. People much prefer to buy rather than be sold.

"If I could show you how I could make you an extra twenty thousand a year, would you be interested?" This could very well be the worst opening on the face of the earth. Many sales books preach this approach to gain the clients interest before the sales pitch. This is a ridiculous question. Of course people are interested in making more money, and you have just revealed to your prospect that you will be selling to them now. Remember, people like to buy, they don't like to be sold. It just sounds like a setup and you're about to launch into a sales pitch without understanding any of the agent's unique needs. In this scenario, the salesperson has already decided what the agent's needs are and is going to meet them with a sales pitch—no self-discovery, no listening, no understanding. This sale is doomed to failure and you get stuck with the lunch bill.

"How can I help you be more successful in your business?" What kind of question is this? You're basically saying that you're smarter than the agent. Even if it's true, there is no need to shove their nose into it. At this stage, you don't even know their strengths, weakness, or needs yet, and here you're ready to provide advice on how they can be more successful. It's a sales pitch. You are building towards a relationship, not a one-time sale.

Scripting

Over the years, we have heard hundreds of different approaches to this moment of opportunity in a budding relationship. This is a powerful moment in any business relationship, and as a sales professional, you should know what to put into this moment to start the relationship off on the right track. Scripting is critical to really knowing what to say. There are many moments during a client sale that we know might come. We know what the client might say and what situation might occur. As professionals, we need to know what to put into moments of opportunity to fully capitalize on it. So what could you say to the real estate agent when you start to talk business?

Here are some suggestions, but really, you need to spend some quality time with yourself, your mentor, your boss, and even others in your target audience to assess how well these approaches work. Fine tuning these moments of opportunity separates the big winner from the mediocre performer. Top salespeople in every industry have learned how to capitalize on these moments to keep the relationship on the right track. This is your sale and it's therefore your accountability to ensure you are in charge of the direction you wish the conversation to take. So what could you say? Write down a few approaches yourself to see how they feel.

"Betty, you've been successful in this business for many years, how have you managed to be a top performer on such a consistent basis?" Notice we've used the agent's name, included a compliment to enhance liking, and asked a wide open question that really could go anywhere. This allows your prospect to explain the business from her perspective and will showcase what she feels is important in her ongoing success. These are her needs, and you should listen carefully for what they are. Everyone loves to talk about themselves, especially other people in sales. Successful salespeople usually have a decent-sized ego. Use this to your advantage. As Betty speaks, you should be noting the things she says that are important to her success so that when you restate, you will choose the ones that open the door for you to provide the right assistance. It's a simple process that works but requires great discipline and patience. Don't ask a second question—find an opportunity to restate.

You might restate something like, "So, you get most of your business from referrals through existing customers." Betty will jump in on this one and explain how service is paramount to her business—the personal touch and making friends with her customers so they have lifelong relationships with her. She offers trust and credibility to clients and she needs to know that her broker and lawyer believe in this same philosophy—a breakdown in the chain of closing affects her credibility. Many salespeople will go for the close right here and usually fail. Identifying one need does not mean you will close; it should signal you to restate to take the conversation where you want it to go next.

Where do you want the conversation to go? Many people will ask a question about the brokers she currently uses. Don't do it. Restate where you want to go rather than ask another question. This is a conversation, not a sales pitch. In conversations, you want to learn more.

You might restate, "Having a team of business partners you trust and who have the same customer philosophy as you is really important to your business." Betty will go off again explaining her philosophy in much more detail and will usually share how her current mortgage person has let her down on deals and it took a lot of effort to salvage them.

We keep moving down the funnel with more specific restatements until Betty finally says, "You know, I have been unhappy with my current broker lately. He just seems to be too busy chasing other realtors and not paying much attention to me." Resist the urge to jump in here. Take a breath, pause, and count to ten. Betty will continue and ask you about your philosophy of customer service or she might even ask if you would like to do her next deal to see how you work together.

The relationship and future business could be sealed over lunch and you only asked one question and didn't sell. You let her buy instead. This is an amazingly powerful tool that very few professional salespeople use effectively. The many principles of influence are at play here and you will be surprised at how effective this can be in both your professional and personal life.

The Close—Helping Your Client Meet Their Needs

This part of the sales conversation is usually where most people like to go quickly. We all love to help people solve their problems and we all love to close a sale. Well, we're finally here after a very fruitful listening and restating strategy.

The close is made up of several distinct phases as follows:

Provide advice – Every good salesperson should give value to their client and should act in an advisory capacity. You bring knowledge and expertise to the situation and clients expect to hear your advice. If you cannot provide good solid advice, you are in the wrong business.

Match features and benefits to customer needs – You provide a good framework around your advice by understanding the client's needs and matching specific needs to your product or service. Using exact words and phrases previously used by the client to express their needs adds tremendously to the credibility of your advice.

Ask for the business – Since we are humble people and usually hint at the business rather than ask for it, be bold and ask for what you want. Apply the principle of concessions here if necessary. Just be sure you know what you want, because you just might get it.

Gain a commitment – Asking is one thing, but getting an answer is something completely different. You need to cement the deal with a commitment, and the best commitment is a written commitment. People really do live up to what they write down.

Overcome objections – During the close, you might face an objection. It might be price, service levels, or even timing. Be ready with your approach to overcoming objections. A good salesperson usually knows likely objections in advance and should be ready with a well-scripted approach. This is a huge moment of opportunity and we know it's coming. Be ready!

Deliver the goods – This final stage is the actual delivery of the product or service and payment. If it's a new widescreen TV, help the client load it into their van. If it's a commitment from a realtor to send you business, get the first client right away.

There is no magic bullet in selling and there are no perfect closing sentences that guarantee a sale every time. There are, however, some specific approaches that are more effective than others in getting your client to say yes to your requests.

The Pareto Principle

In 1897, Vilfredo Pareto discovered what has come to be known as the Pareto principle. He determined that there is an underlying principle to input and output. He was studying the patterns of wealth and income distribution in nineteenth-century England. He quickly discovered that most income and wealth belonged to a minority of the people, but what really interested him was that there seemed to be a consistent mathematical pattern of wealth and distribution. He found that 20% of the population accounted for 80% of the wealth. He could predict that 10% of the population accounted for 65% of the wealth, and only 5% of the population accounted for 50%. He studied various time periods and other countries and found similar patterns.

Studies by various companies and researchers in the '50s and '60s applied this consistent pattern to other areas of life and discovered that the rule applied in general to almost every piece of data they looked at. Teachers will tell you that 20% of the students cause 80% of the trouble, and businesses find that 20% of their customers deliver 80% of their business.

In 1963, IBM discovered that 80% of a computer's time is spent executing 20% of the operating code. The company immediately rewrote its operating software to make the most-used applications more accessible. Using this approach, IBM's computers became faster and easier to use than its competitors and led the computer revolution into home and business use.

The Pareto principle translates into sales as well: 20% of salespeople account for 80% of the business, and 20% of your customers account for 80% of your volume. On a more personal note, the average salesperson asks for the business only 20% to 30% of the time and just hints at the business the remainder of the time. This is why you should identify the top 20% to 30% of your clients and spend more time with them—and actually ask for the business! Business grows from existing customers faster than it does from non-customers. Referrals come from only 20% to 30% of your customers, so work these clients more aggressively and you will get more referrals. The challenge of asking for business has been dealt with earlier in the book, but the Pareto principle will augment the psychology behind it.

The Powerful Request

When making a close, it should look more like a recommendation from an expert in the field. You are that expert and you should clarify your role as a partner in this purchase rather than a simple salesperson. You have spent considerable time identifying the needs, and the client has discovered these needs as well. Now the time is right for the close and the powerful request.

Three words have the essence of power within them and should be used when framing your final sales request; the words are: *recommend, suggest,* and *advise.* We mentioned these words in chapter 5, but they deserve repeating here in the conversation section.

These simple words carry tremendous authority, and as we know, people are influenced by experts in the field and have a tendency to believe what an expert says. These words create a sense of authority in the speaker. We guarantee the client will pay more attention to your close when you use them versus any other technique. If a client pays more attention to you, you have a greater chance of success.

"After reviewing your requirements, I recommend that you invest your money according to this financial plan and consolidate your investments under one roof with us because...." Many salespeople will humbly go halfway with the request and will blow the opportunity. They will say something like, "After reviewing your requirements, I recommend that you consider investing your money according to this financial plan...." The difference is between the definitive "recommend that you invest" and the more humble "recommend that you consider investing." What a difference, and the results would be equally different. Go for the gusto and make a powerful request. What's the worst that can happen? The client might say no, but that will be a moment of opportunity to make a concession and achieve your secondary goal. *Consider* means the client should think it over and maybe get an opinion from another company before they decide. It's a natural tendency for us to give the client an easy out, but this costs you money and costs the client time.

"After listening to what you really need, I suggest you purchase our top-of-the-line model because…." Again, make the powerful request rather than have them consider your top model. The *because* leads you into matching the features and benefits of the product to the specific needs that the client has expressed to you during the understanding section of the sales conversation. This is asking for the business with the right reasons to support your suggestion.

"After weighing the pros and cons of the various options we have discussed, I advise you to select the variable term mortgage for your purchase because…." Can you see what this does for the relationship between seller and buyer? The relationship is based on trust, and the prospect is expecting to get some expert advice before they decide on their purchase. The salesperson who uses one of these magic words elevates the relationship above the norm and the client is much more likely to agree with a trusted advisor than with a person who is selling or, even worse, providing options.

These words are so effective because they immediately change the tone of the dialogue. They imbue a sense of professionalism, authority, and expertise in the person using them. These words enhance your persuasiveness by capitalizing on our tendency to believe in an expert and to want advice from such an expert. We recommend you use one of these powerful words in your next sales conversation with a client when you are ready to close.

Referrals

Asking for referrals is probably the most important activity you can do to keep your business pipeline full. All successful salespeople use referrals to grow their business more so than cold calls. Those who rely on cold calls are usually in another line of work within a couple of years. Cold calling is a stressful and painful way to make a living. A warm call through referrals is much more productive and enriching.

As we've stated many times, we are humble people who usually hint at the business and referrals. In listening to over four thousand sales professionals ask for referrals, we have been surprised at how gentle they are. We usually hear things like: "If you have any family or friends who would be interested in our product, I hope you will hand out one of my business cards." Wow, how subtle can you get? We even risk sounding like we assume they have no family or friends, so we take the humble way out. Is that a powerful request? No it's not, and yet we do this type of thing all the time.

We have also heard, "Here are five of my cards, please hand them out to your family and friends who might be interested in our services." This is better, but still not very powerful. If the client accepts the cards, the odds are very slim that they will remember to hand out the cards. Second, this is a statement and not a question. To be effective, you need to get a response from the client so they will make a verbal commitment to handing out the cards, and they will act consistently with that commitment. Ask a question: "Will you please hand out my cards…?" The client will have to say yes and will be likely to actually do this for you.

However, this is still a far cry from a powerful request. What do you want the client to really do for you? What is the best thing this client could do to help you in your business? Many say they want more business, they want their next deal, they want a referral, and someone will finally say they want a name and a number. Light bulbs pop on in heads around the room and a big *aha* rings out in every group we've talked to. Get a name and number of someone to call. This is a warm lead, and yet most salespeople never ask for this larger request.

There is an even larger request that some will come up with, which is to ask the client if they will introduce you to someone they know will be interested in your services. It doesn't get any better than this. A delighted client will actually bring in a prospect and make a personal introduction. This is the most powerful request you can make when it comes to getting referrals. We suggest you try it and see what happens. You will be surprised at how effective this can be. If they say no, be ready to make a concession. The concession will be to ask for several names. If you want to double your success with this second request, we suggest dropping your eyes a wee bit when asking for the names of referrals. This shyness is endearing to customers, and they find it hard to resist. They will usually deliver a name or two, especially after you have made a concession from the introduction.

In all situations, think of what you really want to see happen and then ask for it.

Objections

You sometimes face objections during the close. This often occurs during the understanding conversation and is merely seen as discovering additional needs and isn't much of an objection at all. When it comes during the close, this could be a much stronger objection. The key to all objections is that they are really an expression of interest in buying; otherwise, the client would just walk away. This is a real opportunity to close. The client is interested enough to express their concerns to you, and that's good news.

Objections are often the method that clients use to gather additional information that might not have been divulged during the understanding phase. It might also be a way for a client to ask for clarification. Always look at an objection as an opportunity. Many objections simply pinpoint a client's major needs and key areas of interest. Generally, a client's objection is a call for help. They need additional information and the objection is a signal that they are getting closer to buying. If you get defensive or take the objection personally, you immediately lose any chance you have to influence the decision-making process and you can watch the sale float out the window into the waiting arms of your competitor. Accept the fact that objections are good and a part of your sales plan to win the day.

Acknowledgement

The first step in dealing with an objection is to acknowledge it. Don't try to resolve it immediately. The client has a right to an opinion and you should be delighted they feel confident enough in the relationship to express it to give you an opportunity to resolve it. In many cases, sales are lost because clients don't express their objections and keep them hidden and merely walk away from the sale. If an objection is emotional, you need to deal with the client's feelings first. You can never get to logic if emotional barriers are in the way.

Feelings First

Think of an objection situation between husband and wife. Emotions escalate usually because one of the partners doesn't appreciate the emotional response of the other and deals with the situation at a different level. Have you had a fight with your spouse only to forget what you were fighting about? We often forget the cardinal rule of objections: Take care of feelings first so you can move on to the actual situation at hand. Identify the emotion—"You seem upset"—and the client will continue the conversation.

So what can you say to an objection? As you know, scripting is an integral part of every successful salesperson's repertoire. You know what moments of opportunity will occur during a conversation and you should you be ready to maximize your influential impact on the relationship. Practice some lines on family and friends until they feel and sound good to you. They need to come from your heart and not from a book. We suggest including some phrases such as, "I can understand you're frustrated with this," "I appreciate your concerns with this issue and would like to know a bit more about how you feel about this," or "That is an excellent point you have raised and I can hear your concern, tell me more." Try a few on for size, and even make some objections when your out buying to see what others are practicing on you. Be an observer of life and you'll be surprised at what you can learn.

Clarify

Once you have taken care of the client's feelings, you need some clarification about the issue or objection and what it means to your client. You need to gauge the importance of the objection: Is it a deal breaker or a negotiation point to get you to lower your price or provide additional services? Is it simply a misunderstanding of the features and benefits that you provide? In any case, you do need to show respect for your client's perspective by investigating it further. You need more information before you can help. This is much like the needs-analysis section, as you have discovered another need that requires investigation. The restatement technique works very effectively here.

The danger for the novice salesperson is to look at an objection and immediately jump to resolving it before you fully understand the nature of the issue. Jumping to close is one of the deadly sins of selling. Listen to understand so you can more effectively match your features and benefits to these new needs. Only then can you provide a recommendation to close. Choose the part of the objection that you want to investigate further and simply restate that part and pause. This is much more effective in getting the client to talk openly than firing back a question.

Never say, "You don't understand the nature of our offering; let me clarify for you what we have." This is a lost opportunity to understand—it's simply selling. Let the customer sell themselves first. Restate something like, "So, you are concerned about our warranty period" or "I hear you say our price is a little higher than our competitors'." Price is always a tough nut to crack and requires some real practice. We are not ready to argue price just yet, so let the customer talk; it's surprising what they will say about issues other than price if you give them a chance.

Many salespeople ask a question here such as, "What else other than price is important to you?" This isn't bad, but we prefer to allow the customer to express themselves freely and we are always surprised at what they say and how they convince themselves that price is really not the issue at all. Again, script out some samples and practice, practice, practice. This is another moment of opportunity, and you know it's coming, so be prepared to deal with it productively. If you're not prepared for this objection, you're really not ready to sell.

Recommendation

After the objection has been fully clarified, it's time to make your recommendation. You should revise your advice to this client based on their objection and provide a slightly different product or service that more accurately meets their needs. This is where the three magic words again come into play and will have a positive impact on the outcome. You understand the client's needs and objections, and they know you can help them fulfill their need. Add some authority to your sales close by saying, "After having discussed your needs in more detail, I recommend you purchase because…" and then match features and benefits to the client's newly expressed requirements. This simple system works, but it does require a great deal of discipline and patience. You will be rewarded with more sales and higher volumes.

Once you make your recommendation, pause again. You will hear an affirmative on the order, so wait for it. Don't jump right in and check to see if this recommendation is okay, and certainly don't second guess yourself before your client has time to mull it over. If the client wants to think it over rather than give an immediate purchase, treat this as an objection and go through the process once again. This sometimes happens, so be ready for it. It's another moment of opportunity waiting for you to be more persuasive.

Retention

The final step in the sales conversation is retention. It's much simpler to get more business from an existing customer than from a new customer and it's much easier to get referrals and introductions from a happy customer than from a stranger. It's all about the relationship, and the role of every successful salesperson is to build on the initial relationship that allowed the sale to go through in the first place. You're not selling products or services, you're selling the relationship. This stage is made up of three components: Check for satisfaction, thank the client for their order, and follow up for future business and referrals.

Check for Satisfaction

This means simply ensuring your client is happy with their purchase. Their happiness with you and the product will determine the amount of new business you can generate from the relationship. The client's level of delight is directly related to your future income.

Thank the Client

Thanking the client for the business seems like a statement of the obvious, but it is surprising how many times a humble salesperson will not do this well enough. Thank them and offer a compliment, which will make them feel they made the right decision for themselves rather than simply made you happy as a salesperson. A compliment means they will like you a bit better in the process, and if a client likes you, this leads to more money in your pocket.

Saying goodbye is a lost art for most people. It seems we just want to escape the room with our sale under our belt and rush outside to scream how happy we are and celebrate. Be gracious, be nice, and show gratitude.

Follow Up

When is the best time to follow up on a customer after you have just had an appointment with them in their home or office? In our review with over four thousand salespeople, we have heard things like, "I follow up in the next several days," "I send an email within two weeks," "I document for follow-up several times over the next three months," and some even say, "I wait for them to call me, and if they don't, I drop them an email after thirty days." What is your normal follow-up procedure currently?

We are amazed at how erratic the sales follow-up process is for most people and companies. No one seems to have a consistent approach to handling their follow-up process and few realize how critical this aspect is to building relationships. It seems people are just so happy to make a sale that they don't see the need to follow up. Many salespeople believe they are selling a product or service and not themselves. They don't want to bother the client too much. The most successful salespeople don't think this way; they believe in the value they bring to the sales exchange. People buy from people, especially from people they have a relationship with.

So, when is the best time to follow up on an appointment? The best time is while you're still in the parking lot. That's right, follow up with a phone call from your car in the parking lot. This is an immediate surprise for your customers, and surprises make people memorable. But why so quickly? You are certainly not alone if you turn your nose up at such a direct and forceful approach. Most people we speak to about this strategy come up with all the reasons why it wouldn't be a good idea. They say things like, "The client will be angry at being bothered so quickly," "Why would I call, I have nothing new to add?" "I don't like people doing this to me, so I couldn't do it to a client," "I would be embarrassed to make the call," "I don't like to irritate my clients by being so aggressive," or "I prefer to wait a few days and send an email. Besides, I wouldn't know what to say."

We can understand how you feel about the forwardness of this approach. Maybe it's not your style; many would prefer the easy route of an email with minimal personal risk and no fear of receiving a negative response as with an immediate phone call. But, anyone who has actually tried this approach has been amazed at how thankful the client was for receiving a phone call to ensure everything was okay. In fact, we have had some reports that the salesperson was invited back into the house or office for a larger sale on the spot or an introduction to someone else in the office who also wanted the services.

It's tough to put yourself on the line with this approach, but it works wonders. A quick follow-up call reveals that you care about the client as a person. It shows an interest in them and their purchase. The fact that no one else does this will certainly separate you from your competitors. Be bold, be different, and be successful!

So what can you say when you make the follow-up call? This is another moment of opportunity that you can be prepared for. We suggest you practice this one as well. Practice with co-workers and family, and then practice with live clients and assess what happens. You will be surprised and delighted by the response.

You can say things like, "Hello, George, it's John Brown from ABC company. I just wanted to make sure everything was clear in today's meeting and to thank you for the opportunity of meeting with you today," "Hello, George, John Brown from ABC company, I just wanted to thank you for taking the time today and to say how much I enjoyed meeting you and discussing how we can help. Have a great day," or "Hello, George, John Brown again. Just a quick follow-up to make sure you received all you needed from today's meeting. It was a real pleasure to meet you today and I look forward to working through this deal with you."

One or two sentences is all you need—short, sweet, and to the point. You will often get voicemail, which is okay too. It's easier for you to deliver your message, but it's still quite effective. The key is to make the call within five minutes after the meeting.

A second option is a handwritten note, thanking the client for the time, given to the receptionist to hand to your client later. Handwritten notes are much more effective than email.

Another approach would be to call later in the day or the next day. A phone call is often the most effective.

Finally, you could send an email. The only problem with this approach is that every other salesperson you're competing with will do the same thing. Differentiate yourself if you want to build relationships and make more money. Email is a rather weak follow-up strategy in new relationships. It's almost as bad as not following up at all.

Best Practices
Greeting
1. Do your homework. Pre-call planning should include details

about who you're seeing.

2. Show some teeth in the mirror while pumping yourself up before you leave the car.
3. Review the objective of your meeting. Make sure you actually have an objective.
4. Use the client's name twice in the first minute of meeting them.
5. Hand out a business card at the beginning of the meeting.
6. Find some similarities, give a compliment, and get client to like you quickly.
7. Check to proceed to gain a "yes" and show respect for your client's time.
8. Set the stage for the questions and discussions.

Understanding

1. Appreciate that understanding is the most difficult aspect of selling.
2. Ask open-ended questions.
3. Listen, listen, listen, and don't interrupt.
4. Forget about closing. Seek to understand.
5. Restate the client's key phrases to gain more understanding.
6. Don't fire a series of questions at your client.
7. Pause to let the client think about their answer for at least ten seconds.
8. Practice with your watch to determine how long ten seconds really is.
9. Be patient—this is a conversation to build a relationship.
10. Objections are your friends—take care of feelings first.

Closing

1. You can finally close, but if you did the understanding part correctly, the client is already sold.
2. The three magic words: *recommend, suggest, advise*.
3. Make a powerful request.

4. Don't hint for the business, ask for it.
5. Be prepared to make a concession if your hear "no."
6. Get a verbal commitment from the client—a written commitment is even better.
7. Be prepared for objections—take care of feelings first.
8. Practice scripting out the various close approaches.
9. Always ask for a referral.

Retention

1. Make sure the client is satisfied with their purchase or commitment they just made.
2. Thank the client for the business.
3. Give the client a compliment—make them feel that they made the right decision in buying from you.
4. Avoid buyer's remorse through positive reinforcement.
5. Ask directly, "What else can I help you with today?" rather than, "Is there anything else I can help you with?" Open-ended questions are better than closed.
6. Make sure you can meet your obligations on this transaction and follow up to ensure things are on track and on time.
7. Follow up with a phone call within five minutes after the appointment.
8. Your voice is much more powerful relationship builder than an email.
9. Be bold and different.
10. If you can't phone, leave a handwritten note of appreciation with the receptionist.

The Final Word

Congratulations! You have covered a great deal of material in the "Life Is Sales" journey. Your challenge now is to integrate these new strategies to bring lasting change and results to your life. We promise that as you implement these new approaches, you will notice an improvement in your results. We expect these wins will inspire you to try out more and more of the lessons from this book.

Nothing will happen unless you take the first step. Make a commitment right now to change your life for the better. Your first challenge is to gain control over your own thoughts. You do have the ability to choose how you react and you can choose what it is you really want in life. The self-fulfilling prophecy will come into play to help you move in the direction of your choice. What you look for you will find—both the good and the not so good. Nothing happens overnight, so persistence in maintaining your dream is paramount. Thinking you can accomplish amazing results is one thing, but actually believing you can achieve amazing results will take you to the next level.

When you decide what you want for your life and make powerful requests of yourself and others, you will get what you want. This is the critical first step in building your future. Decide, commit, believe, and live into your future. Your results will surprise you. *Life Is Sales* provides the foundation for change in your life and business. These practical suggestions will require fine-tuning to match your own personal style.

We firmly believe in scripting. Countless moments of opportunity occur every day. The challenge is to recognize these moments of opportunity and then be prepared to fill that moment with your carefully scripted words in order to be more influential and persuasive. Most of us don't even notice these opportunities and let them slip through our fingers. There is a lot of noise out there in our world and many appealing distractions. It will take a new discipline for you to hear and see these opportunities anew.

When deciding to write this book, we had to make a major commitment of time. We really had no idea how much work was involved in writing a book. We had a vision, a message we are passionate about, and a commitment to share it. So how did we find the time in our hectic lives? Connie decided to look at this creation as a part-time job. She gave herself permission to reallocate her precious time, which gave her the incentive and focus to get the writing completed. Gary, on the other hand, decided to reduce his TV watching and instead do something productive with an hour or two every night. It was interesting to observe how, before this new commitment, TV could actually overtake entire evenings. We used two different approaches to meeting a commitment and both worked exceptionally well to keep us on track and on vision.

Be focused on your goals and don't be distracted by frivolous activities that might blur your vision for your future. This takes conviction and hard work because the world is full of distractions. People and organizations that create seven to ten strategic goals rarely attain their goals. We simply can't focus and deliver on too many goals: Keep your goals to just a few. Make your goals simple to maintain your focus and get the results you want.

We encourage you to experiment with the various best practices we have suggested. Discover your own strengths in communication and influence and build on them. You will be more successful by building on your natural strengths than you will ever be trying to focus on your weaknesses. Our natural tendency might be to focus on weaknesses first, but by building on your strengths and focusing on what you are already good at, you will discover that the weaknesses really have little impact on your performance. Professional baseball pitchers rarely spend time practicing how to hit home runs. They usually build on their best pitch first and then add to their repertoire. Discover your strengths and turn them into a powerhouse.

In the sales game, what are you really selling? You are selling yourself first. People buy from people first and then they buy the product or service. The suggestions in *Life Is Sales* provide you with the tools to sell yourself first. It is now up to you to deliver this in the real world. Persistence, initiative, and assertiveness are key to your success.

We hope you enjoyed reading this book as much as we enjoyed writing it. Learning is a lifelong commitment and we hope this book inspires you to reflect on your life and recognize opportunities before you. Opportunities will unfold for you in new and exciting ways and help you to be more proactive. We have provided the tools for you to become more influential and persuasive in your life: They work at home, in the office, in sales, and in all aspects of your life. You can change your life and get what you want. You can find true happiness and fulfillment in all aspects of your life. The choice is now yours. Make a commitment, write it down, share it with your friends, and take your first steps. If you want it bad enough, the law of attraction and the self-fulfilling prophecy will take over and you will meet your goals. Success is unlimited.

It is up to you. Find your magic in life and your dreams will come true.

Notes

1. KFC Corporation—Corporate History. www.fundinguni-verse.com/company-histories/KFC-Corporation-Company-History.html

2. "Lincoln's 'Failures'?" From ed. Don E. Fehrenbacher. 1992. *Selected Speeches and Writings: Abraham Lincoln* by New York: Vintage. http://showcase.netins.net/web/creative/lincoln/educa-tion/failures.htm

3. "Steve Paul Jobs"—Short Biography. J.A.N. Lee, 1994. http://ei.cs.vt.edu/~history/Jobs.html

4. Gelman, Eric and Rogers, Michael. 1985. "Showdown in Sili-con Valley." *Newsweek* 30 (September) pp. 46-50.

5. Dr. Madeline Daniels' Homepage. www.drmadeline daniels.com

6. Kulka, R. A., & Kessler, J. R. 1978. "Is justice really blind? The effect of litigant physical attractiveness on judicial judgment." *Journal of Applied Social Psychology*, 4, pp. 336-381.

7. Aronson, E., Wilson, T. & Akert, R. 2005. *Social Psychology*. Fifth Edition. Toronto: Prentice Hall.

8. Kunz, P. R. and Woolcott, M. 1976. "Season's Greetings: From My Status to Yours," *Social Science Research*, 5 pp. 269-278.

9. De Cooke, P.A. 1992. "Children's understanding of indebtedness as a feature of reciprocal help exchanges between peers." *Developmental Psychology*, 28, pp. 948-954.

10. Regan, D. 1971. "Effects of a favor & liking on compliance," *Journal of Experimental Social Psychology*, Vol. 7 pp.627-39.

11. Cialdini, Robert. 2000. *Influence: Science and Practice.* New York: Allyn & Bacon.

12. Milgram, Stanley. Dec. 1973. "The Perils of Obedience." *Harper's Magazine.* pp. 62-66, 75-77.

13. Erickson, Lind, Johnson & O'Barr. 1978. "Style and Impression Formation in a Court Setting: The Effects of 'Powerful' and 'Powerless' Speech," 14 *Journal of Experimental Social Psychology.* p. 266.

14. Shedler, J., & Manis, M. 1986. "Can the availability heuristic explain vividness effects?" *Journal of Personality and Social Psychology*, 52, pp. 26-36.

15. Langer, E.J. 1978. "Rethinking the role of thought in social interaction" in Harvey, Ickes, & Kidd. *New Directions in Attribution Research.* Volume II. Philadelphia: Lawrence Erlbaum Associates, Inc.

16. Freedman, J.L. & Fraser, S.C. 1966. "Compliance without Pressure." *Journal of Personality and Social Psychology.* Aug; 4(2) pp. 195-202.

17. ibid.

18. Moriarty, T. 1975. "Crime, commitment, and the responsive bystander: two field experiments." *Journal of Personality and Social Psychology*, 31 pp. 370-376.

19. Tuckman, Bruce. 1965. "Developmental sequence in small groups." *Psychological Bulletin*, 63, pp. 384-399.

20. Mortensen, Kurt W. 2004. *Maximum Influence: The 12 Universal Laws of Power Persuasion*. San Francisco: AMACOM Div American Mgmt Assn.

21. Gansberg, Martin. "Thirty-eight who saw murder didn't call the police." *New York Times*. March 27, 1964.

22. Rosenthal, A.M. 1999. *Thirty-Eight Witnesses: The Kitty Genovese Case*. Berkeley: University of California Press. p. 82.

23. Latane, Bibb & Darley, John. 1970. *The Unresponsive Bystander:Why Doesn't He Help?* New York: Appleton-Century Crofts.

24. Wenner, Melinda. "Everyone Agrees." *Psychology Today*. November, 2007. p. 13.

25. Weaver, Garcia, Schwarz, & Miller. "Inferring the popularity of an opinion from its familiarity: A repetitive voice can sound like a chorus." *Journal of Personality and Social Psychology*, Vol. 92, No. 5 (May 2007), pp. 821-833.

26. Mortensen, Kurt W. 2004. *Maximum Influence: The 12 Universal Laws of Power Persuasion*. San Francisco: AMACOM Div American Mgmt Assn.

27. Prendergast, Mark. 1994. *For God, Country and Coca-Cola: The Definitive History of the Great American Soft Drink and the Company That Makes It*. Jackson: Basic Books.

28. Matthew, Blair. "Coca-Cola's Big Mistake: New Coke 20 Years Later…" *Soda Pop Dreams*. June 16, 2006. www.sodaspectrum.com/36_newcoke.htm

29. Oliver, Thomas. 1987. *The Real Coke, The Real Story*. New York: Penguin.

30. Stephenson, Michael., Witte, Kim., Vaught, Charles., Quick, Brian., Booth-Butterfield, Steve., Patel, Dhaval. & Zuckerman, Cynthia. "The Influence of Positive, Negative, and Neutral Messages on Voluntary Hearing-Protection Behaviors Among Miners" Paper presented at the annual meeting of the International Communication Association, New Orleans Sheraton, New Orleans, LA, May 27, 2004.

31. MacKenzie B. "When sober executives went on a bidding binge." *TV Guide*. June 22, 1974.

32. Seligman, Martin E. 2006. *Learned Optimism: How to Change Your Mind and Your Life*. New York: Knopf Publishing Group.

33. ibid.

Life Is Sales

Seminars and Workshops

Life Is Sales offers unique sales and effectiveness training and workshops as well as keynote speeches to clients. Programs include "Life Is Sales," a program designed to enhance influence and persuasive skills in every environment. We tailor these programs to each client's needs. Topics on sales conversations, asking for referrals, customer service, and more, build success with sales reps. These programs deliver an interactive and fun approach to learning. We bring psychological research into why people say yes to requests, and this approach significantly changes the way participants interact with their clients for astounding improvements in their success ratios.

We have delivered programs to RBC; TD Canada Trust, Avalon Healing Centers, California; Leon's; CitiFi; Home Life Realty; BMO; BNS; First Canadian Title; and many others. Over four thousand salespeople have enhanced their persuasive skills by attending one or more of our seminars. We are approved for continuing education credits for CAAMP, IMBA, and RECO.

www.lifeissales.ca

Testimonials

"Gary's enthusiasm and passion for the customer combined with his winning desire for everyone to be successful at selling is infectious."
—Doug Dawson, vice president, BMO

"*Life Is Sales* has captured the essence of selling and why people buy. Truly impactful."
—Gary Laughlin, vice president, RBC

"This was one of the best presentations I have ever hosted for my audience of realtors. I had a line of folks thanking me for inviting them to this presentation."
—Brenda Manning, marketing development manager, Scotiabank

We can improve the sales results of every sales team with simple yet effective persuasive techniques that can be implemented immediately. We will increase your success both professionally and personally.

Receive more information on the programs available by going online to www.lifeissales.ca